ANALECTA BIBLICA

INVESTIGATIONES SCIENTIFICAE IN RES BIBLICAS

107

The Destruction of Jerusalem According to Luke's Gospel: A Historical-Typological Moral

ROMAE
E PONTIFICIO INSTITUTO BIBLICO
1985

CHARLES HOMER GIBLIN, S.J.

Fordham University
Bronx, New York

The Destruction of Jerusalem According to Luke's Gospel: A Historical-Typological Moral

ROME
BIBLICAL INSTITUTE PRESS
1985

ISBN 88-7653-107-6

© Iura editionis et versionis reservantur

PRINTED IN ITALY

GREGORIAN UNIVERSITY PRESS
BIBLICAL INSTITUTE PRESS
Piazza della Pilotta, 35 - 00187 Rome, Italy - Tel. 06/678 15 67

To my mother
(née Jessie Wruck)
on her eightieth birthday

PREFACE

While teaching Paul's Epistle to the Romans in Jerusalem as a visiting professor at the École Biblique et archéologique Française from January to June, 1974, a few months after the Yom Kippur War, I relaxed by reading privately a less polemic, even irenic NT writer, Luke. To my acute discomfort, I found that this Evangelist, whom Dante called *scriba mansuetudinis Christi*,* placed on Jesus' lips the harshest predictions of Jerusalem's fate and the lot of its people on record, not only in the Gospels, but in the rest of the NT as well. At first, In Luke's childhood narrative (1,5 – 2,52) and in the opening third (3,1 – 9,50) of his account of Jesus' adult ministry, all seemed to be sweetness and light. In the second third (9,51 – 19,27) of the public ministry, ominous passages appeared here and there. In the climactic third (19,28 ff.), Luke seemed to go out of his way to stress the dire fate for Jerusalem, not just as a city, but as the capital of a nation and its people, including women and infants. Could this frightful prospect reasonably be explained exegetically and theologically?

There was, indeed, ample evidence in Luke's Gospel (and in Acts) which showed that Luke's remarks about Jerusalem were not dictated by overt or latent anti-Semitism. Moreover, in at least one of the judgmental passages leveled against the inhabitants of Jerusalem (19,41-44), Luke's Jesus, in a quite rare display of emotion, was portrayed as himself weeping over the city because of what lay in store for it. Nevertheless, why was Luke almost preoccupied, in the climactic portion of his narrative of Jesus' adult ministry, from his entry into the temple until his death on the cross, with the destruction of this city? In Acts, apart from what may be inferred from accusations brought against Stephen (6,11-14), not from Stephen's speech itself, nothing is said about the event.

Over the subsequent years, I reflected on the problem as various teaching commitments allowed. In the Fall Semester of 1983, as visiting professor at the Pontifical Biblical Institute in Rome, I taught a course concerning Luke's Jerusalem narrative (19,28 – 24,53) with emphasis on the topic of the destruction of Jerusalem. This monograph results from that course and from previous reflection. It is not intended as a tale of two cities. Personally, it may be such. Perhaps for Luke himself it could be. The one city is impermanent, its destruction a sign to be fulfilled for the nations; the second, the center of Luke's known world,

---

* Dante, *De Monarchia* I, xvi, 2. Underlying the statement is the traditional imagery of Luke as the "ox"; cf. *Ep.* VIII, 14 [to Henry VII, King of the Romans], *"bos noster."*

and later a so-called "eternal city," is liable to the judgment on the inhabited world which the fate of Jerusalem portended (Luke 21,24b-26).

Monographs customarily not only use an inductive approach but also tend artificially to hold the reader in suspense by this method until he reaches the conclusion of the study. To proceed otherwise might call into question one's professional integrity. For the "thesis method," a fairly clear statement of one's position at the outset of an honest inquiry, seems still to be discountenanced. It smacks too much of deduction—which is true, in large measure, if one loads the statement of the thesis with technical terms. On the other hand, why pretend to leave one's reader in suspense and treat him as a docile student who must read every chapter carefully in turn before looking at the last pages? Scholars regularly read conclusions first, the better to perceive or critically to review the argumentation.

At the outset, then, I offer a prefatory statement of my "thesis." Doing so should serve both to indicate the basic position taken and to orient the reader to follow the Table of Contents.

According to Luke's Gospel, Jesus' views concerning the fate of Jerusalem begin, in the course of Luke's narrative, with the second (9,51 – 19,27) of three stages of his adult ministry, and are clearly judgmental only in the third stage (19,28 – 24,53). The narrative progression becomes essential to the clarification of a sequence of key texts concerning this topic. The topic entails another mode of interpreting Luke's Gospel, complementing other accepted modes (apologetic, pastoral-hortatory, doctrinal) and aptly described as "historical-typological." This further mode is grounded in the preface (1,1-4) to Luke's presentation of his Gospel as a kind of history. It respects the narrative progression of Luke's Gospel, including some attention to the way in which he conditions his typed audience to reflect upon and personally to apply the intended lesson. The fate of Jerusalem is brought about by two major factors. First, the people are insensitive to the terms for peace. Although they are ostensibly favorable to Jesus' teaching (as "impressed unbelievers" have been hitherto), and are warned rather than condemned, they will, as a matter of historical reality, perish for the more serious sins of others. Second, the rulers of the people (the Romans not excepted, but not considered as primarily responsible) have committed injustice and thus bring about the ruin of the people. The fate of Jerusalem, however, is not ultimately weighed as an event in itself; it is a sign for others, and is expressly related to times for (judgment of) nations.

All this proves to be relevant, parabolically, to Luke's readership, a man of affluence and influence, educated, who is expected to perceive in "a history" what should be done and what should be avoided, to discern models of good and of evil, with their consequences for society as he knows it. In effect, Luke's lesson apropos of his account of Jerusalem's destruction is to be construed as a question prompted in the typed reader's mind: If this is what happened to Jerusalem because of the way Jesus and those who represent him, his disciples, were treated, what will happen to my city / nation / society if he (and his followers, who stand for him) are treated similarly? What am I, as a respected man with some influence, expected to try to do?

Table of Contents

DEDICATION V

PREFACE VII

TABLE OF CONTENTS IX

CHAPTER I. **Introduction** 1

CHAPTER II. **Luke's Typing of His Audience and of His Gospel (Luke 1,1-4)** 10

    A. Luke's Typing of His Reader 12
    B. What is Expected of the Typed Reader 14

CHAPTER III. **Luke's Conditioning His Reader's Perception** 19

    A. Narrative Episodes 19
    B. Narrative Progressions 24

CHAPTER IV. **Prospects for Jerusalem in View of Jesus' Journey (Luke 9,51 - 19,27)** 30

    A. Luke 9,51-55 31
    B. Luke 10,1.10-16 33
    C. Luke 11,29-32; 13,1-5 34
    D. Luke 13,31-35 37
    E. Luke 17,37; 19,11-27 43

CHAPTER V. **Jesus' Immediate Approach to Jerusalem (Luke 19,28-44)** 47

    A. Introduction and First Stage 48
    B. The Second Stage 50
    C. The Third Stage 55

CHAPTER VI. **The Parable of the Wicked Tenants (Luke 20,9-19)** 57

    A. The Proximate Narrative Context 57
    B. Luke's Redactional Reworking of the Parable 61
    C. The Parable as Contributing to the Historical-Typological Moral 73

CHAPTER VII. **Jesus' Final Discourse in the Temple (Luke 20,45 - 21,36)**   74

    A. The Over-All Structure of Luke 21,5-36   78
    B. Luke 21,20-24   87

CHAPTER VIII. **The Judgment Oracle on the Way to the Cross (Luke 23,26-32)** . .   93

    A. The Opening and Closing Verses   94
    B. Luke's Prophetic Judgment Oracle   95

CHAPTER IX. **Concluding Reflections**   105

APPENDIX: **The Reticence of Acts Concerning the Judgment Against Jerusalem** . .   108

SELECT BIBLIOGRAPHY   113

INDEX OF TEXTS   117

    A. Old Testament   117
    B. New Testament   118
    C. Other   121

INDEX OF AUTHORS   122

I. Introduction

Few points in the literary analysis of the Gospels have received the consensus of scholars as has Luke's special interest in Jesus' movement towards the temple and Jerusalem. Over twelve centuries ago, Venerable Bede, not noted for original biblical scholarship, expressed the consensus eloquently when he wrote of this evangelist, symbolized by the ox: [*qui*] ... *circa templum maxime et Hierosolimam narrationis suae diversatur incessu.*[1] Luke's childhood narrative (1,5–2,52) partially fulfills its introductory function by drawing the reader's attention to Jerusalem and the temple as a fitting place for prophetic disclosure and for Jesus' own maturing concerns.[2]

Major stages of Jesus' adult life move with progressive clarity (especially from 9,51 onwards) to its fulfillment in Jerusalem and the city's immediate environs. Although scholars differ concerning precise, major divisions of the text,[3] three basic stages of Jesus' adult ministry may be discerned: 3,1–9,50; 9,51–19,27; 19,28–24,53. To sketch them at the outset of this study should prove helpful to the investigation of its specific theme. First (3,1–9,50), there occur the immediate prophetic preparation for Jesus' coming and his prophetic anointing (3,1-38)[4] followed closely by two inaugural scenes disclosing Jesus' messianic purpose and his activity on his own, before his calling the disciples (4,1-13 and 4,14-44),[5] and

---

[1] *Bedae Venerabilis Opera*, CChr 120, *In Lucae Evangelium Expositio* 2,41, 71.2038-2042.

[2] Cf. Francis D. Weinert, *The Meaning of the Temple in the Gospel of Luke* (Fordham University Dissertation, 1979; available from University Microfilms International, Ann Arbor, Michigan 48106) 307-16.

[3] J. A. Fitzmyer claims that there is general agreement among commentators about six major divisions of the public ministry, of which 9,51–19,27 is one; *The Gospel According to Luke (I-IX)* (AB 28; Garden City 1981) 134. He goes on to concede: "It would in the long run make little difference if the whole section 3:1 to 9:50 were to be regarded as one part." Ibid., 135. He retains three major divisions after 19,27, even though all of these portions of the text (19,28–21,36; 22,1–23,56a; 23,56b–24,53) locate events in Jerusalem and its immediate environs. Ibid.

A. George treats 19,29–24,53 as a single major part; "La Construction du troisième Évangile," *Études sur l'oeuvre de Luc* (EBib; Paris 1978) 15-41; 25-32.

[4] That Jesus' baptism is a prophetic anointing may be construed especially from the direction of his activity by the spirit (4,1; cp. 4,14) which has descended on him (3,21-22), from his address in Nazareth (4,17-19.21), and from Acts 10,37-38.

[5] Both scenes are similarly introduced (ὑπέστρεψεν plus reference to the spirit); both deal with a clarification of his conscious purpose; each ends with mention of Jerusalem (4,9-13) or Judea (4,44), thus extending the purview of Jesus' mission beyond Galilee.

then by an account of the Galilean ministry entailing the call and formation of disciples in an ever-widening ministry. This first stage, developed with the beginning of 5,1, contains three major movements: *a*) (5,1 – 7,50), the call of disciples in the context of a prophetic ministry of preaching, healing, and forgiveness; [6] *b*) the formation of the Twelve in the context of three short journeys (8,1-21; 8,22-56; 9,1-17); [7] *c*) a sequence of three episodes (9,18-27.28-36.37-50) highlighting passion-predictions. [8]

Jerusalem is not mentioned in any Lucan texts from 3,1 to 9,50 except the following: 4,9, the place of the climactic, diabolic test, whether the Son of God expects God to preserve him from death or bodily harm; 5,17, where Jesus' audience includes Pharisees and lawyers from Jerusalem; 6,17, where crowds from Jerusalem as well have flocked to hear him; and 9,31, when Moses and Elijah speak about Jesus' ἔξοδος, which he is to fulfill in Jerusalem. Luke borrows only one of these texts (6,17) from Mark (3,8), [9] and omits Mark's references to scribes,

---

[6] This proceeds in three major stages: First, after the call of Simon Peter (with notation of his contrite disposition, 5,8), there occurs a pair of miracles directed to the attention of Jewish authorities (the priest, representing the "religious board of health," 5,12-16; and the Pharisees, 5,17-26, where the cure is an attestation of Jesus' power to forgive sins). Second, the call of Levi and a dinner in his house, representing the call of sinners (5,27-39), is followed by a pair of sabbath scenes (6,1-5.6-11). Lastly, the choice of a core-group of Twelve apostles is followed by the sermon on the plain (6,12-49), a pair of miracles—one, for a gentile man, the other, for a Jewish woman (7,1-10.11-17), and consequent upon the latter (cf. 7,16-17), two further episodes concerning Jesus' role as a prophet: the discussion with emissaries from John and Jesus' evaluation of John (7,18-35) apropos of Elijah-typology and the forgiveness of the sinful woman, an action transcending that of any OT prophet, in the house of Simon the Pharisee (7,36-50).

[7] The threefold structure is not difficult to discern once one notes Luke's redaction of Mark. For instance, the first journey, with notation of an expanding group of followers (8,1-3) is one through cities (8,1.4); mention of the lake is avoided. The second journey brings Jesus outside Galilee (8,26), across the lake, and back (8,40). The third is a training program for disciples, both in sending them out (9,1) and in enjoining them, upon their return (9,10), care for the multitude (9,13).

[8] Again, redactional changes vis-à-vis Mark ground this threefold structure, helped by the Lucan repetition of ἐγένετο (9,18.28.37). In particular, Luke incorporates a reference to the passion (Mark 9,9-13) within the scene of the transfiguration (9,31) and, avoiding any change of locale, incorporates in the third scene a prediction of the passion (9,43b-45), omitting the lesson in Mark 9,28-29 and shortening the Marcan discussion following this prediction (Mark 9,38-50), thus setting in relief the prediction itself.

[9] Here, building on Mark, Luke changes Ἱεροσόλυμα to Ἱερουσαλήμ, which he almost always uses in his Gospel (21 times as against 4 times for Ἱεροσόλυμα) and prefers in Acts (39 times as against 24). No theory to date satisfactorily explains the difference in Lucan usage if, indeed, there is any besides a preference for the usage of the LXX; cf. Arndt–Gingrich–Danker, *A Greek-English Lexicon of the New Testament* (Chicago ²1979) 373. The latest effort, by Dennis D. Sylva, "*Ierousalēm* and *Hierosolyma* in Luke-Acts," *ZNW* 74 (1983) 207-29, attractively suggests that Luke is clarifying for his reader's benefit his concept of the city as "Holy Salem," but depends too heavily for parallels on poetic

Pharisees, or people from Jerusalem in Mark 1,5 (describing the activity of John the Baptizer),[10] Mark 7,1 (part of Luke's "Great Omission"), and Mark 3,22 (the Beelzebul controversy, which Luke reserves for his central section, cp. 11,15). Where he adds references to Pharisees and lawyers from Jerusalem (5,17), Luke does so without a harshly polemic note, which he has excised from other portions of the first third of his Gospel.[11] In Luke's account of the forgiveness and cure of the paralytic, even the Pharisees and scribes are hardly to be excluded from the glorification of God given by all (ἅπαντες), who go on to attest things contrary to their expectation (Luke 5,26, παράδοξα). For Luke has deliberately peopled the room with these professors (Luke 5,17; contrast Mark 2,2 and, in 2,6, "some scribes sitting there").[12] References to Jerusalem in Luke 3,1–9,50 (and, all the more so, in Luke 1,5–2,52, cf. 2,38) are not polemic. Indeed, his modification (6,17) of Mark 3,8 places the Jerusalemites and Judeans more integrally in the context of a receptive people (λαός—not the quite diverse Marcan "crowd") which, however, may here include people of undetermined ethnic origin from outside Palestine (Tyre and Sidon) as well.[13] Luke's additions in 4,8 and 9,31 orient the whole first stage of Jesus' public ministry to a forthcoming test (4,8) but prophetically successful fulfillment (9,31) in Jerusalem. No foreboding knell at all is sounded for Jerusalem itself in this first stage of Jesus' adult ministry.

---

texts, and does not even discuss the probably unaspirated form of Ἰερουσαλήμ, which is relevant to a play on ἱερός.

[10] For Luke depicts John not in a fixed position near Jerusalem, but as engaged in itinerant preaching in the whole region of the Jordan.

[11] Luke even omits the unfavorable comparison with the scribes (Mark 1,22c). He softens the sabbath conflict in 6,1-5 by having the Pharisees direct their question to Jesus' disciples (6,2; cf. W. Grundmann, *Das Evangelium nach Lukas* [THKNT 2; Berlin ⁹1981] 135) and by modifying the number of the Pharisees (6,2: τινές; cf. Fitzmyer, *Gospel According to Luke [I-IX]* 608). He strikes mention of Jesus' anger in 6,10 (cp. Mark 3,5) and points up the Pharisees' irrational anger (ἄνοια), avoiding mention of their plot to kill him (6,11; cp. Mark 3,6). Luke phrases Jesus' appeal to Scripture in a less blunt way (6,3; contrast Mark's castigation of their ignorance, 3,25: "Haven't you *ever* read?"). He has also omitted the Marcan diatribe against Pharisaic customs and attitudes (Mark 7,1-23; 8,11-15).

[12] Luke may have drawn attention to those religious leaders partly to present this scene as a testimony to another group of religious authorities, more clearly pairing it with the cure of the leper, which was intended as a proof for the priests (5,14). The two scenes are paired on other grounds and are linked by the reference to Jesus' prayer in 5,16; cf. Ludger Feldkämper, *Der betende Jesus als Heilsmittler nach Lukas* (St. Augustin bei Bonn 1978) 51-81.

[13] The "great multitude" in Mark includes people even from Idumea and Perea. In Luke, the term λαός (followed by only one prepositional phrase, ἀπὸ κτλ.) has a smaller compass. Fitzmyer, *Gospel According to Luke (I-IX)* 624, sees in Tyre and Sidon a reference to Gentiles, which I. H. Marshall admits, since these cities symbolize heathenism (10,13-14), in spite of Luke's inclusion of them under the term λαός; I. H. Marshall, *The Gospel of Luke* (Exeter 1978) 242.

At the very onset of the second stage (9,51 – 19,27), the reader is faced with Jesus' determination to move onward with his disciples towards Jerusalem. The reader has been conditioned to expect this, if not by the locale of the climactic temptation (4,9) — for the point made there looks ominously to a future, opportune time for the major messianic test (4,13) — then at least by the prophetic dialogue in the scene of the transfiguration (9,31). The literary structure of this central portion of Luke's Gospel does not as yet seem to have yielded itself to a clear outline after its introductory section.[14] Suffice it to note that general agreement obtains that Luke placed most of his Q source in this section, that he redacted at least certain portions to give them more coherence, and that he placed everything under an over-all rubric of movement towards Jerusalem, even while ignoring detailed geographical progression until the very end of this journey.

During this stage of Luke's narrative, one finds that Jesus' relationships with the people of Jerusalem begin to take on a foreboding tone. Not a few [16] have seen even in Jesus' "setting his face to go to Jerusalem" (9,51) a sign or attestation of coming judgment against the city. In the context of a warning from some Pharisees that Herod, the tetrarch of Galilee, has designs to kill him (13,31), Jesus replies that it is not acceptable (sc., to God) that a prophet die outside of Jerusalem. He proceeds prophetically to address the city as one which has not accepted his concern for it (13,34-35). Jerome Neyrey takes this apostrophe to the city as a judgment oracle against it,[17] an interpretation which will call for modification, especially given the progression of Luke's narrative. Nevertheless, this text stands as the first definitely negative view of Jerusalem in Luke's Gospel, and surely as the first negative view of its status ("your house is left to you[rselves]"). Furthermore, the passion prediction given in 18,32 (occurring in that portion of the journey to Jerusalem in which Luke has returned briefly [18,15-43] to follow Mark for the most part) ties the fulfillment of the prophets' writings concerning the Son of Man to Jesus' going up to Jerusalem. In 19,11-27, at the very close of this journey, Jesus

---

[14] The minimal introduction is provided in Luke 9,51-56 (followed by mention of what happens *en route,* 9,57). If there is a larger introductory section, as Michi Miyoshi holds, *Die Anfang des Reiseberichts, Lk 9,51 – 10,24. Eine redaktionsgeschichtliche Untersuchung* (AnBib 60; Rome 1974), it must not be cut short (as in Miyoshi's study) at 10,24, but extended to 10,37 to include Jesus' answer to the lawyer, before the next indication of progressive movement (10,38), and especially to alert the reader to further controversies with lawyers, Pharisees, etc., which become more prominent in this central section (cf. n. 11, *above*).

[15] Cf. J. A. Fitzmyer, *Gospel According to Luke (I-IX)* 825. The only relatively detailed geographical progression begins with mention of Jericho (18,35.36.40b; 19,1.4.11) as the immediate point of ascent to Jerusalem (cp. 18,31; 19,11.28).

[16] Craig A. Evans, "'He Set His Face': A Note on Luke 9,51," *Bib* 63 (1982) 545-8; J. H. Davies, "The Purpose of the Central Section of St. Luke's Gospel," *SE* II (= TU 87 [1964]) 164-9.

[17] Jerome H. Neyrey, "Jesus' Address to the Women of Jerusalem (Lk. 23. 27-31) — A Prophetic Judgment Oracle," *NTS* 29 (1983) 74-86, 79-80, 83.

corrects the false impression that the kingly rule of God will be made manifest when Jesus arrives in Jerusalem, and tells a parable highlighting the theme of a future, final reckoning. In this case, the reckoning looks not only to the royal servants, but also to members of the city who did not want the nobleman to become their king.

The preceding hints of a severe judgment against Jerusalem come to the fore in the third stage (19.28 – 24,53) of Jesus' ministry, particularly in its first half (his entry and his teaching in the temple, 19,28 – 21,38) and, in the second half (22,1 – 24,53), at the close of the passion narrative, just before the crucifixion on Calvary. Four key texts command attention here, especially when one compares Luke with Mark. The first consists of the entry into Jerusalem, which proves to be an entry into its "forum," the temple area in which Jesus contacts all the people of the city and their leaders. This text includes a prediction peculiar to Luke concerning the city's destruction (19,41-44). The fourth text, also proper to Luke, consists of a direct address to the sympathetic daughters of Jerusalem (23,27-31) and quite poignantly makes the same basic point. Luke recasts the second of these four texts, the parable of the wicked tenants (20,9-19), which alludes to the counterproductive Israel of Isa 5, notably by nuancing the intended audience(s) and by adding a closing development of the stone-imagery to suggest ineluctable judgment. In the third text, the so-called "eschatological discourse," Luke revamps the Marcan schema on a number of counts, particularly by depicting not the profanation of the Jewish cult-center but the destruction of the capital city, Jerusalem, the plight of its people, and, indeed, the ruin of the whole nation.

That Luke takes special pains to draw attention to Jesus' prophetic words concerning the devastation in store for Jerusalem is evident. On this score, no other Evangelist or NT writer comes comparatively close to Luke's statements in his Gospel.[18] Luke's reasons for taking this negative view of Jerusalem, however, have not satisfactorily been clarified.

Usually, only one or other text has been subjected to close examination. Understandably, different reasons are assigned for the fate of Jerusalem in dealing with texts examined mainly in themselves. Fridolin Keck, for example, in the most thorough study to date of Luke 20,45 – 21,36, finds the fate of Jerusalem attributable not to Jesus' death (as is generally held), but to the treatment of his disciples.[19] This conclusion, however, does not account for and has not been shown to cohere with Luke 19,28-44, which refers to the Lord's visitation as an event which has just occurred and is not recognized by the people, or to 23,27-31,

---

[18] Matthew and Mark are concerned with the destruction of the temple and the profanation of its cult, but say nothing about the city as such. John gives a strictly Christological interpretation of the destruction of the sanctuary (2,18-22). No other writer speaks of its ruin, even John of Patmos; cf. C. H. Giblin, "Rev 11. 1-13: Its Form, Function, and Contextual Integration," *NTS* 30 (1984) 433-59, 438-40, 445-6, 457 n. 47.

[19] Fridolin Keck, *Die öffentliche Abschiedsrede Jesu in Lk 20,45 – 21,36. Eine redaktions- und motivgeschichtliche Untersuchung* (FzB 25; Stuttgart 1978) 254.

where Jesus himself, en route to his death, is the occasion for the women's lamentation and is the point of reference for his response to them concerning their coming lot. No one, to my knowledge, has examined all the relevant texts with reference to their coherence on the redactional level.[20] No one seems even to have examined a combination of the relevant texts in the context of Luke's ongoing narrative, from its beginning to its climax in the passion narrative. This monograph, then, attempts to meet the need for a more perspicacious, complexive study of all the texts which bear on the problem of accounting for Luke's concern with the fate of Jerusalem.

The need for a more perspicacious study also arises from the fact that none of the theories which does try to assign a reason for Luke's concern with the destruction of Jerusalem takes precisely into account the kind of audience for which he wrote. By and large, these theories discuss the basis for the judgment itself. They draw attention to the specific aspect of guilt and/or to the specifically guilty parties, whether high priests, elements among the people, the Romans, or some combination of these.[21] Such interests are not idle inquiries. Nevertheless, they never address the issue of precisely what it was that Luke intended to do. Was he merely interested in "placing blame," and, if so, why? What did he expect his reader to see or infer?

Investigation of Luke's marked interest in the destruction of Jerusalem has never taken seriously the distinctive preface which Luke provides to type his kind of Gospel narrative, to type his reader as well, and, accordingly, to suggest what he expects his reader to perceive in the kind of evangelical communication which Luke offers him. How are these dire predictions of the fate of Jerusalem conceivably relevant to Luke's educated readership, "Your Excellency, Theophilus" (1,3)? To press the point, how are they relevant to Christians today, who accept them as God's effective word, a word transcending the first century production-context of Luke's Gospel?

Not that the destruction of Jerusalem is the main theme of Luke's Gospel or must determine the principal mode of interpreting it! Luke's work is so rich that several levels, or, lest that term seem pejoratively to connote degrees of value, several modes of interpretation are called for. No one of them suffices to cover

---

[20] Lloyd Gaston, *No Stone on Another. Studies in the Significance of the Fall of Jerusalem in the Synoptic Gospels* (NTS 23: Leiden 1970) 244-369 covers most of the texts from the standpoint of his espousal of the theory of Proto-Luke. As we shall see below, it is not evident that all the explicit references to the destruction of the city are to be found in the special material of the Gospel of Luke, much less that the significance of any of the texts is to be determined on the level of the composition and *Sitz im Leben* construed for Proto-Luke. Besides, Gaston does not treat Luke's significant modifications of the parable of the wicked tenants (esp. Luke 20,15b-19).

[21] As, for example, in the discussion about 23,27-31; cf. A. Plummer, *The Gospel According to S. Luke* (ICC; Edinburgh ⁴1913) 529; J. Neyrey, "Jesus' Address to the Women of Jerusalem," 78-9.

everything Luke's Gospel contains, but a basic variety invites reasonable classification. No one mode excludes any other. Nor, indeed, can any one be typed in terms of a particular exegetical school, although one or other may be more prominent in certain commentaries or exegetical studies. The apologetic mode[22] stresses Luke's concern to portray Jesus himself not as a rival to Caesar or as a social revolutionary, and to make clear that his followers are therefore not to be taken as a threat to civil (sc., Roman) power.[23] The pastoral-hortatory mode highlights Jesus' example as a model for his disciples to admire and follow.[24] The doctrinal mode is many-faceted, but tends to set in relief Jesus'.work as prophet and savior[25] or, more specifically, as the just man who suffers unjustly and by his prayer—especially his prayerful death—brings forgiveness of sins. This latter mode of interpretation goes quite far in elucidating the messianic imperative as Luke develops it: the Messiah must suffer and die to achieve his mission, for such is the role of a prophetic Messiah.[27]

Each of these three modes of interpretation gravitates, as does the Gospel itself, towards the climactic encounters of the passion narrative.[28] It is in that portion of the Jerusalem narrative (19,28 – 24,53) in particular, the final passion prediction and its fulfillment (22,35 – 23,49), that Jesus' relationships to the Roman authorities, his model conduct for disciples, and his salvific mission in bringing about repentance and forgiveness of sins find their common focus: the death of the wrongly accused Just One.

Another mode of interpretation, however, is called for by texts concerning the destruction of Jerusalem. Their frequency, concentration, and focus in Luke's Gospel can hardly be intended apologetically to exonerate Roman unbelievers

---

[22] Cf. Henry J. Cadbury, "The Purpose Expressed in Luke's Preface," *Expositor* 21 (1921) 431-44; S. MacLean Gilmour, "The Gospel According to Luke," (IB 8; New York 1952), 5-6.

[23] Recently, renewed interest has been shown in the political relevance of Luke-Acts; cf. *Political Issues in Luke-Acts,* ed. R. J. Cassidy and P. J. Scharper (Maryknoll 1983). The perspective which Luke provides, however, is not a socio-political program; cf. J. Y. Thériault, "Les dimensions sociales, économiques et politiques dans l'oeuvre de Luc," *ScEs* 26 (1974) 205-31.

[24] A. Vanhoye, "Structure et théologie des récits de la Passion dans les évangiles synoptiques," *NRT* 89 (1967) 135-63; B. E. Beck, "*Imitatio Christi* and the Lucan Passion Narrative," *Suffering and Martyrdom in the New Testament* (FS. G. M. Styler; [ed. W. Horburg and B. McNeil] Cambridge 1981) 28-47; G. Schneider, *Die Passion Jesu nach den drei älteren Evangelien* (Munich 1972) 164-9.

[25] A. George, "Le sens de la mort de Jésus pour Luc," *RB* 80 (1973) 186-217; W. F. Arndt, *The Gospel According to Luke* (St. Louis 1956) 29-30.

[26] G. Schneider, *Das Evangelium nach Lukas. Kapitel 11-24* (Würzburg ²1984) 437-9.

[27] Richard J. Dillon, "Easter Revelation and Mission Program in Luke 24:46-48," *Sin, Salvation, and the Spirit* (ed. D. Durken) (Collegeville 1979) 240-70, 248-51.

[28] The resurrection functions as essential for revealing the value of the passion, but in no way eclipses the importance of the passion; the latter guarantees the fact that Christianity is not a religion of evasion. Cf. A. Vanhoye, "Structure et théologie," 135-6.

(much less justify the action of Christians). Jesus sympathizes with the lot of his people, demonstrably so in 19,41, and probably so in 23,27-31. Even when indicating the cause of the calamity, Luke never justifies its perpetrators. Nor does he present in these passages a model for Christians to follow or an occasion for righteous gloating. Nor is any doctrinal theme in evidence (other than references to scriptural fulfillment regarding· the calamity) either to ground the universal preaching of the Gospel on the condition of Jerusalem's destruction or to ground hope for the ultimate conversion of the Jews.

The additional mode of interpretation, a historical-typological mode, may be found by considering the key texts concerning the fate of Jerusalem in the light of Luke's intended communication as set forth in his preface (1,1-4). Luke's preface must be characterized as a kind of historical preface because of elements which it shares with that recognizable type of writing (e.g., reference to previous writers, claim to "historical accuracy," indication of purpose). To be sure, it is the preface to a religious history, not to a secular history, and the method which Luke follows may aptly be termed "imitative" historiography.[29] Nevertheless, it introduces Luke's Gospel as a kind of history. Thus, it "types" the kind of narrative which is offered to the reader.

The reader, too, is typed. Luke's address to Theophilus (whether the latter is to be taken as a real person or as a fictitious one) is not, as is generally assumed,[30] a phrase of dedication, as is, for example, Josephus's address to Epaphroditus in *Against Apion,* I,1.1, but a specification of his audience. The change of persons from Luke 1,1-2 ("they to us") with the main clause and its development in 1,3-4 ("I to you [sg.]") substantiates this specification. The respectful form of address (κράτιστε) further shows that Luke is not directing his work "to any man in the street" or even to just anyone in a Christian community, but to a person of assumed affluence, influence, and education.

Now, what is expected of such a reader when he is presented with a religious history? To read history in Luke's day was to learn what should be done and

---

[29] This characterization would accord, for instance, with J. A. Fitzmyer's view of Luke's historical writing; *Gospel According to Luke (I-IX),* 14-8, 28-9. Robert Maddox, *The Purpose of Luke-Acts* (Göttingen 1982) 16, speaks similarly of "theological history."

Charles H. Talbert, *Luke and the Gnostics* (Nashville 1966) 98-110, seems to confuse modes or aspects of interpretation with "alternative" categories for determining Luke's purpose. "Theological history" is broad enough to cover many specific interests, none of which needs to exclude another. At the same time, a certain mode of interpretation may need to be determined to handle a whole sequence of texts which attest to one among the author's various, special interests. Luke's catholic concerns are not amenable, however, to univocal classifications; witness his use of titles for Jesus.

[30] Even by Fitzmyer, *Gospel According to Luke (I-IX)* 299; cf. G. Schneider, *Das Evangelium nach Lukas. Kapitel 1-10* (Würzburg ²1984) 39-40.

Nevertheless, some move a bit beyond this assessment by noting that Theophilus "represents" a wider audience; e.g., Fitzmyer, ibid., 300, and Paul S. Minear, "Dear Theo. The Kerygmatic Intention and Claim of the Book of Acts," *Int* 27 (1983) 131-50, 132.

what should be avoided in the light of various situations which the given history recounted. Religious history of a biblical character, notably that in the Deuteronomic tradition, would demand this attitude even more so than secular history. The directly personal address, moreover, which Luke provides from the outset, supposes personal reflection. Many Hellenistic historians tended to moralize for the reader's benefit. Luke does not do so. He subtly conditions the reader to think parabolically about his own situation and avoids didactic or reflective comments of his own.

Given the assumptions of the historical genre as Luke employs it, the reader will come to see the whole written account as parabolically applicable to himself and to his own circumstances — social as well as personal. Confronted with the fate of Jerusalem and its apparent causes, as the narrative will have progressively disclosed them, he should well ask himself whether Jerusalem's fate is not a case in point — indeed, a primary model, a type — for what may will happen to his own city or people or nation, and to the gentile world at large. What action he takes, if any, can be left to the working out of reflections prompted by Luke's narrative.

The method of working out the discovery and clarification of the historical-typological moral requires that the relevant texts be studied in their narrative contexts. This approach helps obviate the bias that may well arise from a logical, topical development dictated by an exegete's ingenuity. In addition, it more closely respects the way in which Luke himself has approached his typed readership. Accordingly, the lineup of the chapters of this monograph, indicated in the Table of Contents, will move from Luke's preface, through further reflections concerning his conditioning of the reader's perception, to the prospects for Jerusalem in view of Jesus' journey towards that city. In the central section of Luke's narrative (9,51 – 19,27), problems concerning the city's fate (and Jesus' own death there) begin to emerge. The four major texts, all placed within the compass of the Jerusalem narrative (19,28 ff.), will be investigated singly, but, again, in terms of the connections suggested by the narrative. After the general conclusion to the study of these texts in Luke's Gospel, a brief appendix will consider why the fate of Jerusalem is so notably absent in Acts, except for Stephen's speech in response to charges concerning the destruction of the temple and of "this place."

II. Luke's Typing of His Audience and of His Gospel (Luke 1,1-4)

When he reexamined Luke's preface in 1973, W. C. van Unnik could still complain that he had never come across a commentary in which Luke 1,1-4 was taken seriously so as to give a guideline for understanding the Gospel (and perhaps Acts).[1] To some extent, J. A. Fitzmyer has remedied this deficiency by noting that Luke intends to write systematically, that is, in a given literary order, periodized, and guided by promise and fulfillment.[2] What is more, constructively contrary to van Unnik's position that this Hellenistic historical preface contains nothing characteristically Christian,[3] Fitzmyer judges Luke's basic mode of writing history to be far more like that of OT biblical history, and to contain from its outset a Christian perspective.

True, the scope of Luke's exceptionally short preface cannot fully be determined simply by a study of the preface itself. Prefaces function in terms of the whole work to which they provide a foreword. Nevertheless, the preface provides a solid basis for previewing Luke's project, especially his Gospel.[4] In particular, it helps disclose that Luke did not invent a category of *Heilsgeschichte* which rationalized and institutionalized the kerygma, but rather that he intended to demonstrate the bond between the sacred history of promise and fulfillment, on the one hand, and the present situation of Christian belief.[5]

In working out the scope of Luke's preface, most of the studies devoted to it detail the meaning of the terms which Luke employs. To a considerable extent, Dillon's examination provides an exception. It corrects the myopic perspective which one runs the risk of taking in limiting the inquiry to a discussion of the specific terms in the preface, especially the more problematical ones. For Dillon considers such details under four points which respect both the structure of the sentence and its genre as a historical preface: first, the context of Luke's endeavor (v. 1) — regarding his forerunners and tradition(s); second, the closely-associated subject matter (v. 2) — highlighting its ultimate sources as the eyewitnesses who became ministers of the word; third, the procedure and

---

[1] W. C. van Unnik, "Once More St. Luke's Prologue," *Neot* 7 (1973) 7-26, 7.

[2] J. A. Fitzmyer, *The Gospel According to Luke* (AB 28; Garden City 1981) 289-90.

[3] W. C. van Unnik, "Once More...," 8.

[4] R. J. Dillon, "Previewing Luke's Project from His Prologue (Luke 1:1-4)," *CBQ* 43 (1981) 205-27.

[5] Ibid., 227.

standard of the work (v. 3) — its kind of historicity; fourth, the purpose of the "orderly" composition (v. 4).[6]

Earlier, J. Wijngaards[4] tried to clarify the general scope of Luke's preface by moving beyond analysis of specific terms to a delineation of the elements of the genre known as "historical preface." He singled out six elements: a phrase of dedication; indication of the subject matter; reference to foregoing writers; formulas of modesty; declaration of purpose; and claim to historical accuracy. Although helpful, Wijngaards' analysis can be faulted on a number of counts. In Hellenistic authors, the "formulas of modesty" are not uncommonly polemic, self-justifying, even boastful statements disparaging other authors.[8] The "phrase of dedication" is frequently lacking, and it would be wiser to speak instead of "reference to prospective readers."[9] What is more, Wijngaards somewhat woodenly conceives the claim to historical accuracy. For historical writing in the Hellenistic period was largely a function of rhetoric,[10] and its concern for accuracy — undogmatically but critically — would usually be construed as a serious attempt to avoid mistakes or to avoid writing on the basis of mere hearsay.[11] Nevertheless, the key elements of the genre emerge: the reference to foregoing writers and an indication of the subject matter; a claim to historical accuracy; and a declaration of purpose (regularly, with an indication of the intended audience, whether general or specific).

Thanks to studies like those briefly reviewed above, it becomes unnecessary here to reopen debate concerning all the philological details in Luke 1,-1-4. Other aspects of Luke's preface, however, which have passed completely or relatively

---

[6] Ibid., 206, 211, 217, 223.

[7] J. Wijngaards, "Saint Luke's Prologue in the Light of Modern Research," *Clergy Monthly* 31 (1976) 171-9, 251-8.

[8] Cf. Josephus, *Jewish War*, I, 1-5 §§ 1-16; *Against Apion* I, 1.; and historians (Anaxamenes and Theopompus) referred to by Dionysius of Halicarnassus, *Roman Antiquities*, I, 1 §§ 2-3.

[9] As, for example, in Dionysius of Halicarnassus, *Roman Antiquities* I, 6 § 5, who writes for all who take pleasure in the contemplation of great and noble deeds, and to express his thanks to the city of Rome, or Polybius, *World History*, IX, 1, who addresses himself to the politically-minded.

[10] Cf. W. C. van Unnik, "Éléments artistiques dans l'évangile de Luc," *L'évangile de Luc. Problèmes littéraires et théologiques* (Mémorial Lucien Cerfaux; [ed. F. Neirynck *et al*] Gembloux 1973) 129-40, 135-6. A certain elasticity in the range and affinities of historical writing of the period is sketched by C. K. Barrett, *Luke the Historian in Recent Study* (Philadelphia 1970 [repr. of 1961 ed. with supplemental references]), when he notes different norms for historical writing, admitting that, in some sense, Luke is definitely a historian, but then goes on to observe that the Hellenistic romance, with its interest in tracing the hero's fortunes through suffering to success, may make some claim to being the literary setting of the Lucan writings (ibid., 9-15).

[11] W. C. van Unnik, "Once More St. Luke's Prologue," 18, who adduces Hellenistic parallels contrasting the data of "hearsay" and what is known either ἀσφαλῶς and / or ἀκριβῶς.

unnoticed, command attention. For these, too, bear directly on the way in which Luke intended his reader to approach his "Gospel as history," and especially how he began to guide him to construe passages concerning the historical fate of Jerusalem. Two major points should prove to be necessary and sufficient for the scope of this current study: first (A), how the structure and form of address in this historical preface type Luke's readership; second (B), how the genre of this preface conditions such a typed reader to construe the destruction of Jerusalem in the course of Luke's narrative.

A. Luke's Typing of His Reader

In this single periodic sentence (Luke 1,1-4), the pivotal point occurs with the main clause at the outset of v. 3. The following, schematic arrangement of the Greek text [12] should facilitate further discussion of it:

v. 1a   Ἐπειδήπερ πολλοὶ ἐπεχείρησαν

 1b   ἀνατάξασθαι διήγησιν περὶ τῶν πεπληροφορημένων ἐν ἡμῖν πραγάτων,

 2   καθὼς παρέδοσαν ἡμῖν οἱ ἀπ' ἀρχῆς αὐτόπται καὶ ὑπηρέται γενόμενοι τοῦ λόγου,

 3a ἔδοξε κἀμοὶ
        παρηκολουθηκότι ἄνωθεν πᾶσιν ἀκριβῶς,

 3b καθεξῆς σοι γράψαι, κράτιστε Θεόφιλε,

 4   ἵνα ἐπιγνῷς περὶ ὧν κατηχήθης λόγων τὴν ἀσφάλειαν.

Fitzmyer has already noted the balance between protasis (vv. 1-2) and apodosis (vv. 3-4) on three counts, in three parallel phrases.[13] He finds a formal contrast between "many" (v. 1a) and "I, too" (v. 3a); between "to compile an orderly account" (v. 1b) and "to put [them] systematically in writing" (v. 3b); and between the secondary subordinate clauses, "just as..." (v. 2) and "so that..." (v. 4).

The personal references, however, also require attention, even primarily so. For they serve to unify the whole sentence, to render more coherent its major, two-stage progression, and to impart to the composition a characteristically Lucan emphasis: Who has done what for whose (ultimate) benefit? "Many," alluding to foregoing writers, probably including Luke's written sources (e.g., Mark and Q), compiled an account concerning things brought to fulfillment among "us" (v. 1b), that is, among members of the Christian community.[14] The first person pl.

---

 [12] The text followed is that of *NA*[26].

 [13] Fitzmyer, *Gospel According to Luke (I-IX)*, 288.

 [14] Although the first pl. pron. in v. 1 covers the "many writers" and "the eyewitnesses who became ministers of the word," whereas in v. 2 it refers to Luke and other third

reappears in the following clause (v. 2), which mentions the tradition(s) employed by foregoing writers. Significantly, this prior stage of communication, attributed to eyewitnesses who became ministers of the word, was also directed "to us," Thus, Luke situates his own contribution within the framework of concerns for the community. He by no means suggests that he disparages either of these previous stages [15] even though he himself is not writing "for a community." Rather, the positive progression which he introduces in his main clause (v. 3), "it seemed good to me, also," brings out his concern for a new, personally individual communication. Vv. 3b and 4 (unlike the parallel lines, vv. 1b and 2) employ the second person sg. ("to write ... you," "that you may know ..."). What is more, v. 3b contains the vocative singular, which directly addresses Luke's audience. Thus, the general movement of the preface runs from "they" (many writers; also, ministers of the word) in relation to "us" (as those, respectively, who experienced the fulfillment and as those who were the beneficiaries of the earliest stage of tradition), to "I" in relation to "you (sg.)," sc., Theophilus as the intended reader of Luke's own contribution.

Regularly, commentators regard the words κράτιστε Θεόφιλε as a phrase of dedication.[16] If Theophilus is not a fictitious person, there may be some truth in this assumption. Even if he is regarded as fictitious, one might argue that, in addressing him, Luke makes use of a conventional, if unnecessary element in his preface. If he is not fictitious, it seems strange that no mention of him occurs in early tradition, apart from what seems to be "a worthless legend of later date." [17] In any event, Luke's form of address, given its placement in the preface, can by no means adequately be accounted for as a phrase of dedication. Luke has indicated repeatedly in vv. 3-4 that he is writing *for* Theophilus. Whether this man is a

---

generation Christians, both instances imply a continuity of faith within the living community.

[15] The phrase πολλοὶ ἐπεχείρησαν (v. 1) is better understood in terms of modified two-source criticism, not as a disparaging or pejorative remark; cf. R.J. Dillon, "Previewing Luke's Project ...," 207. Dillon effectively refutes G. Klein, "Lukas 1,1-4 als theologisches Programm," *Zeit und Geschichte* (FS. R. Bultmann, [ed. Erich Dinkler] Tübingen 1964) 193-216. 195. Luke's κἀμοί, "to me, *too*," implies that he appreciatively builds upon the efforts of his predecessors. Cf. also W.C. van Unnik, "Once Again...," 15.

[16] See above, Ch. I, n. 30; cf. also Heinz Schürmann, *Das Lukasevangelium: Erster Teil: Kommentar zu Kap. 1,1–9,50* (HTKNT 3/1; Freiburg 1969) 2; Gerhard Schneider, *Das Evangelium nach Lukas. Kapitel 1-10* (Gütersloh ²1984) 39.

[17] So J.A. Fitzmyer, *Gospel According to Luke (I-IX)*, 299, referring to the Ps. Clementine *Recognitions* (10.71), which are usually dated between A.D. 211 and 231.

On the other hand, the name is apparently not symbolic, sc., "beloved of God," for, philologically, this would suppose the voc. Θεοφιλές, For the discussion, cf. Fitzmyer, ibid., 299-300. One need not therefore suppose, however, that the name represents an actual individual, but only recognize that Luke has in mind more than merely a symbolic figure or "abstracted personality." To exemplify somewhat: "Dear John" is not "Dear Grace of God." Luke is not writing like St. Francis de Sales.

fictitious individual or not, he represents a type of reader: an individual, almost surely of some affluence, influence, and education. Although the term κράτιστε is not reserved to one who occupies an official, much less governmental position, it is not the formula of address which would be used of an ordinary or non-privileged member of society.

Comparison with phrases of dedication elsewhere, particularly in Josephus's *Against Apion,* I,1 § 1; II,1 § 2, establishes the distinctiveness of Luke's mode of direct address. Josephus's "Most excellent Epaphroditus," is indeed no more than a phrase of dedication to his interested patron, who, presumably, will at least peruse his protégé's composition. Josephus's intended *audience,* however, consists of the malicious anti-Semites who have attacked his *Antiquities,* of the ignorant, and of whoever is interested in learning the truth about the ancient origin of the Jewish race. The opening of the second volume of his apologetic history (II. 1 § 1) pursues more briefly the same aim and assumes the same sort of readership. Luke, on the other hand, indicates no other audience but the man whom he addresses directly; he directs personally to him, and / or, to the type of reader Theophilus represents, his orderly account and stated purpose.

B. What Is Expected of the Typed Reader

How would the genre of this preface condition Luke's typed reader to understand his work, particularly the passages which deal with the destruction of Jerusalem? Two basic considerations, subsequently to be developed, may be outlined here. First, distinctive features of this preface show that Luke is presenting his reader with a kind of religious history, which is meant, moreover, to stimulate his personal reflection concerning the religious knowledge he has already received. Second. Luke is adapting his version of the Gospel-as-history to an educated Hellenistic reader. Such a reader, faced with a kind of written history, would be expected to discern moral implications in the story, particularly those aspects which develop its relevance for his own cultural milieu and his personal involvement in it. For instance, he would not be expected to regard an event like the destruction of Jerusalem, to which Luke will devote considerable attention in the climactic portion of his Gospel, as simply an unfortunate event in the recent past, or as merely Jesus' prophetic prediction of a matter of fact, devoid of moral relevance for the reader of this kind of book. Rather, it is likely that he would be expected to ponder its relevance to his own social situation. Examination of key texts themselves will, of course, be required to bear out these assumed attitudes on the part of Luke's reader. It is advisable, however, to explore at the outset the reasonableness of these assumptions regarding Luke's typed audience.

Indications that Luke is writing a religious history are evident from key expressions which color interrelated phrases. Ministers of "the word" (v. 2) clearly evokes the notion of the Gospel message (cp. Luke 8,11; Acts 6,4) and would be thoroughly out of place in a preface to a secular history. Preceding this, in speaking of transmitted accounts which relied upon ministers of the word (καθὼς παρέδοσαν), Luke mentions "events fulfilled among us." If only because of the personal point of reference ("among us"), the events can hardly be construed as general occurrences of a non-religious character. What is more, the use of the ampler term πληροφορεῖν, especially as subsequently articulated in the work thus prefaced,[18] should be construed as the realization of prophecy, not merely as "events which have transpired."[19] Closing phrases in the purpose clause (v. 4) support the tone of religious history. "Assurance / truth (ἀσφάλεια)." in Luke's understanding of the term is best paralleled by the adverbial form which Peter uses in addressing the Jews on Pentecost (Acts 2,36): "Let the whole house of Israel, then, know assuredly (ἀσφαλῶς) ..." The context shows that Peter is insisting on the conclusion befitting prophetic testimony. Whether or not "the words concerning which you have been instructed" (v. 4) refers to evangelical catechesis remains doubtful. For the term κατήχεσθαι does not seem to have carried at this early date the technical, connotation of formal, elementary instruction in the faith, sc., "catechesis," though it moved in that direction.[20] Nonetheless, it assumes a knowledge of the general subject matter, and presumably of the kind of sources Luke mentioned in v. 1 or even in v. 2.

The ultimate point of reference for the tradition underlying Luke's predecessors' accounts and his own adaptation of them to a new audience suggests that the key notion of Deuteronomic history, fulfillment according to God's word, is by no means alien to his thinking. The preface itself does not establish this point. Later passages, at least according to Fridolin Keck's study of Luke 20,45 – 21,36, may serve to do so. The possibility, however, deserves to be borne in mind.

Another aspect of the religious orientation of the preface elicits attention. For it seems to be unparalleled not only in Hellenistic prefaces but even in OT historical books: the writer personally addresses another individual as his intended audience. What helps cast this form of address as religious is Luke's personal interest in supplying Theophilus with grounds for genuine knowledge of the religious tradition on which his writing is based. Luke's reader, however, is a man of the Hellenistic world. How would he be supposed to construe his role as Luke's reader?

[18] The Greek verbs πληροῦν and πληροφορεῖν are synonymous; cf. Arndt–Gingrich–Danker, *A Greek-English Lexicon of the New Testament* (Chicago ²1979) 670, although πληροφορεῖν seems to convey a further note of personal assurance and / or human instrumentality, which would be quite appropriate in this context.

[19] Cf. Dillon, "Previewing Luke's Work...," 209 and n. 12, 211-2. For a still fuller discussion, cf. Fitzmyer, *Gospel According to Luke (I-IX)*, 293.

[20] The wide spectrum of the term and its relatively non-technical meaning in Luke's day, can be perceived even within the NT: "report, inform" are attested by Acts 21,21.24, but "instruct, teach basics" can be justified by Acts 18,25 (notably as teaching ἀκριβῶς); Gal 6,6; Rom 2,18; 1 Cor 14,19 (where Paul speaks of grasping the meaning of five intelligible words, sc., a clear, concise statement).

Most studies concerning the Hellenistic quality of Luke's writing, notably that by Plümacher,[21] treat exclusively his second volume, Acts. Regarding the historical cast of his Gospel, very little has been written apart from discussions of the historical preface.[22] This is understandable, if only because Jesus' discourses, unlike the speeches interspersed throughout Acts, neither have the traits nor serve the *ad hoc* function of speeches in Hellenistic histories.[23] Nonetheless, the preface itself sufficiently attests Luke's concern for a basic feature of contemporary historical writing above and beyond the claim to historical accuracy and to careful investigation of sources.

From the very fact that it is a recognizable form, a historical preface alerts the reader to what is expected of himself as a reader. In brief, he is to discern the moral implications of the account. Dionysius of Halicarnassus, a literary critic as well as a historical writer, made quite clear the supposition that history contains an implied moral. He considered truth and justice "to be the aim of every history" and looked to the interests of "all who take pleasure in the contemplation of great

---

[21] Eckhard Plümacher, *Lukas als hellenistischer Schriftsteller. Studien zur Apostelgeschichte* (Göttingen 1972).

[22] Neglect of attention to this matter is striking, as can be seen from the scholarly contributions extensively reviewed by François Bovon, *Luc le théologien. Vingt-cinq ans de recherches (1950-1975)* (Neuchâtel 1978) 19-84, and "Du côté de chez Luc," *RTP* 115 (1983) 175-89. Later discussions seem to bear out the neglect of Luke's Gospel itself or of the need for special attention to it.

For instance, Schuyler Brown, "The Role of the Prologues in Determining the Purpose of Luke-Acts," *Perspectives in Luke-Acts* (ed. C. H. Talbert) (Edinburgh 1978) 99-111, struggles with the relationship of the exegesis of the "two prologues" and the purpose of Luke's "two-volume" composition. I think that this approach tends *de facto* to compromise study of the historical quality of the *major,* first volume, and even to "equate" the two volumes. I also question the assumption that a dominant purpose in either or both volumes must be discerned other than the general one of writing theological history (*see above,* Ch. I, n. 29), which is indicated by the preface to Luke's Gospel. At the same time, I readily admit that Luke 1,1-4 must somehow serve as the preface both to the Gospel and to its "confirmatory" complementary volume, Acts (cf. W. C. van Unnik, "The 'Book of Acts'—The Confirmation of the Gospel," *NT* 4 [1960] 26-59), if only because *Acts 1,1-2 is not, in form, a historical preface.* It serves rather to allude to the foregoing book with the preface which constitutes an integral part of that book—which is the *major* book, because it is integral in itself and because, without it, the second volume has no theological or historical *point d'appui.* In Acts 1,1-2, the Gospel is referred to in the μέν clause, and Acts itself apparently constitutes the implied δέ clause.

[23] No doubt, close adherence to traditions that Luke received from Mark or from Q dictated this.

In Acts, Luke composes missionary speeches in imitation of the LXX, but with dependence on Hellenistic models and techniques as he creatively adapted these to his own subject-matter, the "holy origin" of the apostolic word; cf. E. Plümacher, *Lukas als hellenistischer Schriftsteller,*78-9, 138-9.

and noble deeds." [24] Accordingly, Dionysius extended his history to include an accurate account of periods untouched by other historians and dealing with the accomplishments of good men in order to provide standards of value and models of conduct for their present and future descendants.[25] Diodorus Siculus declares that the knowledge of history, by raising the hope of immortal glory, prompts leading men (ἡγεμόνας) to attempt the noblest good deeds and, by the fear of everlasting reproach, to deter the wicked from the impulse to do evil.[26] He repeats this theme in similar terms later on in his work.[27] Diodorus of Agyrium discourses at length in a similar vein,[28] and provides a kind of summary of his encomium of history by writing: "Know her by her fruits, and you will find her making for righteousness, denouncing every evil, eulogizing the good, and, in a word, endowing those who study her with the sum of human wisdom." [29] More dryly, but more succinctly, Polybius expressed the value of history by speaking of the knowledge of past events as "the sovereign corrective of human nature." [30]

One must recognize, of course, radical differences between Luke and these pagan authors. Luke does not offer hope for renown among men. Nor does he find a guiding principle for history in Fortune (Polybius) or in a rather impersonal Providence (Diodorus of Agyrium). Nor does he indulge in a moralizing tone either in his preface or by way of making personal comments in the course of his work. A single, possible exception, interesting for its uniqueness, may be found in the parenthetical comment made in 7,29-30.[31] Unlike the pagan historians, Luke personalizes his approach; he addresses his typed readership as an individual, and directs his educative aim to him personally, building upon the religious information which Theophilus already possesses.[32] Nonetheless, he makes use of a form (the historical preface) which orients his reader to a kind of *composition* which that reader must reasonably suppose has a moral dimension, as did other historical works of this period.

Of itself, Luke's personalized approach would not prove the presence of a historical moral in his work. Proximately, it suggests what has been termed Luke's

[24] Dionysius of Halicarnassus, *Roman Antiquities,* I, 6.§5.

[25] Ibid., I, 6. 2-4.

[26] Diodorus Siculus, *Historical Library,* I, 1.5.

[27] Ibid., XI, 1.1.

[28] Diodorus of Agyrium, *Universal History,* I, 1-5.

[29] Ibid., I, 2; trans. by A.J. Toynbee, *Greek Historical Thought. From Homer to the Age of Heraclius* (New York [10]1952) 50.

[30] Polybius, *World. History,* I, 1. Cf. the instructions Polybius gives for the serious student, ibid., IX, 2.

[31] The parenthetical remark seems to be dictated by the need to specify the group targeted in 7,31-35, lest the reader get the impression here that "this (quarrelsome) generation" refers to the people at large.

[32] Whether or not "the *words* of which you have been informed" allude to oral instruction or to what Theophilus has learned from written or oral tradition, Luke surely intends to build upon and further attest the religious information in question.

pastoral-hortatory concern in the narrative. Thus, the reader is expected to learn to apply to himself subsequent accounts of religious attitudes, models of conduct, and the like. Once again, however, Luke's preface supplies the general context of a *type of writing* which itself alerts the reader to perceive a "historical moral" when he is presented with episodes which repeatedly ground inferring it. Given the occurrence within Luke's narrative of certain oustanding historical events like the predicted lot of the nation's capital city and of its people, the "pastoral-hortatory" mode of interpretation will need to be complemented by specifically attending to the "historical moral" of the event. in particular, this will prove necessary insofar as the predictive character of the events in question looks beyond even the horizons of the reader's own cultural and social circumstances to take in, for instance, the perspective of the end of the world. At the same time, one may surmise that the educated, sympathetic reader will be expected reflectively to grasp that moral and its relevance to his own life and culture without being given the author's own didactic reflections. For Luke does not treat his reader condescendingly, nor does he write as a theorist.

Luke does not, however, leave his reader adrift to find his own bearings in the course of the narrative. Subtly, without instructional asides, he conditions him to perceive events in relation to his own world. Luke shows at least a modest effort to "inculturate" the Gospel in a new, Hellenistic environment, and to condition his reader to a personally reflective mode of thinking. It may prove helpful, then, to survey some signs of this effort before proceeding to examine the key texts which are most pertinent to the historical-typological moral.

III. Luke's Conditioning His Reader's Perception

Following the line of inquiry suggested at the close of the preceding chapter, it seems advisable to survey certain ways by which Luke conditions his typed reader to perceive the historical-typological moral included in his narrative. Key texts regarding that moral will deal with Jesus' attitude towards Jerusalem. These texts, however, do not begin to appear until the central third of Luke's Gospel. To defer to that portion of Luke's Gospel study of his conditioning of the reader's perception might distract attention from the matter at hand. Doing so might also fail adequately to situate these texts in the ongoing narrative context. That context consists of the progression of Jesus' prophetic ministry and the main lines of its acceptance or rejection. In dealing with any narrative, particularly one which is cast as a kind of history, the exegete should respect that progression.

Needless to say, only a brief survey can be offered here. Moreover, this survey will cover some features which are not solely or even directly illustrative of Luke's conditioning his reader to perceive a historical-typological moral. On the other hand, this kind of overview may shed light on the way Luke has carried out the educative aim indicated in his preface and thus provide a better framework for understanding Luke's specific concerns with Jerusalem as these emerge in the central and final portions of his Gospel. Two major considerations should suffice: First to be noted (A) are narrative episodes (particularly those betraying Luke's hand) which help orient Luke's reader to personal, cultural assimilation of this Gospel. Second (B), features of the narrative progression of Luke's Gospel emerge which contribute to an understanding of Jesus' prophetic mission, particularly in its context of an ongoing ministry through cities.

A. Narrative Episodes

Luke makes certain editorial changes to adapt his Gospel to his intended audience which are of quite minor importance in themselves, but which nonetheless show some concern for cultural adaptation. For instance, Greek rather than Palestinian buildings are supposed in Luke's describing the tile roof of the house in which the paralytic is forgiven and cured (5,19; cp. Mark 2,4), in depicting the prudent man's work in building his house, sc., with a foundation (6,48; cp. v. 49 and Matt 7,25), and perhaps even in the positioning of the lampstand, sc., in the reception area of a Greek house (8,16; cp. Mark 4,21).[1]

---

[1] Cf. Joachim Jeremias, *Die Gleichnisse Jesu* (Göttingen ⁶1962) 22-3. Jeremias also notes Luke's use of πράκτωρ in 12,58 (*Büttel,* bailiff) — instead of what Matt 5,25 has, sc., ὑπηρέτης, *Synagogendiener;* ibid., 22 n. 2.

Probably to be included among such adaptations is Luke's marked preference for "dinner scenes" as the occasion for conversations entailing different, conflicting points of view (e.g., 5,27-39; 7,36-50; 11,37-54; 14,1-24).[2]

Other redactional changes or original compositions are considerably more pertinent. Two reworkings of episodes are Luke's explanation of the parable of the sower (8,15) and his portrayal of the ἄρχων who addresses Jesus in 18,18 concerning everlasting life. Pertinent, too, is the unique narrative episode of the walk to Emmaus (24,13-35), which is parabolic of a current situation known to the reader (sc., the celebration of the Eucharist). Although the latter passage occurs towards the very end of Luke's narrative, and accordingly after the texts concerning the historical-typological moral, it illustrates Luke's thought-provoking composition, especially in the concluding portion of his Gospel, where the reader has already been conditioned "to think parabolically."

Admittedly, I am about to probe Luke's text for some significantly allusive elements in his way of telling his own story about Jesus and those he taught, with a view to indicating the perception which Luke expects of his reader. Allusions are notoriously elusive if one tries to prove exegetically that the text *demands* such and such an interpretation. Nevertheless, allusions can be grounded with solid probability if one reasonably assumes that the author is writing for an intelligent reader who is expected *to look to the way the story is told,* and to reflect upon it according to the writer's personal interest in effecting a literary and religious perception of his narration. The storyteller functions as a teacher precisely in the way he tells his own tale, whether that tale is not already known or, preferably, if it already is. Some exegetical control, moreover, is provided either from the author's use of a known source or by analogy with other accounts, whether given elsewhere or included in the course of the same author's integrated narrative. Lastly, the more the author respects his audience as he narrates his tale, the less he should be expected intrusively to indicate the conclusions to be drawn. An implicit "Let him who reads understand!" (not unlike Jesus' own: "Let him who has ears to hear, hear!") suffices.

Regarding Luke's interpretation of the parable of the sower, perhaps the most important parable in the synoptic tradition, if only as a programmatic parable concerning the effect of Jesus' teaching, especially regarding his disciples, not a few notable alterations from Mark deserve special attention. Mark first alerts his reader to sudden perils to the seed (cf. εὐθύς in Mark 4,15.16.17) and then to obstacles which aggressively "enter in" (v. 19, εἰπορευόμεναι) to choke it. At the concluding climax, Mark speaks of the miraculous yield among those who hear the word and acknowledge it. Luke, however, presents the successful results of the sowing in qualitative, not quantitative terms, and builds up to these by introducing two patterns which outline a "long term" progression, one doctrinal, the other

---

[2] Cf. X. de Meeus, "Composition de Lc., XIV et genre symposiaque," *ETL* 37 (1961) 847-70; E. Springs Steele, "Luke 11:37-54—A Modified Hellenistic Symposium?" *JBL* 103 (1984) 379-94.

moral in scope. Thus, regarding the first two classes (the seeds sown on the pathway and those on rock, 8,12.13), he introduces and develops the three-stage, doctrinal pattern of hearing — believing — being saved.[3] The first class does not reach even the second stage; the second class does not perdure in that stage. With the third of four classes the pattern shifts to moral conduct: hearing, going on one's way through life, coming to maturity. This group is suffocated en route (as *they* go on their way, πορευόμενοι, contrast Mark 4,19) by the cares, riches, and pleasures of life and does not reach fruition. Luke's climactic, fourth class hears the word "in a noble and good heart," holds it fast, and bears fruit in patient endurance (ὑπομονή, the prosaic, "day-to-day" practical living-out of what is more sprightly expressed as ἐλπίς).

In speaking of the "noble and good heart" (ἐν καρδίᾳ καλῇ καὶ ἀγαθῇ), Luke offers a good example of inculturating into a Hellenistic milieu the notion of receptivity to the Gospel. A reader of Theophilus's assumed background would hardly be insensitive to the Greek ideal of the καλὸς κἀγαθός.[4] The combination of these adjectives regularly suggests the Greek equivalent of what seventeenth to nineteenth century England termed "the gentleman." He was the man endowed with everything: good family background, education, handsome appearance and good manners, wealth without excess, respect from his peers, etc. Using this expression would help Luke bring home to the educated reader the appeal of the Gospel in terms of his reader's own culture. The "noble and good man," however, like the "gentleman," for all his physical, intellectual, and cultural assets, and perhaps because of them, could be a snob. In any event, he would certainly be a member of a distinct, superior social class, and would no doubt be aware of his special status. In alluding to this type, however, Luke effectively factors out elements which would conflict with his understanding of the universal Gospel. For he speaks of an interior disposition of mind (the heart), not of qualities characteristic of social prestige. Also, by employing the phrase of those who hear the word, retain it, and bear fruit with perseverance, he clearly dissociates the seed on good ground from a specific economic or political stratum of society.[5]

---

[3] At the same time, he deliberately avoids the Marcan emphasis on sudden peril by eliminating εὐθύς each of the three times it occurs in Mark 4,15-17.

[4] E. Klostermann, *Das Lukasevangelium* (Tübingen [3]1975) 97, raised the question of an allusion to the Greek concept of καλοκαγαθία; Fitzmyer, *Gospel According to Luke (I-IX)* (Garden City 1981) 714, referring to Grundmann, *TDNT* 3, 540-3, notes Luke's joining the human reaction to God and his promptings to the classic Greek expression of noble generosity. The expression needs to be evaluated further, however, in the light of the intended, typed audience. For Luke's Hellenistic reader, as even a cursory examination of the word groupings under καλοκαγαθ- in Liddell–Scott–Jones, *Greek-English Lexicon* (Oxford 1968) 869 will show, the phrase could hardly be taken in the watered-down sense ascribed to it by I. H. Marshall, *The Gospel of Luke* (Exeter 1978) 327, especially as the climactic conclusion to the explanation of the parable.

[5] Luke's concern to dissociate the idealized, Christian receptivity to the word from the issue of social status may help account also for his insistence on God's special concern for

Luke's modification of the dialogue beginning in Mark 10,17 (Luke 18,18) likewise attests adaptation of the account to the kind of reader typed in his preface. Mark does not call the questioner a young man (as Matt 19,20 does), but he does represent him as a somewhat impetuous person.[6] Luke introduces him as an ἄρχων, for which the best modern equivalent may be "an executive." Be that as it may, he appears to be a man of recognized social position as well as one of considerable wealth.[7] In Luke's account, the man's reaction to Jesus' call to put personal allegiance to him above all his possessions is not depicted as shocked rejection. Although saddened (v. 23), he does not become appalled or gloomy (contrast Mark 10,22) at Jesus' word. Nor does he go away (Mark 10,22). He remains "on stage," apparently for the rest of this scene, and it is directly to him that Jesus presses home the parabolic lesson concerning the obstacle which riches pose to those entering God's kingdom (18,24, unlike Mark 10,23). Thus, Luke's version of the story has more telling personal relevance to the sort of man he has addressed in his preface.

Jesus' teaching in parables challenges discernment not only on the part of Luke's narrated audience, but on that of his reader as well. To some extent, this has been illustrated by the two foregoing texts. Another example, combining narrated introduction and parabolic discourse in Luke 15, further supports this observation and helps one perceive, too, how the whole unit, as narration, functions to stimulate personal appreciation of Jesus' message.

The concise narrative (15,1-3) introducing the sets of parables (the double parable in vv. 4-10 and the main one in vv. 11-32) sets up a triangular relationship which is repeated in the parables. Publicans and sinners (*a*) draw near to hear Jesus (*b*); Pharisees and scribes (*c*) complain about his festive reception of them (*ab*). Obviously, they do not think that such conduct is justified. Jesus addresses those

---

"the poor" (*'ānāwîm*). He must bring his typed audience to realize that God's blessings and concerns are not to be construed in terms of accepted socio-economic structures, but as personal concerns which cut through the latter, culturally-determined framework of human society. In short, Luke's attention to "the poor" is not dictated by an ideological idealization of "poverty," but by his concern for the need of the affluent reader to whom he directs his Gospel to recognize God's way of breaking through human socio-economic structures to deal with human beings on a universal basis. Those who are actually "poor" in Luke's two-class society concretely represent the "mass" of mankind, but they are not presented primarily in the light of their socio-economic status.

[6] Mark 10,17 describes him as προσδραμών (cp. 9,15) and γονυπετήσας (cp. 1,40).

[7] Luke 18,23 describes him as πλούσιος σφόδρα. The characterization of the man as an ἄρχων may be an inference from the man's great wealth, as Creed opines, *The Gospel According to St. Luke* (London [1930] 1965) 225; cf. also Klostermann, *Lukasevangelium,* 183. Even so, why would Luke have made the inference if not for the sake of the reader he has in mind?

Pace G. Schneider, *Das Evangelium nach Lukas Kapitel 11-14* (Würzburg ²1984) 369, Luke does not present the man as the ruler of a synagogue (as in 14,1) or a representative of Jewish *Gesetzfrömmigkeit,* or even as a judge (12,58).

who find fault with his action. Throughout the parables which follow, an evident, unifying motif lies in the invitation to share in the joy over finding what was lost (vv. 6.9.24.32).[8] Corresponding to the narrative element at point *a* are the parabolic elements of the lost sheep, the lost coin, and the prodigal son; to that at point *b,* the man and woman who search for what is lost and the father in the main parable; to that at point *c,* the neighbors invited to share in the finder's happiness and the reluctant elder son.

The major, climactic parable (vv. 11-32) merits special attention. When the younger son has lost his inheritance by his immoral life, he has, in effect, been excommunicated from the family. He is "dead."[9] He can make no claim for help; the best he can hope for is to be hired as a servant. Nevertheless, his father takes the initiative in welcoming him back and juridically restores him (through a kind of investiture[10]) to the status of sonship. The elder son obtains a preliminary explanation from one of the servants, then angrily decides not to enter. In the dialogue which follows, where the father again takes the initiative, the elder son discloses his legalistic attitude as well as his non-recognition of the prodigal as his brother. He complains that he himself has not been rewarded even as a loyal slave might have been,[11] although he has worked like one, and makes quite clear that he does not think that this other son has deserved the reception accorded him. His father replies that the elder son is not in a position to be paid; his father shares everything with him. This one, however, the elder son's brother, was dead and has been brought to life, was lost has been found. Whether or not the elder son will change his mind ("repent") depends upon him. That conclusion the reader must construe. If the elder son does respond positively, he will enter after making his own the father's viewpoint, which amounts to seeing justice not in terms of payment for services rendered but as an expression of love which transcends contractual obligation or claims. If he does not, the feast will go on without him.

---

[8] Cf. C. H. Giblin, "Structural and Theological Considerations on Luke 15," *CBQ* 24 (1962) 15-31, 18-23.

[9] K. H. Rengstorf, *Die Re-Investitur des Verlorenen Sohnes in der Gleichniserzählung Jesu Luk 15,11-32* (AFLNW 137; Cologne 1967) 21-6, 67.

[10] Rengstorf, ibid. The motive for the father's action is, of course his love; cf. Luise Schottroff, "Das Gleichnis vom verlorenen Sohn," *ZTK* 68 (1971) 27-52, 39-44. A juridical context for the manifestation of this love by no means creates an undue tension, especially if one recalls Paul's juridical presentation of God's justice as God's love in the course of the full sweep of his argumentation from Rom 1,16 to 8,39. "Juridical" is not to be identified with "legalistic" (as Luke 15 makes clear in story form, and as Rom 1,16 – 8,39 dialectically, argumentatively demonstrates).

[11] That a kid goat was customarily given to a devoted servant or slave for a private feast with his friends has not, to my knowledge, been documented. It seems, however, to be a quite reasonable inference, especially for what must be supposed to ground the elder son's argument. His father does not reproach him for being unreasonable; rather, he offers his own wider, interpersonal perspective that supposes transcendence of a self-centered, servile mentality.

Although partly intended as a response to the Pharisees and scribes depicted in the opening narrated situation, the parable has a much wider scope. Together with the narrated situation, as word complementing event, it functions as a challenge to the reader's discernment. The reader can hardly fail to place himself somewhere in the picture. Obviously, he is meant to see things from the point of view of Jesus (and, accordingly, that of the father in the major parable). Conceivably, he may find himself in the position of the prodigal, either before or after his rehabilitation. More likely, given the open-ended close of the parable, he is supposed to correct any narrow, self-justifying attitudes like those which characterize the elder son. In any event, however, the reader faced with this narrative of Jesus' actions and words is confronted with a *whole parabolic situation* (the narrated event and the word explaining the event) which provides him with ample food for personal reflection and application.

The walk to Emmaus (24,13-35) also constitutes a parabolic situation. It is meant to prompt the reader to reflect on the meaning of the resurrection as he himself may be expected to share it in the Christian community. The narrative concerns relatively ordinary disciples like Cleopas and his unnamed companion. It is not intended as an apologetic proof of the resurrection,[12] if only because the two disciples bring no new information to the community (cf. v. 24). What they do contribute is the personal report of their experiences on the road and how Jesus was made known to them in the breaking of bread. They have been filled with joy through the Christian interpretation of the Scriptures (vv. 25-27.32), here put on Jesus' lips,[13] and they came to recognize him in the breaking of bread. For the perceptive reader, the story as a whole parabolically suggests the celebration of the Eucharist—in word and sacrament—as the occasion for one's personal participation in the joy of the resurrection.

Thus far, this survey suggests that Luke subtly conditions his reader to appropriate by personal reflection the narrated deeds and words of Jesus. It should not come as a surprise, then, later to find Luke depicting the fate of Jerusalem in such a way as to prompt his reader to seek out and to apply to himself and to his own situation the implications of the narrative.

B. Narrative Progressions

In preparing his reader for Jesus' journey to Jerusalem, Luke takes care to situate the first part of Jesus' ministry mainly in the context of a journey through cities. The city where he grew up, Nazareth, becomes the scene of his inaugural address and the point of departure for his journey elsewhere.[14]

---

[12] Contra R. Bultmann, *History of the Synoptic Tradition* (trans. John Marsh) (Oxford 1963) 286, 288-90, 302.

[13] Cf. Jacques Dupont, "Le pèlerins d'Emmaüs (Luc. XXIV, 13-35)," *Miscellanea Biblica B. Ubach* (ed. Romualdo Ma. Díaz) (Montserrat 1953) 349-74, 357-61.

[14] Cf. U. Busse, *Das Nazareth-Manifest Jesu. Eine Einführung in das lukanische*

Although the initial reaction at Nazareth to Jesus' explanation of his mission seems to be quite positive (4,22), his countrymen's response may best be construed as that of "impressed unbelievers." [15] What is more, their identification of him as Joseph's son, while not hostile (as in Mark's account), but even in accord with the genealogy which Luke has given as Jesus was beginning his public ministry (3,23-38), apparently conveys a sense of self-interest. Since Jesus is known to them as one of their own, the "home town boy" who has become a success, they expect special favors. This attitude does not emerge from their remark in v. 22b, considered by itself, but from Jesus' own remarks which immediately follow it. For, in effect, he reads their thoughts (v. 23).[16] From his point of view, no prophet is acceptable, namely, acceptable *to God,* in his own homeland.[17] The term δεκτός (v. 24) picks up the theme stated in Jesus' sermon that he is to herald the year acceptable to the Lord (v. 19) and serves as the point of reference for the probative examples of the prophets Elijah and Elisha which he proceeds to cite. Not those in Israel, but foreigners were the beneficiaries of their miracles. In particular, Elijah was not "sent" to anyone in his own country (v. 26).[18] Likewise, Jesus' mission, at least insofar as it entails miraculous deeds, will look beyond his own homeland.

The Nazarenes' murderous reaction becomes intelligible in the light of their disappointed self-interest. No doubt, Luke has deliberately exaggerated it (as he has heightened the placement of their city to make plausible their murderous designs in wanting to throw Jesus off the "cliff"). Luke's reason is not difficult to discern in the context of his whole composition. The genuine prophet, who looks to what is acceptable to God, will suffer violence and eventually death at the hands of men, although his death is not "acceptable" (οὐκ ἐνδέχεται) outside of Jerusalem (13,33).

Jesusbild nach Lk 4,16-30 (SBS 91; Stuttgart 1977). Busse also points out Luke's use of Greek historical writing, ibid., 116, cf. 52-62, even in such a detail as Jesus' passing through the crowd (4,30; cf. Dio Chrysostom VI, 60), ibid., 46.

[15] John Nolland, "Impressed Unbelievers as Witnesses to Christ (Luke 4:22a)," *JBL* 98 (1979) 219-229, 225-229.

[16] Luke notes other instances where Jesus adverts to what his hearers think (5,22—without, however, mentioning the inner perception stressed in Mark 2,8, τῷ πνεύματι αὐτοῦ), but with attention to others' inner dispositions, ἐν ταῖς καρδίαις ὑμῶν, 6, 8 (not paralleled in Mark); 7,39-40; 9,47; 11,17. In other cases, "reading of hearts" is not expressed. Nevertheless, Jesus responds to an attitude he detects in another's statement: for example, 14,15-24 (the parable is stated in challenging reply to the complacent attitude platitudinously expressed by one of the guests, 14,15).

[17] Cf. David Hill, "The Rejection at Nazareth," *NT* 13 (1971) 161-180. One should also bear in mind what Jesus later says about the prophet's death, namely, that it is not acceptable (οὐκ ἐνδέχεται), sc., to God, outside of Jerusalem (13,33).

[18] In v. 26, especially, the language (ἐπέμφθη) echoes the theme of prophetic sending (ἀπέσταλκέν με) in Jesus' reading of Scripture concerning the acceptable year of the Lord (vv. 18-19).

Next, in Capernaum, Jesus is received by the people with unqualified enthusiasm. They even want to retain him, to possess him as their own. To account for Jesus' continuance of his journey, Luke places on Jesus' lips a reiterated statement of his prophetic purpose (4,43). Jesus then continues his preaching activity throughout Palestine, mainly in Jewish religious centers (4,43-44).

After the call of the disciples on the Lake of Gennesareth, Jesus' journey through cities continues to occupy Luke's attention (5,19 – not in Mark; note also Luke's omission of the sea in 5,27, and cp. Mark 2,13). Luke expressly notes this urban preaching as part of the context for the widening circle of followers that includes women (8,1) and as the setting for Jesus' teaching in parables (8,4, contrast Mark 4,1). Even in the second of the cycle of three journeys, Luke notes the urban provenance of the Gerasene demoniac (8,27; cp. 8,39), and, in the third, the preaching of the Twelve in villages (9,6 – not in Mark), and the city, Bethsaida (9,10b) as the goal of his retirement with the disciples (not Mark's "deserted spot").[20] The reader cannot fail to get the impression that cities form the major theater of Jesus' contacts with people and their positive or negative responses to him.

In the first third of Luke's account of Jesus' ministry, even conflicts with Jewish religious leaders are handled in a relatively low-keyed manner. The note of rejection or of acid controversy on the part of Jewish leaders, so obtrusive in Luke's Marcan source, becomes remarkably muted, until it is mentioned, almost unexpectedly, in the first passion prediction (9,22), which closely adheres to Mark. Luke even omits Mark 1,22c, in which the crowds speak disparagingly of the scribes. He does not seem to exclude from eventual praise of God (5,26) the temporarily disaffected scribes and Pharisees (5,21) who pack the room in which Jesus has been teaching (5,17). He has Jesus add a wry comment in 5,39, suggesting that his questioners may have to acquire a taste for what they are not accustomed to or initially inclined to accept. Characteristically, Jesus' proof from Scripture as given to his learned objectors calls to their mind a biblical text (6,3: "Have you not read this...?") rather than unmasks their ignorance (as in Mark's "Haven't you

---

[19] "Judea" in v. 44 may refer to a specific region, but it seems preferable to take it in the comprehensive sense of the country of the Jews; cf. Fitzmyer, *Gospel According to Luke (I-IX)*, 557-8; Martin Völkel, "Der Anfang Jesu in Galiläa. Bemerkungen zum Gebrauch und zur Funktion Galiläas in den lukanischen Schriften," *ZNW* 64 (1973) 222-37. 226.

[20] Luke retains mention of a "deserted spot" to explain the lack of provisions (9,12). Apparently, Jesus and the disciples had not yet reached Bethsaida. Nonetheless, the episode is city-oriented.

With the cycle of the three passion-predictions, however, Luke drops mention of Jesus' activity in urban areas (cp. Mark 8,27, "the towns of Caesarea Philippi") in favor of occasions and places for private instruction of the disciples (Luke 9,18.23.43b-44; omission of Mark 9,33).

[21] Cf. Odil Hannes Steck, *Israel und das Gewaltsame Geschick der Propheten. Untersuchungen zur Überlieferung des Deuteronomististischen Geschichtsbildes im Alten Testament, Spätjudentum und Urchristentum* (WMANT 23; Neukirchen-Vluyn 1967) 257-60.

ever read...?" 2,25), and drops a polemic reference to their oppressive application of teaching concerning the sabbath (Mark 2,27). In particular, Luke omits mention of Jesus' anger at the scribes and Pharisees (Mark 3,5; Luke 6,10) and their expressly hateful intent, in league with the Herodians, to kill him (Mark 3,6). Instead, Luke points out their irrationality (ἄνοια, 6,11) and leaves unspecified what they spoke of "doing to Jesus." When proclaiming the beatitudes and woes, Jesus draws attention to the fact that his hearers, as a prophetic people, will have to suffer persecution (6,23.24), but he does not indicate the agents of this persecution (as he will do in a subsequent part of his Gospel, 11,49).

Admittedly, Pharisees and lawyers are singled out for their refusal to accept God's plan for themselves by accepting John's baptism (7,30), and personal controversy with a representative Pharisee is soon sharpened when Jesus addresses his rude host, Simon (7,40-47). By and large, however, throughout Part One of his account of Jesus' public ministry, Luke has toned down Jesus' confrontation with the Pharisees as contained in his Marcan source. He has omitted from this portion of his Gospel the Beelzebul controversy (Mark 3,20-30) and, among other Marcan passages, Jesus' incisive attack on the traditions of the Pharisees and scribes from Jerusalem (Mark 7,1-23) and on the leaven of the Pharisees and of Herod (Mark 8,15).[22]

Furthermore, apart from the "programmatic rejection scene" at Nazareth, Luke recounts in most of Part One no directly unfavorable reaction on the part of the people. Jesus' remark about the centurion's faith is not prejudicial to the inference that he found a favorable response on the part of Israel (7,9).[23] The Galileans are even said to have recognized God's visitation of his people (7,16), and the people as a whole are commended for their contrite reception of John's baptism (7,29). That they are not given the grace to understand the parables (8,9-10)[24] is not an occasion for finding fault with them; for example, with their failure to be converted. Even when foreigners ask him to leave their territory, Luke explains their request as motivated by fear or religious awe at the prodigy (8,37); he levels no condemnation at these pagans. Lastly, although those mourning the death of Jairus's daughter laugh at Jesus, Luke avoids suggesting that Jesus

---

[22] Luke may have omitted some of these passages partly out of preference for the version of them which he found in Q. Nevertheless, in omitting the Marcan version of them, he also restructured his own narrative and altered the general tone of his Gospel vis-à-vis Mark's before Jesus moves towards Jerusalem.

[23] Contrast Matt 8,10b: "From no one have I found in Israel such faith." The pejorative tone in Matthew is no doubt a feature of his own redaction of the non-Marcan source, given his further addition (from Q) in vv. 11-12.

[24] "Understanding the parables," precisely insofar as it involves acquiring a knowledge of the mysteries of God's kingdom (which are not mere "puzzles"), necessarily entails wisdom and practical discernment in applying the teaching to one's own life. A merely intellectual grasp of the "intended point(s)" of tropical speech hardly comprises what the evangelists suppose "understanding the parables" means.

expelled them from the house, even though he takes care to note the restricted audience for the miracle (cp. Luke 8,51-53 with Mark 5,37-39).

Only with the first passion prediction, which specifies the elders, high priests, and scribes as the agents of Jesus' suffering and rejection, do Luke's remarks about Jewish leaders take an ominously decisive turn (9,22). Only in the second prediction is the place for the prophetic fulfillment of Jesus' death and resurrection mentioned, namely, Jerusalem (9,31). Only in the third prediction are his adversaries generalized to include "men" in general (9,44). All three predictions are directed specifically to disciples, as in Mark, but the third is so phrased as to offset the evident acclaim of his deeds on the part of all. Accordingly, it may include a veiled reference to "the people" or "the crowds," notwithstanding the more pronounced emphasis on "authorities" which is here implied by speaking of those into whose hands Jesus will be betrayed.

Thus, Luke has alerted his reader to the focal point of opposition to Jesus: Jerusalem, particularly as involving the elders, high priests, and scribes. Not out of keeping with Lucian's advice that the historian should avoid abrupt transitions,[25] Luke brings to a close the first part of his account of Jesus' public life by announcing for the reader's benefit the movement of subsequent portions of his Gospel. The murderous hostility towards the prophet, first shown on the part of his townspeople in a suggestively programmatic way, will be carried out by religious leaders in Jerusalem.

One may surmise that, to some extent, Luke's avoidance in Part One of virulent opposition to Jesus by the Jewish leaders is correlated to his development of the theme of the kingdom. In Part One, the kingdom seems to be an unmixed blessing. Its temporal polarity, "already,... but not yet fully" remains undeveloped in Jesus' public utterances before Part Two, and so, accordingly, does the theme of decisive judgment connected with the realization of the kingdom. The apparent exception consists of the promise to his followers of a vision of the kingdom for some of them during their lifetime (9,27). These followers, however, notwithstanding the term "all" in 9,23, are those "on stage," namely, the disciples (9,18). The promised vision is the anticipatory one of Jesus in glory, which is dated as occurring a week later (9,28-32). Even this vision, however, conveys no overtones of judgment on Jesus' adversaries or on those of his disciples, like texts which we shall find in Parts Two and Three. Throughout Part One, Luke consciously omits the note of an imminent judgment. He suppresses the programmatic theme of Jesus' preaching of repentance in view of the proximity of the kingdom (Mark 1,14-15). Likewise, he drops Mark's references to a divided kingdom (Mark 3,24),[26] to the mysteries of the kingdom (Luke 8,10) as entailing growth to a judgmental harvest or worldwide consummation (Mark 4,26-29.30-32), and the stern warning about entering the kingdom as an alternative to gehenna (Mark 9,47).

---

[25] Lucian, *How to Write History*, § 55.

[26] True, the kingdom discussed is that of Satan, but Luke intends to go on to discuss antithetically the current anticipation of God's kingdom; cp. 11,17-20.

For Luke, Jesus' preaching of the kingdom in Part One is characterized rather by the message of forgiveness (4,43, picking up 4,18-19), a promise to the poor (6,20),[27] and an announcement of blessing correlated with the ministry of healing exercised both by Jesus himself and by his disciples (9,2.11). Luke even notes Jesus' correction of John's apparent expectation of an imminent judgment (7,18-23; cp. 3,17) by appealing to merciful healing.[28]

With Part Two, however, and the movement towards Jerusalem, the reader can begin to perceive a marked change of tone with regard to the consequences both of not accepting the message of the kingdom and of not accepting Jesus himself. The absence in Part One of condemnatory statements and of the fully eschatological perspective of the kingdom (with its negative aspect of punitive judgment as the alternative) serves to prepare Luke's reader to perceive Jesus' ministry anew. After winning his reader's interest in Jesus' benign work of forgiveness and cures, Luke will give him more sobering food for thought in Jesus' subsequent pronouncements to all his hearers.

---

[27] Although by parallelism with the other beatitudes and by contrast with the woes the word ἐστίν in 6,20 has a future import, the present tense suggests rather a general definition of the disciples' blessedness rather than an effort temporally to determine the realization of the kingdom. The Lucan Gospel does not bring out here the expectation of the eschaton so much as the contrast between one's earthly lot and one's lot after death. Cf. J. Dupont, *Les béatitudes* (3 vols.; Louvain, 1958, 1969, 1973) II, 100-9.

[28] "In effect, his [Jesus'] answer is, 'Yes, I have come, but not in the sense that you mean it, not as a fiery reformer.'" Fitzmyer, *Gospel According to Luke (I-IX)*, 667.

IV. Prospects for Jerusalem in View of Jesus' Journey
(Luke 9,51 – 19,27)

As he opens the central section of his account of Jesus' adult ministry (9,51), Luke announces not only the fuller perspective of Jesus' forthcoming passion—so as to include his ascension,[1] but also his decided movement towards Jerusalem. This portion of his Gospel is not accurately labeled "Luke's Travel Narrative." He has already narrated three journeys of smaller compass which were led by Jesus or enjoined by him.[2] In this large, central portion, moreover, stages of the movement towards Jerusalem are stated perfunctorily,[3] with no clear tracing of a route until the sequence of episodes marking the immediate ascent from Jericho. These, in turn, seem to be noted largely to bring out the temporal proximity of Jesus' movement to Jerusalem. This journey as a whole does not concern Jesus' activity in Perea.[4] In spite of the mention of a Samaritan town at the outset of the journey (9,52) and again in the course of the journey (17,11), it need not be construed even as a journey to Jerusalem routed principally through Samaria. For, besides the mention of Galilee in 17,11,[5] a Galilean perspective to the journey is supposed by Jesus' instructions to the seventy-two (*see below* concerning 10.1.10-16) and suggested by the Pharisees' warnings about Herod (13,31). What does emerge from

---

[1] This term of his journey (ἔξοδος) was adumbrated in 9,31.

[2] Cf. 8,1-21; 8,22-56; 9,1-17; *see above*, p. 2.

[3] Notably at 9,51; 13,22; 17,11; 18,31; or simply as being en route: 9,57; 10,38; 18,35 (to Jericho); 19,1 (through Jericho); 19,11 (near Jerusalem).

[4] Cf. Fitzmyer, *The Gospel According to Luke (I-IX)* (Garden City 1981) 824-5.

[5] The phrase διὰ μέσον Σαμαρείας καὶ Γαλιλαίας is a well-known *crux interpretum*. One or other geographical term (probably the reference to Galilee, which comes second and is "out of order" geographically) may well have been added in view of the following conversion-account of the Samaritan leper; the other nine, presumably, were Galileans. In any event, the order of Samaria and Galilee is surely not what one would expect were Luke trying to indicate a specific route. There is no need to suppose he is as ignorant of geography as Conzelmann would make him. It may suffice to say that Luke is concerned with Jesus' movement towards Jerusalem. He is definitely not in Judean territory (before he comes to Jericho), but is moving about elsewhere in line with his intended, ultimate arrival in Jerusalem.

[6] Although Herod's jurisdiction also covered Perea, Luke does not seem to take note of it (even in 3,1), so he can hardly suppose his reader will assume that that area is intended (the *v. 1.* in 6,17 is unauthentic). He deliberately seems to avoid mentioning the area in directing Jesus towards Jerusalem; cf. Fitzmyer, ibid. [n. 4, *above*].

the regular indications of Jesus' movement towards Jerusalem is the *intended, over-all direction* of his journey, not his itinerary or even his route.[7]

Luke's notation of the direction of Jesus' movements will help account for the way in which he presents Jesus' attitude towards Jerusalem in 9,51b and in 13,31-35. As Luke's narrative stands, Jesus is prophetically headed towards the city. With only two, non-pejorative exceptions (6,17; 5,17), he has not as yet encountered its people or their principal leaders. At the same time, one or both of Jesus' statements about this particular city may have an ominous ring. Another set of texts, regarding the fate of typed cities or of people within them, has an even clearer judgmental tone (10.10-16; 11,29-32; 13,1-5; 19,14.27). This tone, a new aspect of the kingdom-motif, may also partially be accounted for by the concise introduction in 9,50-51.[8] For Luke has there extended the passion-resurrection theme to include Jesus' ascension, his enthronement with the power of judgment.[9]

Both the texts dealing with Jerusalem and those which treat the fate of other cities or of the inhabitants of cities will be discussed as they occur in Luke's narrative. For, even in this loosely-knit central section of his Gospel, something may well be gained from respecting the sequence of relevant passages in the ongoing account.

A. Luke 9,51-55

A few scholars, most recently Craig A. Evans, regard Jesus' "setting his face" in 9,51 as an indication of judgment as well as determination.[10] Evans admits a key argument against his position, namely, that the Lucan "idiom" does not

---

[7] The movement towards Jerusalem differs significantly in this respect from the travel narrative in Acts 27-28. Luke 9,51-19,27, moreover, curiously indicates no precise sequence of "days" except those which are to be taken metaphorically or metahistorically (9,51a; 13,33). The "hours" or other temporal links serve only to tie together certain pericopes (10,21; 11,37; 13,31). Luke shows a recurring interest at times in the size of Jesus' following, especially in 11,29; 12,1; 14,25, but mainly as an occasion for challenging addresses regarding allegiance; he does not develop this feature throughout the journey.

[8] This minimal introduction may suffice. Michi Miyoshi, *Der Anfang des Reiseberichts Lk 9,51-10,24: Eine redaktionsgeschichtliche Untersuchung* (AnBib 60; Rome 1974) takes it as part of a larger introductory passage. If so, however, the latter must be extended to 10,38. For the next indication of movement on the journey (after 9,57) begins with 10,38. What is more, without the inclusion of 10,25-37, the so-called introduction would fail to alert the reader to Jesus' dealings with Jewish authorities, an element of no little importance in the remaining portions of the journey towards Jerusalem.

[9] That the ascension connotes for Luke Jesus' enjoyment of the prerogatives of divine messiahship, including judgment, should be clear from Jesus' reply to the Sanhedrin (22,69—which drops the Marcan indication of the parousia, "coming with the clouds of heaven" in favor of a reference to the ascension, "seated at the right hand ...") and Acts 2,32-36.

[10] C. A. Evans, " 'He Set His Face': A Note on Luke 9,51," *Bib* 63 (1982) 545-8.

contain the preposition ἐπί (with acc.).[11] He tries to lessen the force of the objection by appealing half-heartedly to Ugaritic parallels.[12] More subtly, he rhetorically shifts the sense of middle terms: an option between "towards" or "against" becomes an instance of "dispatch," which becomes "commission to oppose," and then "go with a message of judgment." His procedure certainly looks like exegetical sophistry. Furthermore, the lexicographical issue is not merely the lack of ἐπί (with acc.), but rather the construction of the whole expression: "He set his face to go towards Jerusalem." Luke follows αὐτὸς τὸ πρόσωπον ἐστήρισεν not directly with a preposition but with the articular infinitive indicating purpose (τοῦ πορεύεσθαι, "to journey [onwards]") and then by a prepositional phrase indicating the intended term of this journey, εἰς Ἰερουσαλήμ. Moreover, in specifically explaining the Samaritan town's unreceptive attitude (v. 53), Luke rephrases Jesus' purpose in almost the same words: ὅτι τὸ πρόσωπον αὐτοῦ ἦν πορευόμενον εἰς Ἰερουσαλήμ. If there were a judgmental tone regarding the Jewish capital in Luke's phraseology in v. 51, it would be very strange for Luke immediately to note the Samaritans' hostility and then to repeat practically the very words of v. 51 to explain their hostility to Jesus as he proceeds "against" Jerusalem. In line with Luke's forthright clarity of expression, the text demands and allows for nothing beyond an announcement of Jesus' firm determination[13] to journey towards that city, which has not figured in his journeys before this point.

Besides, to opt for a judgmental overtone in Jesus' setting his face to go towards Jerusalem amounts to reading back into this passage prophecies dictated by events yet to unfold, and smacks of theological determinism. Luke elsewhere gives no indications of judgment without also giving grounds for it in terms of stated, culpable actions. Here, Jesus does not so much as hint of a fault on the part of the people of Jerusalem. Even the manifestly hostile Samaritan village does not incur his ire. As at Nazareth,[14] Jesus moves on to another town. At times, therefore, even an actually belligerent audience does not meet with the threat of judgment. Much less does judgment appear to loom over Jerusalem at this juncture.

---

[11] Ibid., 547. Evans takes as "the Lucan idiom," "to set his face." This begs the question. Is not the prepositional complement an essential part of "the idiom," as contrasted with a mere "phrase"? Cf. *Webster's New Dictionary of Synonyms* (Springfield, MA ⁵1978) 608, "phrase ..."

[12] Ibid., 547.

[13] Cf. Fitzmyer, *Gospel According to Luke (I-IX)* 823, 828.

[14] Here, however, there is no murderous hostility. What is more, the rejection of Jesus is depicted as rejection of him *through those whom he sends* to prepare for him (9,52-53). The identification of Jesus with others, announced to the disciples themselves at the close of Part One (9,46-48) figures more prominently in Part Two (10,1-16; 11,48b-49; 12,8-12).

B. Luke 10,1.10-16

In a suggestively universal perspective, Luke recounts the mission instructions to seventy-two disciples.[15] They are to prepare "every city and place" (10.1) for Jesus' personal coming. Thus, the journey to Jerusalem takes on a kind of typological scope. It prefigures the universal Christian mission after Jesus' ascension[16] as well as preparation for his coming to cities which lie ahead and his ultimate arrival in Jerusalem. The instructions given in vv. 10-11 to this wider circle of disciples include not only the symbolic gesture of their shaking the dust off their feet when they leave a city which does not accept them (cp. 9,5), but also the suggestion of forthcoming judgment in view of the advent of the kingdom (10,11). Similar instructions for the earlier mission of the Twelve in 9,5 spoke vaguely of "witness against them," (ἐπ' αὐτούς), but the mission seems to have met with no actual rejection, considering the Lucan addition in 9,6 (esp. πανταχοῦ). The severity of the later warning and particularly its eschatological consequences are underscored by unfavorably likening the city to pagan Sodom on the day of judgment (10,12).

The woes which Jesus utters against Chorazin and Bethsaida and his apostrophe against Capernaum (10,13-15) do not stand as an interlude between the sending out of the seventy-two and their return.[17] Luke's narrative gives no grounds for retrospective reference to Jesus' own earlier work in Galilee concerning these cities. Nothing has hitherto been said about Chorazin. Bethsaida and Capernaum showed no signs of antipathy towards Jesus in Part One, and, given Jesus' own activity in those cities, are hardly to be inferred as the unnamed cities to which he sent the Twelve. Rather, the address to these cities in 10,13-15 forms part of Jesus' commission to the seventy-two who are to prepare for his own future coming. This conclusion follows from his continued address to these missionaries in v. 16, where he identifies acceptance or rejection of them with acceptance or rejection of himself and of the one who sent him. Such a

---

[15] The number, symbolic of the nations of the world, is based on Gen 10 (70 nations according to the MT; 72 according to the LXX). The better-attested number in Luke is 72, and accords with his general dependence on the LXX.

[16] This observation may be supported by the curious phrasing in 9,51; literally: "when the days of his ascension were being fulfilled." A *twofold* perspective seems to fit here: first, the period of Jesus' earthly life, as he moves towards Jerusalem and the accomplishment of his journey through death-resurrection-ascension; second, the period during which he "is ascended" but has yet to come to every city and place which will have been prepared for his coming, sc., the period of the worldwide mission of the Church. Surely, the perspective of the mission of 72 disciples (10,1) strikes a metageographical and metatemporal note, which is confirmed by the "end-time" perspective that emerges in Part Two both in this connection and in Luke 12 and 17.

[17] As does, for example, the brief passage concerning Herod (9,7-9) in the course of the training exercise for the Twelve.

pronouncement assumes that the seventy-two have not as yet departed. Without indicating an interlude, then, Luke mentions their return in 10,17.

Some of the cities to which the seventy-two are sent may be assumed to be pagan or Samaritan cities, rather than places with a notably or predominantly Jewish population. For the journey to Jerusalem, particularly as it foreshadows a worldwide mission in the days when his ascension was (to be) completed, commences with mention of a non-Jewish town. The comparison with Sodom, therefore, though it types these cities' sinfulness to the point of exaggeration, comes as no great surprise. On the other hand, the cities to which these missionaries are dispatched must also, in accord with vv. 13-15, include Galilean cities and market-towns. Here, the typing of their culpable impenitence or prideful self-assertion becomes quite striking, both on the score of the pagan character of the points of comparison and on the score of the places' size. Tyre and Sidon were major commercial centers of the civilized world and legendary models of worldly concerns, but figure as models of receptivity compared with small market-towns like Chorazin and Bethsaida. As for Capernaum, the largest of the three, but hardly world-renowned, the point of comparison is none other than Babylon, the world-city, represented by its king, according to the text cited (10,15) from Isa 14,11-15. These Galilean cities are addressed in judgmental tones because of Jesus' prophetic vision of their non-acceptance of his emissaries (v. 16).

The manner of typing cities and the populace represented by them should be borne in mind when one confronts Jesus' oracles regarding the fate of Jerusalem itself. For already, in the journey towards Jerusalem, Luke is conditioning his reader to perceive an actual, historical city of his own day on a metahistorical plane, as representing moral wrongdoing in a social dimension, and thus as liable to judgment. Furthermore, the identification of treatment of Jesus' disciples with treatment of Jesus himself reenforces the metahistorical quality of the typological model and renders it applicable to other cities and times.

Jerusalem itself will shortly be addressed in a similarly typological perspective (13,34-35), although as yet without comparison to pagan cities. Before examining that text, however, it seems wise not to neglect intervening passages which reenforce the typological presentation of the judgment motif observed thus far and, at the same time, suggest personal reflection and application on the part of the reader to whom Luke presents Jesus' challenge as a challenge to "this generation."

C. Luke 11,29-32; 13,1-5

In the ongoing journey (10,38 – 13,21), at a stage when crowds increasingly gather about him (11,29a), Jesus perceives an undue interest on their part in seeking a sign. Their interest arose from his exorcism of a deaf mute (11,14b). That

---

[18] Cf. J. M. Creed, *Gospel According to St. Luke* (London [1930] 1965) 162.

miracle prompted some to misconstrue the source of his power, and others to seek an even greater, apocalyptic sign (11,15-16). His reply centered on explaining his miracle as the anticipation of God's kingdom by God-given power (v. 29). He was not an ally of Beelzebul any more than were their own adherents (vv. 17-19), but he, a mightier one, had overcome him, and demanded a thoroughly committed following (vv. 21-23). The pericope (vv. 14-28) closed, in response to a woman's praise of his mother (v. 27), by extolling those who hear God's word and guard it (v. 28), thus preventing a diabolical state worse than what had obtained before the cure (vv. 24-26).[18]

Against the background provided by the foregoing pericope, Jesus goes on to indict the crowd for their preoccupation with a sign (sc., a miracle or heavenly portent). He stresses the need to accept the word, specifically, the sign that calls for repentance, the sign of Jonah. That sign is the prophet himself as the bearer of God's message (vv. 29-30.32b). Jesus, as Son of Man, is to be the sign for this generation. "This generation," of course, stands not only for the men and women living at the time at which Jesus is among them and addresses them, but typologically represents all those of any biologically-determined "generation" who, when confronted with his teaching, look instead for signs and wonders. The sign of Jonah has two eschatological points of reference: its vindication in final judgment and its current presence.

The future tense in 11,30b (ἔσται), especially as used with the "Son of Man," permits the interpretation that Luke is thinking of the resurrection or, more likely, in view of the perspective of general judgment evoked in vv. 31-32, of the final, public reckoning at the parousia.[19] The Matthean version of the sign (Matt 12,38-40, and its parallel in 16,1-4) looks to the resurrection, and was most probably conceived as a "sign of disappearance" as far as the scribes and Pharisees were to be given one.[20]

On the other hand, reference to the current situation as well is by no means to be excluded. Ἔσται can easily refer to the "consequential present," as a proximate verse (11,36) proves. In this event, the future judgment by the Son of Man would be presented as being "in the making." What is more, vv. 29-32 as a whole, particularly as developing the foregoing pericope (vv. 11-28), require, to some extent at least, concern for thr present activity of the Son of Man. For two sets of comparative eschatological judgment (that involving the Queen of the South's "rising up" [ἐγερθήσεται] and the "rising up" [ἀναστήσονται] in a judgmental situation vis-à-vis this generation) are related to what each had heard in their days on earth. The point of each comparison is rendered explicit in the case of the OT examples (hearing Solomon's wisdom; repenting at Jonah's preaching). By

---

[19] Cf. I. H. Marshall, *Gospel of Luke* (Exeter 1978) 485; Marshall admits, however, the sense of a logical future, parallel to δοθήσεται in v. 29; ibid.

[20] C. H. Giblin, "Structural and Thematic Correlations in the Matthean Burial-Resurrection Narrative (Matt. xxvii. 57 – xxviii. 20)," *NTS* 21 (1975-76) 406-20, 415-9.

implication, the generation confronted with "something greater (πλεῖον) than Solomon ... [and] ... than Jonah," namely, the wisdom of Jesus and the preaching of Jesus,[21] is also being confronted in its own time on earth, not afterwards.

The sign of Jonah, therefore, refers to the current prophetic activity of Jesus among men as well as to its future vindication on the day of judgment.[22] His audience, preoccupied with signs rather than concerned with seeking wisdom or responding to preaching that leads to repentance, has its guilt stigmatized by adverse comparison with OT types of a pagan seeker after wisdom and the repentant men of the pagan city, Nineveh. Thus, in yet another way during the course of the journey to Jerusalem, Luke conditions his reader to perceive an immediate judgmental situation (in which Jesus is blaming his unreceptive auditors) in the light of a future one, and this whole complex, in turn, in the light of typological points of reference based on Scripture. The relevance of Jesus' words to the audience he actually addressed is by no means lost. His speaking to them, however, requires a further, metahistorical perspective to be grasped fully and rendered applicable to one's own life by Luke's reader.

* * *

A further stage of Jesus' journey, beginning with a still wider following (12,1), includes among a set of warnings to the crowds (12,54 – 13,9)[23] a development of the prophetic demand for repentance. On information brought at the time at which he is speaking to the crowds (13,1), Jesus draws a double analogy: from the lot of Galileans slain by Pilate and from the fate of those crushed by the tower of Siloam in Jerusalem, to the end which lies in store for the unrepentant (13,1-5). Mercifully, however, he modifies the warning with a parable concerning the unproductive fig tree, which the gardener asks be spared for this season, giving it one last chance to prove productive (13,6-9).

---

[21] The neuter (πλεῖον) may be accounted for by the "abbreviated genitive of comparison," somewhat as in Matt 5,20, sc., "than the wisdom of Solomon, ... than the preaching of Jonah" Cf. Blass–Debrunner–Funk, *A Greek Grammar of the New Testament* (Chicago 1961) § 185 (1).

[22] The temporal aspect of the reference may, after all, not be as important as the Christological assessment that Jesus himself will prove to be a "sign contradicted" (Luke 2,34), which epexegetically (καί) and oracularly explains "the fall and rising (ἀνάστασιν—probably with a pregnant sense) of many in Israel."

[23] The structure of the general context is not haphazard. As crowds of people multiply to the point of trampling one another (12,1a), Jesus first addresses his disciples; they, not the huge crowds, remain his major concern. He then replies to a question from the crowd, expanding his answer with a parable (12,13-21). Once again, he turns to his disciples to continue his discourse (12,22-41). When Peter raises the question regarding Jesus' intended audience (12,41), Jesus replies, in effect, that his words are particularly relevant to disciples, notably the most responsible servant. Lastly, he concludes by addressing the crowds as well and additional remarks they have made (12,54 – 13,9).

What helps in this passage to assess subsequent predictions of the judgment of Jerusalem consists in the thematic background it supplies. The calamities reported provide grounds for a warning directed to those who recounted them and, implicitly, to Luke's reader. The calamities did not occur because those who suffered them were especially sinful—although at least general sinfulness would not unreasonably be assumed.[24] The news of these reported facts,[25] however, becomes the grounds for reflection concerning one's own end if Jesus' religious demands are not met.

The next text to be studied, which occurs in 13,22 – 17,10, mid-way through the journey towards Jerusalem, is the first to be examined thus far which looks to the lot of Jerusalem itself.

D. Luke 13,31-35

Luke 13,31-35 includes one of four texts which Jerome Neyrey has called judgment oracles against Jerusalem.[26] Rather than begin by typing its form or debating Neyrey's basis for classifying it, one would do well to situate the text in its immediately foregoing narrative context. For, in any assessment, a judgment oracle supposes actual conduct and a verdict decided on that basis, a verdict which seems generally to be definitive.[27] Jesus, however, has not as yet exercised any ministry within the city or its immediate environs. Currently, he is still making his way towards it through various other cities and villages (13,22). Apparently, these

---

[24] Whether personal sinfulness is assumed to be the *cause* of the calamity is quite another matter. It need not be assumed, much less should it be supposed to have been taught by Jesus or affirmed by him in these analogies concerning the slain Galileans and the men dwelling in Jerusalem. Jesus might well be taking as background for his illustration certain popular assumptions (as, for instance, in Luke 16,22-29).

[25] The historical basis for Pilate's slaying the Galileans is seriously questioned by Lloyd Gaston, *No Stone on Another* (NTS 23; Leiden 1970) 341-2, although he argues mainly from the silence of Josephus, *Antiquities,* XVIII. 55-89, and suggests adaptation of a story concerning Archelaus; cf. Josephus, *Jewish War,* II. 13; *Antiquities* XVII. 216. I. H. Marshall, *Gospel of Luke,* 552-3, following Blinzler, holds that the episode may well be historical.

[26] Jerome Neyrey, "Jesus' Address to the Women of Jerusalem (Luke 23. 27-31)—A Prophetic Judgment Oracle," *NTS* 29 (1983) 74-80, 83.

[27] Admittedly, a *threat* of judgment, allowing for the possibility of conversion in a covenant-context, may be expressed quite strongly, especially if the covenant has indeed been broken; cf. Julien Harvey, *Le Plaidoyer prophétique contre Israël après la rupture de l'Alliance* (Studia 22; Bruges 1967) 53-5, 24. Harvey's study, however, leaves one perplexed concerning the judgment oracle proper and as part of the *rîb* and / or "prophetic lawsuit" (which he seems to use as the equivalent of the *rîb* or as a wider context for it). The use of the "umbrella term," "prophetic lawsuit," has been seriously questioned by Michael de Roche, "Yahweh's *rîb* Against Israel: A Reassessment of the So-Called 'Prophetic Lawsuit' in the Preexilic Prophets," *JBL* 102 (1983) 563-74, 569, 571.

are not Judean towns, but Galilean towns or Jewish centers in an area of Herod's jurisdiction. For, in his words concerning the narrow gate to salvation and the decisive time of its being closed, Jesus warns his audience of being excluded from the company of the patriarchs and all the prophets, and of the paradoxical entry of others into God's kingdom (13,23-30). Certain Pharisees alert him "at that time" concerning Herod's desire to kill him (13,31). Their motives are not impugned, although, judging by Luke's presentation of Herod's attitude elsewhere in the Gospel (9,7-9; 23,6-15), their report may be false or mistaken, and, if one takes a cynical view, they may be trying to force Jesus out of the territory.

In reply, Jesus gives them a riddle for the foxy king and prophetically indicates Jerusalem as the term of his ongoing but brief journey [28] and the only acceptable place of his death. He then proceeds to apostrophize Jerusalem itself (vv. 34-35).

Although later texts in Luke's Gospel, namely, Jesus' words to the city in 19,41-44 and to the daughters of Jerusalem in 23,28-31, may admit being classified as judgment oracles, this one (13,34-35) does not seem to lend itself to such labeling. In any event, it will be shown to have more striking modifications, particularly the prospect of a change of heart which may avert forthcoming doom. This motif of intended repentance, as we have seen in discussing previous passages, expecially within the narrative of Jesus' major journey (9,51 to this point), should give pause to one who readily concludes from 13,34-35 that Jesus condemns Jerusalem in advance of his arrival there. The passage may better be construed as a "case he has against the city," sufficiently grounded in his own prophetic work in the light of biblical patterns, and, accordingly, as an instance of the *rîb* pattern, but not as a definitive, judgment oracle.

Appeal to the form of judgment oracle demands close attention to a frequently-used OT form which Neyrey does not try sufficiently to distinguish from the *rîb*-pattern.[29] One need not, of course, assume that Luke consciously distinguished between these literary forms, or that he was aware of them as "literary forms." Nevertheless, for Luke and/or his sources, there was ample biblical material which presented God's verdict against individuals or against the people, and for his stating his case against them. More careful attention on the part of the exegete to the differences between these modes of address can at least help to clarify the differences that can be discerned in the Lucan texts which approximate OT types of utterance, as he presents them in the context of his narrative concerning Jesus' journey to Jerusalem and his ministry there.

---

[28] As Flender points out, the duplicated logion (vv. 32b, 33a) is intelligible in the light of the Lucan antithesis between miracle and suffering. "Jesus' activity first takes the form of exorcism and healings, then becomes the path to suffering and death. Both are appointed by God and for fixed periods of time (to-day, to-morrow, ...), though these are not to be measured by human standards..." Helmut Flender, *St. Luke, Theologian of Redemptive History*. Trans. R. H. and I. Fuller. (Philadelphia 1967) 32, n. 3.

[29] Neyrey, "Jesus' Address to the Women of Jerusalem," 78, 80.

In his classic study of the OT judgment oracle, Claus Westermann distinguished between judgment oracles which were directed towards individuals and those which were directed to a people, especially Israel.[30] The former, illustrated especially by Amos 7,6-17; 1 Kgs 21,17-19; 2 Kgs 1,3-4,[31] contain a commission to the messenger or a call for attention, followed by the accusation, the messenger-formula, and the announcement of punishment. This type of oracle, restricted to the historical books, is replaced in the writing prophets by a form which is directed to the people and expressed with more literary skill. The main examples, Amos 4,1-3; Hos 2,7-9; Isa 8,5-8; 30,12-16; Mic 3,1-4,[32] follow the same essential lines, but with amplifications. The pattern consists of grounds for the accusation (first, the accusation, then an expansion), the messenger formula (sometimes omitted), and the announcement of judgment (first, God's intervention, then an expansion, bringing out the consequences of this intervention). In clarifying these elements, Westermann goes on to point out that the *order* of the key elements (grounds for the accusation and the announcement of judgment) is sometimes inverted in the oracles directed against the people. This is the case in Isa 3,1-11; Amos 9,8-10; Jer 2,26-28, and elsewhere.[33]

All the instances of the judgment oracle which Neyrey asserts are to be found in Luke (13,34-35; 19,41-44; 21,20-24; 23,27-31)[34] initially seem to fall under the pattern of the judgment oracle against the nations, with an acceptable variation of the order of the announcement of judgment in the last three cases. In Luke 13,34-35, whatever note of judgment one may detect comes last, in an order which is more usual in the OT texts, but which is singular in Luke.

Before discussing further Luke 13,34-35, it is necessary to point out that the instances of the judgment oracle cited by Westermann regularly convey the message of a decided, forthcoming event.[35] Even if conversion may ultimately be intended, the note of the OT judgmental oracle is not conditional. Furthermore, the judgment oracle is not to be confused with the *rîb*-pattern, although the *rîb* moves logically in the direction of the final verdict in the case, and therefore in the direction of divine judgment, so that an oracle of judgment may sometimes appear as the conclusion of the *rîb*.[36] The *rîb* itself, however, is an altercation, the formal beginning or the pursuance of a judicial process, not specifically a declaration of

---

[30] Claus Westermann, *Grundformen Prophetischer Rede* (BEvT 31; Munich 1960) 93-119, 120-142.

[31] Westermann, ibid., 39.

[32] Westermann, ibid., 124-125.

[33] Westermann, ibid., 127.

[34] Neyrey, "Jesus' Address to the Women of Jerusalem," 83.

[35] He allows for some exceptions, *Grundformen Prophetischer Rede,* 146-7.

[36] Westermann, *Grundformen Prophetischer Rede,* 144, admits that these are sometimes closely joined. As Julien Harvey observes, however, the *rîb* does not generally end with a condemnation, but with threats, and one group ends not with threats but with the obligation to fulfill one's duty and to change one's conduct if catastrophe is to be avoided. *Le Plaidoyer prophétique contre Israël après la rupture de l'Alliance. Étude d'une formule littéraire de l'ancien Testament* (Studia 22; Bruges 1967) 24.

punitive judgment. Closer scrutiny of the form of Luke 13,34-35 may incline us to conclude that the passage is a prophetic altercation with Jerusalem rather than a judgment against the city, and that it highlights a warning intended for the city's conversion.

The phraseology of Jesus' address to Jerusalem, which both Luke (13,34-35) and Matthew (23,37-39) have derived from Q, remains remarkably similar in both evangelists. Minor editorial revisions on the part of each of them may be impossible to determine by themselves. What emerge as the more important divergences can better be discerned in the evangelist in question. These divergences, in turn, require watching the progression of thought in the passage.

Matthew employs the text immediately to conclude Jesus' teaching in the temple (cf. Matt 24, 1, καὶ ἐξελθών) and his warning of judgment against the wicked generation typed by scribes and Pharisees (23,13-36).[37] Luke, on the other hand, situates the passage within the context of his major journey narrative and provides a redactional setting in 13,31 ("at that time") to the foregoing, conjoined text regarding the end of Jesus' journey (vv. 31-33). Shortly before (v. 22), Luke has made another redactional notation regarding the Jerusalem-oriented journey through towns and villages.[38]

Although vv. 33-35 are often called a lament,[39] they are phrased more as a complaint directed against the city addressed. The passage does not appeal to the Lord for compassion in one's recognized, deplorably miserable state, much less with a call to repentance for admitted sins, as seems regularly to obtain in the case of a lament.[40] Two major points may be discerned in the formulation of the address: the complaint, along with the opening address to the city (v. 34); the consequences of the city's non-receptivity as indicated by the complaint (v. 35).

The repetitious address, "Jerusalem, Jerusalem," seems to be peculiar to no specific form, but imparts to the address as a whole a special earnestness.[41] The city is first indicted on the count of an assumedly earned reputation as the murderess of prophets sent to her. The indictment is phrased in a distych characterized by synthetic parallelism, but highlighting the notion of the city's rejection of those commissioned by God (v. 34a):

---

[37] Accordingly, ἀπ' ἄρτι, which does not appear in Luke's account, may well be Matthew's addition (23,39a).

[38] Thus, the link between vv. 34-35 and the preceding entails more than a mere catch-word, as I. H. Marshall supposes, *Gospel of Luke,* 573.

[39] Cf. H. van der Kwaak, "Die Klage über Jerusalem (Mt 23,37-39)," *NT* 8 (1966) 156-170. He proceeds to treat the text in Matthew, however, and its Lucan parallel, as a word of judgment; ibid., 157-8 and 157 n. 5.

[40] Cf. Herbert Haag, *Bibel-Lexikon* (Einsiedeln ²1968) 958.

[41] Cf. "Simon, Simon" in the serious warning given to that apostle and others (Luke 22,31); "Lord, Lord," as a professedly earnest, but merely verbal formula of recognition (6,46); and ἐπιστάτα, ἐπιστάτα in an urgent appeal for Jesus' help (8,24).

ἡ ἀποκτείνουσα τοὺς προφήτας
καὶ λιθοβολοῦσα τοὺς ἀπεσταλμένους πρὸς αὐτήν.

From this general indictment, Jesus moves on to express his own frequent desire and its frustration. Here, the basic tension lies between what he has often wanted and what they have not wanted (aor. of θέλειν). Somewhat as in 22,15, where Jesus states an earnest desire to eat the passover with his disciples before he suffers, there occurs no previous indication of an earnest desire on his part except for the prophetic concern indicated matter-of-factly in the foregoing narrative (for 22,15, cf. 22,1-13; for 13,34b, cf. 9,51; 13,32-33). With the image of the mother-bird and a nesting brood, rather than just a gathering of her various (errant) chicks, Luke may be stressing the notion of personal intimacy.[42] With the aor. ἐπισυνάξαι rather than the repeated pres. ind. ἐπισυνάγει (Matt 23,37) he may be underscoring the same image of gathering Jerusalem's children into a protected nest rather than be adverting to an ongoing process. Be that as it may, the basic point is that Jesus' parental, protective concern has gone unrequited (καὶ οὐκ ἠθελήσατε both in Matt and in Luke).

In Matthew's account, the basis for the refusal finds at least some explanation in the foregoing context of controversies with religious leaders (Matt 21, 23 – 23,36), most notably in their exemplification of the attitudes of those who killed the prophets (23,29-31). In Luke's placement of the complaint, on the other hand, the foregoing narrative (even 11,37-53, on which Matthew drew for 23,13.25-36) has offered no basis for construing a negative attitude evinced towards Jesus by the Jerusalemites, even by their leaders.[43] For Luke, the basis for Jerusalem's "not wanting" what Jesus has often desired appears to be rooted in this passage itself, that is, in the *city's typed reputation* as non-receptive to the prophets to the point of being murderously hostile to them (vv. 33a, 33b). Thus, Jesus' complaint, as given by Luke, does not really fault Jerusalem for personal animosity towards Jesus himself, but faults the city for its historical character as a city inimical to prophets. Its reaction to Jesus may well prove to fit into that typed pattern of activity, but it is not the precise point at issue in Luke's recounting Jesus' complaint en route to the city. Rather, Luke is alerting his reader to the kind of place this is towards which Jesus is moving, and to the character of a city portrayed in such a way as to place it above and beyond the context of one, specific, historical occurrence of resistance to the prophetic emissary.

The consequences of the city's non-receptivity to prophets, and therefore its assumed antipathy to Jesus himself, are then stated in v. 35. Their house is left to

---

[42] Cf. Francis D. Weinert, "Luke, The Temple and Jesus' Saying about Jerusalem's Abandoned House (Luke 13:34-35)," *CBQ* 44 (1982) 68-76, 72.

[43] The only possible exception would be some of the Pharisees and lawyers mentioned in 5,17-26; yet even these, who must have been the majority in the room (contrast the Marcan scene) should not be excluded from the universally favorable reaction described in 5,26.

them. The present tense may be construed as futuristic.[44] Nevertheless, insistence on the present tense as describing the current state of affairs makes better sense both in view of the city's attitude as described in v. 34 and in view of a possible, forthcoming change as indicated in v. 35b (*see below*). Most probably, as argued by F. D. Weinert and others,[45] "your house" in Luke's use of the text does not refer to the temple, but to the leadership of Jerusalem and to the city at large, under the image of its own dwelling-place.[46] Even express mention of desolation by the addition of the adjective ἔρημος in some MSS need not be taken to refer to the city's physical destruction; it may be construed as the city's being bereft of Jesus' own presence, an explanation dictated by a perceived reference to Jer 22,5 (εἰς ἐρήμωσιν). Although Luke later recounts Jesus' prediction of the destruction of the temple, he then does so in a clearly future perspective (cf. tenses in 21,5-6). What is more, as Jesus' discourse continues, he does not consider the fate of that particular building apart from that of the city as a whole.

The case may well differ in Matthew's use of this Q passage. For Matthew employs it to describe Jesus' dramatic departure from the temple and, later on in Matthew, Jesus adverts both to the destruction of the temple and to its profanation (Matt 24,2.15). The different viewpoints of each synoptic author are brought out in the amplification of the consequences for the abandonment of the house (Luke 13,35b; Matt 23,39).

Matthew provides a clear-cut explanatory clause, following up ἰδού with γάρ and marking the present as the decisive point (ἀπ' ἄρτι) for the Lord's departure from the temple. NA^{26} brackets the transitional δέ in Luke's text. The omission would well accord with Lucan usage, especially of Q-material.[47] If, on the other hand, δέ is read as part of the text, it may be taken either as slightly adversative or as explicative, but without much perceptible difference of meaning.[48] For, in any event, v. 35b advances the thought of Jerusalem's being abandoned to herself until Jesus is "seen," that is, recognized,[49] which will occur only when she herself welcomes him as God's emissary, that is (cf. the citation of Ps 117,26), as her savior. Short of a voiced change of attitude on her part, the murderess of prophets who shows no inclination to receive Jesus will remain bereft of his parental concern. This bereavement, whether perceived or not, consists not in the physical

---

[44] Blass–Debrunner–Funk, *A Greek Grammar of the New Testament,* § 323 (1).

[45] F. Weinert, "Luke, The Temple and Jesus' Saying about Jerusalem's Abandoned House," 75-6; Luke rarely employs οἶκος to refer to the temple, and when he does, he tends to identify that place as belonging to God.

[46] Weinert, ibid.; cf. Jer 22,1-9.

[47] Cf. 7,9.28; 10,12; 11,8; 15,7.10; and also 18,8; 19,26.40.

[48] Taken as adversative, the sense would be that the situation will not change until ...; as explicative, the sense is that the situation will perdure until ...

[49] The term "see" in prophetic context like this apparently is intended to convey more than the notion of physical contact. The moment of "seeing" suggests the context of a revelation—whether for weal or woe, for salvation or for judgment, as the case may be; a time for momentous recognition (cf. Luke 3,6; 9,27; 13,28; 21,27; Mark 14,62).

destruction of Jerusalem but rather in the state of affairs made clear by the whole of v. 35.

A final point demanding some attention is the phraseology of the temporal clause in Matt 23,39 and Luke 13,35b. Matthew's ἕως ἄν + subj. looks like his adaptation of whatever the source may have had.[50] The phraseology of the *lectio difficilior* in Luke 13,35b, ἕως ἥξει ὅτε + subj. may have been retained, if not introduced, by Luke himself. It is not redundant. The more difficult, longer reading makes surprisingly good sense when the Lucan passage is judged as part and parcel of his whole narrative.[51] Thus: "You shall not see me until the time will come (fut. ind.) when you *may / should* say (subj., dependent on ἕως)..." As Jesus moves towards Jerusalem, his arrival there figures as the actual time of a possible acclamation, certainly an intended one, as the city's messianic savior. When Jesus does reach the city, however, only his disciples voice this acclamation (19,37-40). The people of Jerusalem are silent. He then weeps over the city and declares its fate. Even if ἥξει ὅτε is not read in v. 35b, the subjunctive after ἕως would sufficiently convey the sense of Jesus' not being seen until an *intended* recognition is voiced by the Jerusalemites.[52] As events prove, this does not take place.

The apostrophe to Jerusalem, then, as given by Luke, points up the historical background of its rejection of the prophets rather than its expressed hostility towards Jesus. Jesus' own concern for the city has not been reciprocated by an interest on its own part which has altered its historical reputation. Accordingly, the Jerusalemites are left to themselves, in a self-chosen state of "abandonment." The consequences of this situation are underlined in v. 35b by the prospect of their continuance with regard to Jesus himself until, as he optimistically intends, they may recognize him as their savior. The city is not judged. Its fate is not sealed or lamented, much less is its destruction envisaged at this point of the story. In Jesus' complaint concerning its historical hostility to the prophets, including its non-receptivity of his own concerns for its welfare, the prospect of conversion remains open, even for the city as a whole.

E. Luke 17,37; 19,11-27

The two closing portions (17,11 – 18,30 and 18,31 – 19,27) of the journey towards Jerusalem may contain texts relevant to the theme of the destruction of the city. Two texts, at least, have received some attention from scholars in this connection.

---

[50] Cf. C. H. Giblin, "Theological Perspective and Matthew 10:23b," *TS* 29 (1968) 637-61, 638 n. 3a, 646 n. 22.

[51] Ἥξει ὅτε introduces a nuance, not a scribal conflation; the nuance is not likely to have been a scribal addition.

[52] The note of intention is grounded in the subj., εἴπητε (cp. Luke 12,36, πότε ἀναλύσῃ; Zerwick–Smith, *Biblical Greek* [Rome 1963] § 349).

L. Gaston, *No Stone on Another* (Leiden 1970) 347, ignoring the narrative context, speaks of Israel's not experiencing the parousia until they repent.

Lloyd Gaston detects some allusion to the destruction of Jerusalem in the mention of vultures/eagles (ἀετοί), as alluding to Roman armed forces, in 17,37.[53] Gaston's exegesis can be faulted from the start on the score that he is concerned primarily with supporting the theory of Proto-Luke and with offering an exegesis of that hypothetical document[54] rather than with providing an exegesis for the composition which Luke has actually given us.[55] In the final analysis, the exegetical explanation must focus on what Luke reasonably expected his intended reader to perceive as he reads the narrative which Luke worked out for him.

Furthermore, Luke 17,20–18,8 contains an eschatological discourse addressed to disciples (beginning in 17,20) which stresses the sudden and unexpected coming of the Son of Man. At one point (17,37), when the disciples ask where the survivor will be left, Jesus answers, parabolically, by speaking of where the vultures (ἀετοί) are gathered. His response thus clarifies "being left" as the situation from which those "taken up" (παραλημφθήσεται) are preserved.[56] Granted ἀετοί can mean "eagles" as well as "vultures," the context of this discourse provides no basis for construing v. 37 as referring to the destruction of Jerusalem by Roman legionaries. The tone throughout the discourse is that of private exhortation to the disciples in view of the consummation of Jesus' own passion.[57] What is more, throughout the discourse, the point of crisis is not developed spatially, but temporally (cf. the references to "day[s]" in 17.22.24.26 (bis).27.28.29.30.31). The place of the climactic event, although pursued by imperceptive disciples in v. 37a, is expressly not defined spatially (as "here" or "there," cf. v. 23). Indeed, in the most proximate point of reference for the disciples' question, Jesus has been speaking not of place, but of time (cf. "on this night," v. 34a). After answering the disciples' query concerning place, but only to clarify the meaning of "being taken up" and of "being left," Jesus concludes with a parable concerning constant, unceasing prayer, a swift response to it, and the need for faith at the decisive time of his coming.

* * *

A second text, which concludes the journey to Jerusalem (19,11-27) and refers to a nobleman's hostile citizens, elicits little interest from Gaston.[58] This element

---

[53] L. Gaston. ibid., 352-3.

[54] Ibid., 355, and 244-365 passim.

[55] Cf. esp. 17,24 and the scope of the examples in vv. 26-35; in 12,35-46, on the other hand, the stress lies on preparedness for the unknown day or hour.

[56] Cf. W. Grundmann, Das Evangelium nach Lukas (THKNT 3; Berlin ⁹1981) 345.

[57] Reference to Jesus' own passion appears (12,50; 17,25) in both "eschatological discourses" (12,1–13,9; 17,20–18,8) prior to Jesus' arrival in Jerusalem, but is not mentioned in the third (21,5-36). See below, however, on 21,22 (pp. 88-89), where mention of "fulfillment of all that has been written" may allude to his passion.

[58] L. Gaston judges that the text was already allegorically interpreted in Proto-Luke

in the parable of the pounds merits some attention, however, partly because, in the course of Luke's narrative, the parable finally clarifies the temporal aspect of the kingdom motif just before Jesus' immediate approach to Jerusalem, and partly because these citizens are contradistinguished from the nobleman's servants.

The crowds following Jesus through Jericho constitute basically a Jewish throng: the blind man acclaims him as David's son (18,38-39); the entire people (λαός) gives glory to God at his cure (18,43); Zacchaeus, too (αὐτός), is a son of Abraham (18,9). The crowd expects God's kingly rule (sc., on earth) to be made manifest upon Jesus' arrival in Jerusalem (19,11). Probably they do so because they have misunderstood Jesus' announcement of "salvation this day to this (Zacchaeus's) house." As in the case of Zacchaeus, however, salvation for the city will be determined by personal interest and by practical expression of conversion for those who encounter Jesus. In addition, God's kingly rule will occur fully only with a final reckoning, as the parable intentionally makes clear. Future judgment will touch the nobleman's unproductive servants, but will be even more severe for the citizens who militantly rejected him in the course of his acquisition of kingly power (19,14.27).

That these citizens are meant to stand precisely for the Jerusalemites seems to be an unwarranted inference at this point of the narrative. For, again, no militant hostility on their part towards Jesus has as yet appeared, much less a rejection of him as king. That precise aspect of rejection, and then on the part of the Jewish leadership rather than on that of the people as a whole, comes mainly with Jesus' crucifixion (cf. 23,36-48). Nevertheless, the *prophetic warning* conveyed by this element in the parable sounds foreboding. Future weal or woe will be determined by the reception accorded or refused the prince even before his actual exercise of royal power. The time for that initial test will begin with the very next episode, the opening episode of Part Three of Luke's account of the public life (19,28-44).

Throughout Part Two, at most three texts have emerged which disclose Jesus' attitude towards Jerusalem, although they seem to be strategically placed in the framework of the journey towards that city. The first occurred at the very beginning, and indicated Jesus' determined goal without judgmental overtones. The second, in the middle, highlighted his forthcoming death in Jerusalem and his controversy with that city, murderess of prophets, but hopefully left open the prospects for expected recognition. The third, at the very end, included a general but ominous prophetic warning about the fate of the nobleman's citizens once he accedes to kingly power. In the course of the narrative, Luke also markedly typed cities and / or people's attitudes so that their moral fault of not recognizing him on his own terms appears in a metahistorical perspective applicable to the sensitive reader. Luke does not narrate "for the record" an account of days long past. The

---

and did not form a part of the direct proclamation to Israel, which he holds is represented by Proto-Luke, *No Stone on Another*, 355. The admission weakens his thesis, for the allusion would hardly have been left unexploited if Proto-Luke had been concerned with making a polemic issue of the fate of the city.

generation to which Jesus spoke is addressed still. Lastly, the identification of the response to Jesus' emissaries and to himself with consequences for the judgment of typed cities has also been made plain to see. It is not unlikely that Part Three of Luke's Gospel will help explicate and even integrate these elements contained in the foregoing portion of his Gospel narrative, which has already conditioned his reader to perceive them.

V. Jesus' Immediate Approach to Jerusalem (Luke 19,28-44)

Preceding Jesus' entry into the temple (19,45), Luke announces for the last time (19,28) Jesus' ascent to Jerusalem. He follows this announcement with a three-stage description of Jesus' drawing near (ἐγγίζειν, vv. 29.37.41).[1] The first stage deals with Jesus' appropriation of a colt, and a kind of enthronement by his disciples (vv. 29-34, 35-36). The second stage depicts messianic acclamation by his disciples and Jesus' response to an objection to their conduct voiced by some of the Pharisees from the crowd (vv. 37-38, 39-40). The third stage consists of Jesus' poignant weeping over the city as he beholds it (vv. 41-44).

For the first two stages of Jesus' approach, Luke employs Mark, although, as we shall see, he makes a number of important changes, particularly regarding the identity of those who acclaimed Jesus and the scope of their acclamation. In assessing these alterations, one should bear in mind the likelihood that a given author should be expected to depart more and more from even his major source as he moves towards the climax of his own distinctive account. In short, where a passage in Luke's Jerusalem narrative can plausibly be explained as a rewriting of Mark, no further source need be posited.[2] With regard to the last portion (vv. 39-40) of the second stage and the whole of the third stage (vv. 41-44), determination of a source becomes difficult. Whether Luke composed these verses or made use of a preexisting block of material, as Grundmann thinks,[3] does not

---

[1] The second stage of the division is not reflected by the paragraphing of NA^{26} and seems to have been overlooked by many commentators, e.g., Marshall, Fitzmyer, Creed, G. Schneider. Grundmann, however, does note it, *Das Evangelium nach Lukas* (THKNT 3; Berlin [9]1981) 367. Moreover, it seems required by a study of Luke's relationship to Mark at this point. Luke changes Mark's pl. to the sg. in 19,29 to put Jesus clearly at the head of the line of march, and his additions at the beginning of vv. 37 and 41 echo this interest.

[2] Appropriately, one may apply Occam's razor (*entia non multiplicanda sunt sine necessitate*) to theories like Proto-Luke. Luke surely used sources (notably Mark, Q, and items here and there often vaguely termed "L"), but he does not compose in the manner of a bookish compiler of documents. It is reasonable to suppose that, as an author like Luke progressively develops his *own* story, albeit using Mark and other sources, he progressively becomes committed to freer redactional activity as demanded by the inner coherence of his own tale. Hence, one should expect greater divergences from the author's sources as the author's own story enters its climactic phase.

Accordingly, I am not convinced by Hermann Patsch's argument for a special Lucan source here, "Der Einzug Jesu in Jerusalem. Ein historischer Versuch," *ZTK* 68 (1971) 1-26, 7,10.

[3] Grundmann, *Das Evangelium nach Lukas,* 367. But he thinks that Luke added τῶν Φαρισαίων in v. 39.

notably affect their interpretation. For these verses certainly form an integral part of Luke's version of Jesus' approach to the city, and should be intelligible to the reader from the course of the narrative. Indeed, they form its climax. I prefer to regard them as Luke's own composition.[4] Each of the preceding stages of Jesus' approach builds towards the third.

A. Introduction and First Stage

The introductory announcement (v. 28) stands as a kind of new introduction.[5] In 9,51, Jesus had set his face to journey towards Jerusalem. At this point, unlike Mark 11,1, which employs the plural of ἐγγίζειν, Luke notes Jesus' going on his journey (ἐπορεύετο) at the head of the group (ἔμπροσθεν).[6] Apparently, he has transposed and rewritten Mark 10,32. What is more, he begins this announcement with a phrase (καὶ εἰπὼν ταῦτα) which suggests that the action which follows figures as a dramatic illustration and conclusion of his teaching concerning the coming of the kingdom, notably the sharp distinction between the nobleman's servants and his hostile citizens (19,11-27). One need not expect exact correspondence between the parable and the events which follow. Suffice it to note that the approach to Jerusalem and Jesus' entry into the temple will not be presented as the advent of the kingdom, and that the citizens of the king acclaimed by his disciples, who prepare for his entry, will prove not to share in acclaiming him as they should.

Altering the Marcan plural (Mark 11,1) to the singular (v. 29), in line with his sharper focus on Jesus' own determination in moving towards the city, Luke proceeds to the first stage of Jesus' approach by way of Mount Olivet. Bethphage may well be a district marking the proximate limits of Jerusalem, not just a village.[7] In any event, Bethany, the place of Jesus' eventual departure (24,50-51), which is certainly a village, stands out as the more important place in Luke's narrative as a whole, and is probably the town to which the disciples were sent (v. 30). Interestingly, even in mentioning this town, Luke maintains the perspective of

---

[4] Klostermann, *Das Lukasevangelium* (HNT 5; Tübingen [²1929] ³1975) 190, offers the option of an old Aramaic source (Wellhausen, Bultmann) or Luke's own invention (Loisy). Currently, commentators in general suppose some source for alleged non-Lucan expressions here or there. However Luke's final composition here emerged, it is definitely well-integrated into the whole movement of Jesus' approach to the city and is exceptionally poignant (an aspect of what Klostermann calls *Prophetenschmerz*).

[5] E. Klostermann, *Das Lukasevangelium* (HNT 5; Tübingen [²1929] ³1975) 189.

[6] Klostermann, ibid., notes that this means "before (them)," not, as in Luke 19,4, "onwards, ahead"—or, more exactly (εἰς τὸ ἔμπροσθεν), "to a spot (vantage-point) ahead"—but in the sense of Mark 10,32.

[7] For Matthew, who drops Bethany, Bethphage is clearly a village. Bethany would have been off the main road from Jericho to Jerusalem, i.e., on a spur about 1 km. to the south of the main east-west road in Jesus' day; the present highway runs south of Bethany.

Jesus' own line of movement (by dropping ὑμῶν from Mark 11,2 in Jesus' instruction to his disciples).

Commentators generally agree that unloosing the colt suggests that Jesus is appropriating the blessing of Judah, as in Gen 49,11, an allusion which Justin Martyr rendered more explicit.[8] Luke makes his own Mark's presentation of Jesus' prophetic foreknowledge,[9] although without the characteristically Marcan note of urgent or expeditious execution, for he omits εὐθύς from Mark 11,2.3. Luke centers attention on the Lord's prerogative. For Luke, if not for Mark, ὁ κύριος αὐτοῦ χρείαν ἔχει must mean: "Its owner (Lord) needs it."[10] Mark employs the expression only in 11,3. Luke 19,34 (following up on v. 31) repeats it verbatim after the statement in v. 33 about "its owners'" seeking the reasons for the disciples' action (εἶπαν οἱ κύριοι αὐτοῦ πρὸς αὐτούς, τί λύετε...;). The pronoun αὐτοῦ in vv. 31 and 34 is not to be construed as αὐτοῦ (= ἑαυτοῦ), for doing so would entail a sense unacceptable in this context, "his (Jesus') Lord has need." Furthermore, the objective complement "... needs it," required in an English translation, lest the notion of "need" be unduly stressed (as in "its owner has need / is in need"), should not be judged to be a double translation. For, in Greek idiom, where the objective complement of χρείαν ἔχειν is clear, notably as being identical with a term already mentioned in the sentence, no objective complement is required; compare 1 Cor 12,24 (where D F G syp unnecessarily, but for further clarity, add τιμῆς [cf. v. 23] after ἔχει).

One should observe that, in the context of the relationship between οἱ κύριοι αὐτοῦ (v. 33) and ὁ κύριος αὐτοῦ (vv. 31 and 34), Jesus acts quite unostentatiously, albeit with a clear indication that he is the animal's owner more than "its owners" are. Impressment of animals was a royal prerogative (cf. 1 Sam 8,17),[11] Furthermore, selecting an animal not subjected to man's use (Luke 19,30b) is characteristic of offerings made to the Lord (Deut 21,13-14; Num 19,2; 1 Sam 6,7).[12] These allusions are suggested, but not triumphalistically expressed, even

---

[8] Justin added πρὸς ἄμπελον δεδεμένος (*Apol.,* I, 32). Plummer, *Gospel According to S. Luke* (ICC; Edinburgh ⁴1913) 446, opines that Justin did so in order to make the incident a fulfillment of Gen 49,11. More probably, Justin knew of a traditional explanation and rendered it explicit by a deliberate, clarifying addition.

[9] In any event, the delegation is similar to that for preparation of the passover meal, which begins the second section of the Jerusalem narrative (22,1.7-13), but which probably represents an intended concealment from Judas of the time and place of the meal-scene. An additional motif, at least in Luke, who earlier speaks of the sending of 72 disciples to every place Jesus himself was to come, seems to lie in fitting delegation of preparatory arrangements. These appositely form part of the picture of the disciples' ministry and set in relief Jesus' own conduct at the decisive time.

[10] J. Duncan Derrett, "Law in the New Testament: The Palm Sunday Colt," *NT* 13 (1971) 241-258, 246, translates the phrase without its implied objective complement, thus: "Its owner (its real Lord) has / is in need."

[11] Cf. I. H. Marshall, *The Gospel of Luke* (NICNT; Exeter 1978) 712.

[12] Even for the king's advent in Zech 9,9, the colt is described as νεός.

though Luke does not make use of Zech 9,9, as Matthew does (Matt 21,5). There is no question, moreover, of a striking disclosure of the "messianic secret," as O. da Spinetoli affirms.[13]

The concluding, second portion (vv. 35-36) of the first stage of Jesus' entry depicts a kind of processional enthronement on the part of his disciples. They place their garments on the colt, an allusion to the enthronement procession of Solomon (1 Kgs 1,33; cp. 2 Kgs 9,13) and have Jesus mount the animal (1 Kgs 1,33), again recalling the coronation procession of Solomon; Luke clarifies the point by using the term ἐπιβιβάζειν (not in Mark; cp. 2 Chr 23,20). After this gesture of Jesus' disciples' acknowledgment of their king, Luke once again draws attention to Jesus' own ongoing journey (πορευομένου δὲ αὐτοῦ), omitting reference to the crowds (πολλοί, Mark 11,8). The disciples, who constitute the logical subject of ὑπεστρώννυον (v. 36) are also said to have placed their garments on his way.

One need not be puzzled by Luke's omission of Mark's "leafy branches cut from the fields." Reasons for this omission are not difficult to construe. Luke insistently focuses attention on Jesus' journey towards the city (cf. πορευομένου δὲ αὐτοῦ ... τῇ ὁδῷ, v. 36, in the light of his more solemn introduction, v. 28, and his reuse [3 sg.] and repetition of ἐγγίζειν, vv. 29.37.41). Furthermore, Mark's notation, "(... strewed) leafy branches, cutting them from the fields," introduced as it is by ἄλλοι (Mark 11,8b) after πολλοί (11,8a) is an integral part of the orderly but large "mob-scene" that he continues to describe in vv. 9-10. Luke restricts the reader's attention to Jesus and to his disciples. Earlier, even the ass's owners were so described to set in relief Jesus' being the real owner, and they merely sought the reason for the disciples' action (v. 33). In Mark (v. 5), on the other hand, there occurred a somewhat distracting interchange with a wider group, described as "some of those standing there," who questioned more insistently, perhaps indignantly: "What are you doing, untying the colt?" (Mark 11,5b; cp. 2,24).

B. The Second Stage

In the second stage (vv. 37-40), Luke introduces a larger group, but speaks even of this throng (πλῆθος) as made up of disciples. He now devotes attention to what is said, whereas in the preceding stage, except for the brief interchanges between Jesus and his disciples and between the latter and the ass's owners, he concentrated on what was done. The movement towards the city, particularly at the point of the descent from Mount Olivet, represents a division of the Marcan "crowd-scene" consisting of two groups in addition to the disciples. Once again,

---

[13] Ortensio da Spinetoli, *Luca, Il Vangelo dei Poveri* (Assisi 1982) 605-8.

For Luke, the messianic secret is focused on the imperative governing Jesus' death as a *prophetic* Messiah. Even an elementary understanding of this mystery is not imparted until Jesus is risen (cf. 24,25-27.44-49); the disciples' lack of understanding is clear as late as the final passion prediction (22,35-38).

Luke introduces the new stage by noting Jesus' own movement (ἐγγίζοντος δὲ αὐτοῦ). Acclamation by Jesus' disciples conveys the note of anticipation of what might follow (ἤδη)[14] on a still larger scale, but which, sadly, will not prove to follow on the part of the populace or, especially, some of their religious leaders.

In Luke, otherwise than in Mark, the acclamation of Jesus is purely religious. The disciples joyfully praise God for all the miracles (δυνάμεις) they have seen, and their praise of God finds expression in their acclamation of Jesus. The motif of glorifying or praising God is a familiar one in Luke (cf. 2,9.14.20; 5,25-26; 7,16; 13,13; 17,15.18; 18,43; 23,47). Remarkably, this kind of reaction has not heretofore been limited to disciples, but has been ascribed even to unbelievers who have been impressed by what Jesus has done or said.[15] Accordingly, the acclamation by Jesus' disciples need not be supposed to be a necessarily exclusive response. Rather, in line with the course of the narrative thus far, with its accounts of Jesus' mighty works, the disciples' response invites a corresponding reaction from those who witness this acclamation.

From Mark's account, the reader gets the impression of a procession with Jesus in the center (although this focus is not rendered explicit), and with groups before and after him giving antiphonal responses. Those going ahead (οἱ προάγοντες, Mark 11,9, without an expressed object; cp. Mark 10,32, where Jesus goes ahead of them, sc., the disciples, but the object is necessarily expressed) cry:

"Hosanna!
Blessed is the one coming in the Lord's name!"

Those following him (οἱ ἀκολουθοῦντες, again, without an expressed object, but understandably, as in Mark 10,32) echo this, in chiastic order and with amplifications:

"Blessed is the coming kingdom of our father, David!
Hosanna in the highest (heavens)!"

Luke, however, not only centers the acclamation on the "multitude of the disciples" and concentrates on their visual experience of Jesus' miracles (v. 37) but also completely depoliticizes their verbal declaration (v. 38).

Thus, Luke characterizes the acclamation as praise of God (v. 37). He also heightens the public demonstration, not only by noting that the disciples were a multitude (πλῆθος) but also by saying that their praise was given "in a loud voice." The phrase φωνῇ μεγάλῃ suggests exceptionally strong human emotion. Luke's

---

[14] Ἤδη occurs in an emphatic position with regard to what follows the gen. abs., not as part of the gen. abs. (as in Acts 27,9a). The adverb does not suggest an anticipated arrival, but strategic location vis-à-vis the city; here, Jesus is already at the point of descent towards the city.

[15] Cf. J. Nolland, "Impressed Unbelievers as Witnesses to Christ (Luke 4:22a)," *JBL* 98 (1979) 219-229, 226.

Gospel employs this phrase only when referring to a demon's outburst (after ἀνακράξαι, 4,33 and 8,28) or, more appositely, μετὰ φωνῆς μεγάλης, with the addition of δοξάζων τὸν θεόν in the account of the cure and conversion of the Samaritan leper (17,15-16),[16] and, finally, to describe Jesus' own death-cry (φωνήσας φωνῇ μεγάλῃ) as he voices a prayer to his Father.[17] Luke's phrasing here may prepare for the apocalyptic explanation given in v. 40. At the very least, it sheds light on some Pharisees' demand that Jesus rebuke his exuberant disciples.

Moreover, Luke completely depoliticizes the event. The Marcan version of the acclamations is tinged with irony, which will emerge in his narrative of a fickle, manipulated crowd's demand, a few days hence, for Jesus' crucifixion (Mark 15,6-15). Those who accompany Jesus twice voice the Hebrew victory-shout—nonetheless that for its praise of the Lord—"Hosanna!" In addition, they regard Jesus as the "blessed one" not only because of his being personally empowered with the authority of the Lord ("come in his name"), but also because he embodies their hope for the coming kingdom of their father, David. Undoubtedly, they conceive the latter as a forthcoming political reality, an interpretation which Luke has taken great care to obviate, both by recounting Jesus' parable to the crowds before his immediate approach (Luke 19,11-27, esp. v. 11 in relation to 19,9a) and by recasting the acclamation as a prayer of his disciples. Mark has the crowd speak of the kingdom of David *their* father (πατρὸς ἡμῶν). There is scriptural warrant for speaking of Abraham as the father of the people (Isa 51,2, ὑμῶν) or of Jacob (Isa 58,14), or of God himself as "our Father" (Isa 63,16). The customary designation for a Hebrew king, however, is "David *his* father" (e.g., Isa 38,5; Sir 48,22). A noteworthy exception is the prayer of the Christian community in Acts 4,25, which further qualifies "our father David" as "your (God's) servant." The phraseology used by the cortege in Mark, however, is not prayerful, nor does it find a parallel in the LXX. The Marcan throng interprets Jesus' coming as the advent of the political establishment of a national kingdom, and finds its meaning in terms of the paragon of that establishment, for their own interests.

Luke shuns these politically-charged acclamations. He introduces the disciples as initiating the acclamation (ἤρξαντο, v. 37) as well as voicing it. They hail Jesus in a four-line statement[18] which is better grouped as two couplets:

---

[16] Cf. H. D. Betz, "The Cleansing of the Ten Lepers (Luke 17:11-19)," *JBL* 90 (1971) 314-28, 325-8.

[17] The use of the phrase in Acts remains charged with emotion. It is employed of the exit of demons (Acts 8,7), of Stephen's enraged accusers and his own death-cry (7,57.60), of Paul's salutary shouts to the cripple at Lystra (14,10)—who probably could not understand Greek, so Paul spoke loudly (as if the man were deaf!) and, no doubt, gesticulated—and to the jailer at Philippi who was about to commit suicide (16,28); lastly, of Festus's exasperated outburst declaring that Paul was out of his mind (26,24).

[18] Cf. Grundmann, *Evangelium nach Lukas,* 367.

vv. 38a saying:

38b "Blessed is the one who comes,
38c the King in the Lord's name;
38d in heaven, peace,
38e and glory on high!"

Since ὁ βασιλεύς in v. 38c breaks the sequence of the quoted Ps 117 (MT 118), 26a and since, without it, v. 38c can hardly stand alone, "the King" should be taken as introducing a further, clarifying statement. Ὁ ἐρχόμενος remained at least somewhat ambiguous in Luke 7,19. In that context (cf. the occasion, Luke 7,15-17 and cp. 1 Kgs 17,23), the title probably referred, on the lips of John the Baptist's emissaries, to the messianic precursor, Elijah. Here, however, no doubt in view of subsequent clarifications in Luke's story (e.g., 7,22-28), it serves to designate the Messiah himself. For the added ὁ βασιλεύς makes the designation of a royal, Davidic Messiah unmistakably clear. "In the Lord's name" further conveys the sense of divine authorization and effectiveness, but can reflect a prophetic as well as a royal commission.[19] The second couplet looks to the effect of that coming, both intended and, in some sense at least, actual. For, otherwise, the acclamation must be judged to be unfounded, which is hardly Luke's view in formulating it.

The proclamation of the Messianic king's advent in the context of a message of peace achieved in heaven prepares most immediately for Jesus' lament over the city which has not recognized the terms for peace on earth. Even as attested in his forthcoming "lament" over the city, Jesus does not come to destroy, nor do his disciples, en route with him, understand his purpose otherwise.

The aspect of actual occurrence of peace has to be examined carefully, for v. 38de does not restate 2,14. "Peace on earth" was announced at Jesus' birth as the consequence of God's acceptance ("good pleasure," εὐδοκία, rāṣôn) regarding mankind (Luke 2,14). That, however, was an angelic annunciation. An annunciation also requires a *response* (compare and contrast Luke 1,18 and 1,34). The scope of the annunciation by the heavenly host[20] extended even beyond the shepherds and the λαός they typified. For, moving beyond the scope of Luke 2,10,

---

[19] The prophetic aspect holds at least for Luke, given the placement of 13,35b in the context of his prophetic journey towards Jerusalem (13,32.33). Besides, even in 19,38, where the quotation includes a clear reference to royal messianism, the context (v. 37) refers to prophetic manifestations of power, through which Jesus' royal, messianic work has been made manifest.

For the OT background, cf. H. A. Brongers, "Die Wendung *bešēm jhwh* im Alten Testament," *ZAW* 77 (1965) 1-20. Brongers concludes that it has a complex content: "at the command of the Lord," or "with the authority of the Lord," and that the substantive *šēm* repeatedly has the sense of "force" or "power" and even of "weapon," ibid., 20; in Ps 118,26, it refers to those whose victory in battle is attributable to Yahweh, ibid., 3-4.

[20] Cf. C. H. Giblin, "Reflections on the Sign of the Manger," *CBQ* 29 (1967) 87-101, 101.

v. 13 looked more widely to "human beings to whom God shows his special concern." The response, however, remained unarticulated. In the course of Jesus' ministry, notably on his journey towards Jerusalem, where tensions between Jesus and his opponents escalated and the full realization of the coming kingdom (announced as early as Luke 1,32-33) was deferred to the day of final reckoning (19,11-17), "peace on earth" could no longer be envisaged as a present or shortly forthcoming reality. Indeed, the prospect became that of further conflict, "not peace, but division" (12,51), an ominous turn of events not unforeshadowed as early as the childhood narrative (2,34-35).[21] In the accounts of the ministry of OT prophets as well, the course of events develops, taking a turn for the better or, often, for the worse, as far as the majority of people are concerned.[22] Thus, the need and efficacy of a final or subsequent, manifest divine judgment according to the dynamic prophetic word is called for and foretold or depicted. For Luke, peace in heaven may recall the apocalyptic fall of Satan mentioned en route to Jerusalem (10,18).[23] More likely, since the acclamation is grounded on Jesus' own miracles, it probably refers to these, especially cures and forgiveness of sins acclaimed by all (cf. 5,17-26; 13,10-17; 18,35-43; cp. also 7,11-17). That transterrestrial peace has been achieved. As closely, chiastically coupled with "glory on high," "in heaven, peace" supposes an indicative ("is") rather than an optative ("may there be") or subjunctive ("let there be").[24]

The second stage of Jesus' approach, like the first, contains a second portion (vv. 39-40). Here, however, Luke introduces a comparatively negative reaction to the disciples' acclamation. The crowd itself (ὁ ὄχλος) seems, in general, to be neutral. As a group, they do not oppose Jesus or voice any complaints. Later, in the temple, when described as the people (ὁ λαός), they show intense interest in Jesus' words, and are sharply contrasted with their religious leaders. The problem which Luke's picture of the people poses must be addressed later. Suffice it now to note that, for all practical purposes, the crowd in v. 39 comprises, by implication, the people and all those present who are not disciples, including, prominently, the objecting Pharisees. Some Pharisees (again, Luke shows tolerant reluctance to condemn outright the whole school)[25] demand (imv.) that Jesus rebuke his disciples. A rabbi (cf. διδάσκαλε, v. 39) was considered responsible for his

---

[21] Cf. Pierre Benoit, " 'Et toi-même, un glaive te transpercera l'âme!' (Luc 2,35)," *CBQ* 25 (1963) 251-61, 255-6.

[22] Cf. 1 Kgs 19,4-18; 22,13-28; 2 Kgs 17,5-23; and, of course, the times of Jeremiah.

[23] Mention of power over serpents and scorpions in 10,19 expresses in apocalyptic terms miraculous activity, but is not to be restricted to exorcisms: cf. Pierre Grelot, "Étude critique de Luc 10,19," *RSR* 69 (1981) 87-100.

[24] Cf. *TDNT* 2, 248.

[25] Flender goes much too far, however, in saying that the Pharisees represent that group among the Jewish leaders which is receptive to the Christian message, *St. Luke. Theologian of Redemptive History* (Philadelphia 1967) 108. Luke 19,39 is a case in point; see also 11,37-54; 16,14-15; 18,9-14.

disciples' conduct, at least in a situation involving himself.[26] In replying, "If these keep silence, the stones will shout!" Jesus enunciates a kind of messianic necessity that the meaning of his approach be proclaimed. At the same time, he implies that the alternative to this messianic acclamation which, obviously, he would not want restricted even to the throng that accompanies him, would be a kind of apocalyptic, catastrophic event.

The language which Jesus uses suggests also a judgment to come as the alternative to messianic recognition. For the image of "stones shouting" is not unlike that in Hab 2,11: "For the stone will cry from the wall and the beam from the woodwork respond."[27] This verse from Habakkuk is set in the context of woes against an unjust nation. Although a number of scholars refer to this text,[28] the allusion is admittedly tenuous and requires further justification. Luke uses κράζειν, a stronger word than βοᾶν (Hab, LXX). Nevertheless, he regards the two as roughly synonymous (cp. 18,38-39) and may have transferred the stronger word from Mark 11,9 (κράζειν) to this point, the *a fortiori* part of his own narrative, in order to express the raucous consequences of repression (again, cp. 18,38-39, where κράζειν is a bit more emphatic than βοᾶν). What is more, his use of the plural "stones" (λίθοι), without any mention of a wall (Hab), fittingly evokes the image of the roadway rather than that of the city's bulwarks. The hint of a violent alternative to the disciples' loud cry would fit well with what precedes, and the hint of a cataclysmic event as that alternative would accord well with the "lament" and judgment oracle which immediately follows.

C. The Third Stage

Καὶ ὡς ἤγγισεν (v. 41) inaugurates the third stage of Jesus' approach. Jesus' declaration stands in place of the pilgrims' psalms of joy (Pss 121, 122) as Grundmann observes. Contrary to his view,[29] however, it is not to be classified as a lament. More exactly, it is an anguished, sympathetic, prophetic oracle of judgment. Ultimate hope for the inhabitants is not absolutely ruled out, although the terms for peace (τὰ πρὸς εἰρήνην)[30] are now hidden from the inhabitants' eyes (v. 42b) and the proximate prospects are unmitigated disaster (vv. 43-44). Jesus' oracle contrasts the city and its inhabitants with his disciples: "If (only) you

---

[26] Cp. Mark 2,24; cf. R. Pesch, *Das Markusevangelium* I. Teil (HTKNT; Freiburg ²1977) 180-1.

[27] *2 Esdras* 5,5 speaks of "stones crying out" as part of a description of one of the stages of the eschatological period.

[28] Cf. I. H. Marshall, *Gospel of Luke,* 716. Grundmann, *Evangelium nach Lukas,* 368, grasps the point of the saying: "Diese Wendung der Antwort ist sprichtwörtlich und meint: Durch die Verwerfung der Proklamation ziehen die Verwerfenden das Gericht auf sich, das in der Zerstörung der Stadt über sie kommt."

[29] W. Grundmann, *Evangelium nach Lukas,* 368.

[30] Cp. Luke 14,32 and *Test. Jud.,* 9,7.

knew *on this day, you, too* (καὶ σύ), the conditions for peace!" These conditions are clarified in a twofold way: first, by directly indicating what the city does not know or recognize; second, by setting this lack of recognition against the background of the disciples' acclamation. Thus, the city has not known the time of its visitation. The time of visitation (ἐπισκοπή) is the day on which God makes known the truth about his relationship to his people and is to be glorified by them (cf. Luke 1,78-79; 7,16; 1 Pet 2,12). Jerusalem has not acknowledged Jesus as the Messiah. Even though the crowd as a whole shows no sign of hostility (for only some Pharisees from it are singled out in v. 39), they are at best onlookers. They have missed the "moment of truth," as events have developed thus far. Only Jesus' disciples have acknowledged him as the Messiah who brings heavenly peace, and only they have related his coming to God's glory.

The fate in store for the city is therefore a judgment for its failure to glorify God by recognizing Jesus' messiahship, notably as made known to it through Jesus' disciples. Furthermore, the city of Jerusalem takes on the character of a "worldly city" in its liability to judgment. For its ruin is described typologically. As Flückiger has shown,[31] its destruction is depicted (v. 44) in words reminiscent not of the actual Roman campaign against it, but of the prophecies of Ezek 4,1-2 and Isa 3,26 (against Jerusalem) to which, in particular, should be added the psalmist's portrayal of the fall of Babylon (Ps 137,9). The typing of the city becomes still more perceptible when one reads this oracle against the background of the way in which Jesus has characterized other cities — in reality, mere villages or market-towns—during the course of his journey to Jerusalem (*see above*, pp. 33-34, regarding Chorazin, Bethsaida, and Capernaum). As those towns faced a judgment harder to bear than that in store for Sodom, Tyre, and Sidon, and like that (in the case of Capernaum) against Babylon, so, too, Jerusalem must reckon with judgment as a type of the worldly city, a metropolis which embodies the culture and civilization of a whole people.

A moral for Luke's typed audience lies implicit in Jesus' anguished, prophetic oracle. If such is to be the fate of Jerusalem, what will happen to other cities which do not acclaim him as his disciples did here, but as their inhabitants will not have done? He has made himself known not just by his own coming, but through the articulate and resounding voice of his disciples. His being heralded to the Jerusalemites implies his being made known to "every city and place to which he will come" (cf. 10,1b). The application of the historical-typological moral, however, which the reader may already perceive, will be developed further in the course of Luke's Jerusalem narrative.

---

[31] Felix Flückiger, "Luk 21,20-24 und die Zerstörung Jerusalems," *TZ* 28 (1972) 385-90, 387-8. Apropos of 19,43-44, he is able to point out that Luke does not describe the siege of the temple proper, which was regarded in contemporary descriptions as the decisive phase of the fall of the city. He misses, however, the typological significance of the clearer reference to the fall of Babylon in describing the fate of Jerusalem itself.

VI. The Parable of the Wicked Tenants (Luke 20,9-19)

The parable of the wicked tenants has often been studied in itself, particularly from a form-critical or from a redactional-critical standpoint.[1] Few if any scholars, however, have adverted to its placement and function in the wider context of a given Synoptist's narrative. Benign neglect of the parable's function in Luke's consecutive account should not be allowed, however, in trying to establish a mode of interpretation valid for his well-integrated Jerusalem narrative. For the emphasis of a given passage, if not indeed its inner thematic coherence, may be expected to be more fully disclosed through a progressive series of interrelated events which precede it and follow it. Accordingly, I shall first examine the proximate narrative context of this parable (A), proceed to an exegesis of its redactional reworking by Luke (B), and conclude by attempting to bring out its relationships on the level of the historical-typological moral to what has preceded and to what will follow (C).

A. The Proximate Narrative Context

The parable (20,9-19) occurs as the second of an opening series of three episodes: the question concerning authority (20,1b-8); the parable of the wicked tenants (20,9-19); and the question concerning tribute to Caesar (20,20-26). This opening series, in turn, stands as a first grouping among three: conflict predominantly between Jesus and the high priests and scribes (20,1b-26); interchanges between Jesus and the Sadducees and between Jesus and some scribes (20,27-44); and Jesus' teaching to the disciples in the hearing of the people (20,45–21,36). All three groupings or series of exchanges are set on a "sample

---

[1] Michel Hubaut's principal interest lies in reconstructing the contours of the primitive form of the parable, *La Parabole des Vignerons homicides* (Cahiers RB 16; Paris 1976). Klyne Snodgrass, *The Parable of the Wicked Tenants* (WUNT 27; Berlin 1983) provides the most extensive coverage of the literature to date, esp. pp.3-13. Snodgrass forbears to take either the form-critical or the redactional-critical standpoint, but discusses a wide variety of questions. Although these are concerned with important issues of literary criticism, the working out of the ensemble seems to lack a precise focus. Snodgrass seems especially interested in leaving open the possibility of assigning the parable to Jesus himself; ibid., 2, 87, 103-4, 108,112.

[2] Interestingly, both the first and second halves of the Jerusalem narrative conclude with mention of the temple: ... ἐν τῷ ἱερῷ ἀκούειν αὐτοῦ (21,38); ... ἐν τῷ ἱερῷ εὐλογοῦντες τὸν θεόν (24,53).

day" of Jesus' teaching in the temple (20,1a). Luke notes at the outset (19,47) Jesus' daily teaching in the temple and mentions it again by way of concluding the first half of his Jerusalem narrative (21,37-38).[2] He has employed a not altogether dissimilar kind of temporal framework before, when borrowing from Mark 1,23-38 a sabbath-day at Capernaum and its immediate sequel (Luke 4,31-44). He will make use of it again for the First Day of the Week, a climactic third day, that of the resurrection-ascension, after the immediately preceding days of burial (Preparation) and of sabbath rest (23,54.56b; 24,1.21b.22b.29.33).[3] Although the schema differs in each of the three cases of a highlighted day, it serves in every instance to interrelate a number of distinct episodes, in the interest of unity, coherence, and emphasis.

The sample day of teaching in the temple may also be intended to set in relief Jesus' open, public teaching, as the later, ironic reference to those come to arrest him (22,53) suggests.[4] In any event, Luke takes care to mention Jesus' teaching τὸ καθ' ἡμέραν in the temple just after Jesus has driven the sellers from what he has declared God's house should be: a house for prayer, not the den for thieves which the sellers have made it (19,46-47). For Luke, the temple functions as a kind of sacred forum for the city, a place for worship (prayer, praise of God), prophecy, and religious teaching.[5] He does not share Mark's view of it, that, as appropriated by the Jewish leadership, the temple serves to symbolize a materialistic, idolatrously thing-centered cult.[6] Nor does Luke spatially or theologically

---

[3] A number of factors militate against beginning the Lucan "resurrection narrative" with 24,1: δέ in 24,1 is correlative to μέν in 23,56b and so 24,1 cannot be construed as a separate sentence. In 23,55, the ptc. + δέ is not Luke's way of inaugurating a self-contained literary unit. The remark in 23,54, especially insofar as it announces on two counts (preparation / sabbath) v. 56, is only rather arbitrarily taken as the conclusion of the burial scene. On the other hand, καὶ ἰδού in 23,5 may introduce a self-contained literary unit in Luke (cf. 5,12; 10,25). The women mentioned in 23,55 are the same as those mentioned at the conclusion of the crucifixion-scene (23,49b). The three-day schema seems to begin with the burial of Jesus. Accordingly, it seems better to construe Luke's account in terms of a burial-resurrection-ascension account (23,50 – 24,53).

[4] For "the day(time)" is contrasted with "your hour, and (epexegetic καί, = that is) the (working out) of the power of darkness"—taking ἐξουσία in an active sense.

[5] Cf. F.D. Weinert, *The Meaning of the Temple in the Gospel of Luke* (Fordham University Dissertation, 1979; available from University Microfilms International, Ann Arbor, Michigan 48106) 306-17.

[6] Cf. John R. Donahue, *Are You the Christ? The Trial Narrative in the Gospel of Mark* (SBLDS 10; Missoula 1973) 103-38. Donahue does not seem to have noted, however, how standard biblical imagery for an idolatrous thing, one "made with hands," functions in the Marcan *narrative*. Considering the telling of the story, the false accusation leveled against Jesus shows that, for the Sanhedrin (for whom the false witnesses serve as mouthpieces), destroying "this sanctuary *made with hands*" is damning evidence. The charge itself accordingly suggests to the Christian reader an idolatrous religious outlook and types the mentality of the high priests and the whole Sanhedrin as equivalently pagan.

distinguish the temple from the city (Jerusalem).[7] Indeed, Jesus' entering the temple (19,45a) concludes his ascent to Jerusalem (19,28) and his approach to the city (19,29-44).

For Mark, Jesus' scriptural explanation of his disruption of the temple's business and cultic activity (11,15b-16) is virtually identified with his "teaching" (v. 17). It is this teaching which prompts most immediately both the infuriated reaction of Jesus' adversaries, who heard him so teach (v. 18a) and the response of the whole crowd, which was astounded at his teaching (v. 18c). For Luke, on the other hand, the action of "cleansing the temple" stands by itself, or, rather, stands out as a prophetic action and word presented as a transition linking his approach to the city (and implied entrance into it) with what he will be doing in the temple. Prophetically, the episode serves to declare Jesus' concern for the respect due to God's house. On another count, too, it remains more than a relic of tradition. For this concern of Jesus will prove further to look to God's relationship with human beings, especially his sovereign demands. These will continue to govern what Jesus says as he teaches in the temple, notably in each of the opening series of three episodes (cf. Luke 20,4; 20,15b; 20,25b) and again in the course of each of the next two series (e.g., at least in 20,37-38 and in 21,22). Thus, the Lucan version of the driving of the sellers from the temple because of the respect to be accorded God's house (which, as the reader knows from 2,49 Jesus respects as his Father's[8]) should be taken as befitting Jesus' prophetic teaching in a sacred forum.[9]

Luke then proceeds to situate the sample day of teaching (20,47a) in the context of an ongoing, daily exchange with various audiences. The first set of audiences (specifically, for the initial series of episodes in the triple grouping noted above) finds programmatic expression in 19,47b-48. Jesus' daily teaching precipitates from the outset divided reactions between two groups, the Jewish leaders and the entire people. In distinguishing the reactions of these two groups, Luke calls attention to Jesus' *daily* teaching. Although this point has been made repeatedly, it bears repetition, if only to insist that, unlike Mark, Luke thus leads his reader to attend to what will immediately follow even more than to recall what has just taken place (the "cleansing"). Accordingly, Luke goes on to sharpen the

---

[7] Michael Bachmann, *Jerusalem und der Tempel. Die geographisch-theologischen Elemente in der lukanischen Sicht des jüdischen Kultzentrums* (BWANT 109; Stuttgart 1980) 136, 289, 376.

[8] Cf. Luke 2,49, whether one takes ἐν τοῖς τοῦ πατρός μου as "in matters of my Father's concern" or "*chez mon père.*" This episode suggests in an appropriate way for his age, and according to the genre of childhood narratives, Jesus' transcendent concerns and future ministry; and so, indeed, does his life's story work out.

[9] Although there seems to be no way of proving it, Luke may have viewed the Jerusalem temple-area on the analogy of major forums in the Roman world. These centered on a temple or complex of temples, functioning as the center of civil, cultural, and religious life, and, in large cities, the principal forum was not a common market-place. Cf. *Oxford Classical Dictionary*, ed. N. G. L. Hammond and H. H. Scullard (Oxford ²1970) 445-7.

Marcan distinction between the two groups, rather than to direct attention, as Mark does, to a barrage of attacks by those who engage Jesus in controversy.[10]

Luke includes among those who want to destroy Jesus not only high priests and scribes but also the leaders of the people (οἱ πρῶτοι τοῦ λαοῦ, v. 47c; cp. Mark 11,18a), and draws attention only to their desire to destroy him. The question of the means to be worked out (πῶς, Mark 11,18) is partly deferred to a later period (Luke 22,2, τὸ πῶς ...), although one can perceive a key ploy already at work in 10,2 (cp. its recurrence in 23,2a). At this point, however, Luke contents himself with underscoring the frustration of their intention (v. 48a). He accounts for this not by mentioning their fear of Jesus himself (Mark 11,18b) or, as Mark suggests here (γάρ, v. 18c) and will parenthetically explain later (11,32) their fear of the crowd, but by drawing attention to the fascination of the entire people (ὁ λαὸς γὰρ ἅπας) as they heard him (19,48). Thus, Luke sets in vivid contrast the leaders of the people and the people themselves.

This strikingly antithetical distinction consitutes a dialectical framework for narrating at least the opening series of episodes. Jesus' specific or immediately intended audience will change somewhat in the second and third series, but the *people* remain a constant factor throughout all the exchanges. Certainly they continue to be such according to the summarizing, general conclusion (21,38), and, again, in the final series (20,45), although they are at that point of quite secondary importance. In the intervening, second series, they seem not to be mentioned, but they are surely supposed to be "on stage." Quite probably, Jesus refers to them obliquely by the plural of indefinite subject: "How is it that they [people] say [i.e., take it for granted] ...?" (πῶς λέγουσιν; 20,41).[11] The dialectical framework in the first series moves from Jesus' teaching the people (20,1a) to the silencing of adversaries who have tried to ensnare him in (any) word before the people (20,26). It merits detailed attention, the better to situate the central episode (the parable) as forcefully warning the people, but not as prophetically charging them with a crime or attacking their own current attitude or conduct.

In the first episode, Jesus is not pictured as "walking about" (Mark 11,27), probably because Luke regularly depicts him as walking purposefully, e.g., "journeying" or moving to some specified place(s). In Luke, he is teaching the people and "preaching," a term which, for Luke, implies essentially the call to repentance.[12] The question about his authority, posed by something like a religious coalition ("the high priests and the scribes together with the elders"),

---

[10] Cp. Mark 11,27; 12,13; 12,18; 12,28.

[11] Luke deliberately recasts Mark at this point, omitting reference to the scribes as a group (Mark 12,35; cp. 12,12). The logical subject in Luke 20,41 cannot be the scribes, since the question is addressed to some scribes (v. 39).

[12] The notion of "preaching / heralding the *gospel*" need not be excluded from Luke's understanding of εὐαγγελίζεσθαι. For even in the case of John the Baptist's preaching (3,3-18), a dominant note is the need for repentance, which proves to be a major theme of Jesus' own "evangelization."

arises as an interruption (ἐπέστησαν).[13] After Jesus' counter-question, his objectors consult with (σύν) one another — again, without any hint of divisive debate among themselves (συνελογίσαντο, v. 5) — and express deathly fear of what the people will do (v. 6). In the second episode, Jesus begins to address to the people, not to his questioners in the previous episode (unlike Mark 12,1), the parable of the wicked tenants. In doing so, he does not formulate the parable against the people, but against their rulers, more clearly delimiting them vis-à-vis 20,1 as "scribes and high priests" (20,19).[14] Lastly, in the transition to the third episode, the question concerning tribute to Caesar, Luke avoids Mark's notation of the departure of Jesus' adversaries (Mark 12,12c) and takes care to point out reconnaissance and counterattack by the same group noted at the close of the parable. Here, of course, if only to mask their own designs, they make use of others, somewhat as, before, they enlisted the support of the elders. With Luke's distinctive conclusions concerning their impotence verbally to entrap him in the presence of the people, and their being reduced to silence by Jesus' reply, this well-integrated series of episodes comes to its close. Luke then proceeds to deal with two other sets of audiences (20,27-44 and 20,45 – 21,36), which need not here delay study of the parable of the wicked tenants.

B. Luke's Redactional Reworking of the Parable

When examining this parable in detail, it may help initially to note the basic structural elements of the passage which are shared by all three Synoptics. Doing so should provide a more solid basis both for considering the thematic unity of the parable, a tradition which Mark probably originated, and for more accurately assessing Luke's divergences in matters of detail and perhaps of substance. Structural elements of the parable, however, not the final literary structure(s) of all, of two, or even of one of the synoptic accounts are at this juncture the point in question. The over-all narrative dynamics, specifically those of Luke's version, must await the comparative analysis which will follow this overview. The structural

---

[13] The term is a predominantly Lucan one, used in conversational idiom ("came up"), often in the sense of an interruption of what is going on (ἐπέστησαν + dat. or implied object); cf. Luke 2,9; 10,4; Acts 4,4; Luke 24,4; Acts 12,7. Ἐπί + acc. seems to indicate more aggressive action: Luke 21,34; Acts 10,17; 11,1; cf. Acts 24,12 (ἐπίστασιν ... ὄχλου = disruption).

[14] The delimitation (sc., omission of "the elders" of 20,1) may be accounted for by observing that the high priests and scribes enlist the help of others. The latter are either those who have appeared to be conciliatory towards Jesus, as well as influential (e.g., the elders, cf. 7,3-6a), or those who could camouflage the intentions of their *mandantes* (20,20). Although the "leaders of the people" are mentioned with the "hard core" opposition which dominates the first series of encounters, the connotation of the end of 19,47, in which they appear, may emphatically express amazement, "indeed, the leaders of the people," rather than a specifically distinct group.

elements of all the synoptic accounts of the parable may be indicated as given below. Matthew is included at this point only to support the general schema.

1. An opening transition to the parable (Matt 21,33a; Mark 12,1a; Luke 20,9a).

2. A man's initial relationship to tenants of a vineyard (Matt 21,33b; Mark 12,1b; Luke 20,9b), with scriptural allusion to Isa 5,1 ff.: "planted (ἐφύτευσεν) a vineyard (ἀμπελῶνα)..., and let it out to vinedressers (καὶ ἐξέδοτο τοῖς γεωργοῖς), and went away (καὶ ἀπεδήμησεν)."

3. His sending of servants (Matt 21,34; Mark 12,2; Luke 20,10a): "He sent servant(s) to the vinedressers (ἀπέστειλεν πρὸς τοὺς γεωργοὺς δοῦλον/δούλους)."

4. Their treatment of his servant(s) (Matt 21,35-36; Mark 12,3-5; Luke 20,10-12).

5. The climactic sending of the son with an indication of the man's hoped-for success (Matt 21,37; Mark 12,6; Luke 20,13): "they will respect (ἐντραπήσονται)."

6. The tenants' thoughts and course of action (Matt 21,40; Mark 12,7; Luke 20,15b): out of a desire to possess the vineyard, they encourage one another to murder and do murder: "This is the heir (οὗτός ἐστιν ὁ κληρονόμος), let us kill... (ἀποκτείνωμεν) (and) they killed... (ἀπέκτειναν)."

7. Challenge to infer the consequences (Matt 21,41; Mark 12,9; Luke 20,15b): "What will he do? (τί ποιήσει)."

8. Answer (with or without dialogue with the auditors) (Matt 21,41; Mark 12,9; Luke 20,16): "... he will destroy ... (ἀπολέσει ...)."

9. Jesus' further, questioning statement (Matt 21,42-43[44]; Mark 12,10-11; Luke 20,17-18) entailing a change from vineyard-imagery to stone imagery, with reference to Ps 117 (LXX), 22-23.

10. Concluding remarks by the Evangelist concerning reactions of Jesus' adversaries (Matt 21,45-46; Mark 12,12; Luke 20,19); "sought ... feared ... knew (ζητεῖν ..., φοβεῖσθαι ..., γνῶναι)"—with reference to their fear of the people / crowd(s).

Analysis of the elements of the parable and of their interrelationship is dictated by the scope of this inquiry into Luke's account. Mark is Luke's source here, and therefore deserves more attention than Matthew. Nevertheless, it will probably prove helpful to call on Matthew at times if only to discern more clearly Mark's own distinctive, prior account, and analogously to set in relief Luke's redaction of Mark. The analysis will proceed according to three principal steps. The first requires attention to the redactional frame passages and to the over-all movement of the story, particularly as a double set of Jesus' words forged together into one parable, a unified and coherent narrative form. The second deals with possible or actual options in addressing the third stage, especially the option of (falsely) distinguishing between parable and allegory. The third step will command comparative, exegetical attention not just to redactional changes from point to point but, rather, to the movement of the parable and its interrelated progressions.

With regard to the first step, special attention should be devoted to the frame passages. The opening and closing elements (nos. 1 and 10) are clearly redactional, even in Mark. For the speaker and the auditors in Mark 12,1a must be construed from context. In Mark 12,12, the pronominal references to Jesus and to his hostile adversaries must again be construed from a narrative context prior to the immediate introduction of this parable. On the other hand, in making use of Mark, Luke specifies at the outset the speaker's audience as the people, speaks of a single parable, and presents it as one which is especially apt in the narrated situation: "*this* parable" (τὴν παραβολὴν ταύτην; 20,9; cf. Luke's suggestion of "apposite parable" in 4,23; 12,41; 18,9). He pointedly repeats the phrase in the closing frame-passage (20,19). Furthermore, he there specifies the audience against whom this parable is told (high priests and scribes). Unlike Mark, who notes "the crowd" in attendance, Luke indicates a double audience: those who are warned but not charged (the people) and those against whom the parable is expressly directed. Mark seems to note Jesus' adversaries' ongoing frustration (12,12, ἐζήτουν, impf., recalling the very same form in 11,18) and their attempt to arrest him. Luke suggests a desire occasioned more proximately by this parable itself (aor.), at least when one also notes his addition of "at (that) very hour" (20,19). His fulsome phraseology, moreover, denotes more clearly than the probable connotation of Mark's "arrest him" (αὐτὸν κρατῆσαι) a violent, personal reaction, "lay hands on him" (ἐπιβαλεῖν ἐπ' αὐτὸν τὰς χεῖρας).

Further attention to general redactional features must be paid to the twofold movement of the story. A division or further alteration of this movement occurs in no. 9 of the schema given above. It consists of Jesus' further question (cf. no. 7 for the initial one), which presses home the disastrous consequences for the vinedressers. It is marked by an abrupt and complete change of imagery, derived from a further scriptural reference. Not the "vineyard image," but "rock imagery" suddenly emerges, unconnected even with the imagery of the tower as given in the Marcan account (12,1).

The *Gospel of Thomas,* §§ 65 and 66, contains as separate items a version of two major portions of what now appears in Mark as a literary unit (because of Mark's ongoing narrative, supposition of the same speaker and auditors, introduction of a further question with an adverbial connective [οὐδέ]). There seems to be no question of literary dependence of any of the Synoptics on the *Gospel of Thomas,* or vice-versa.[15] With or without knowledge of Mark, the logia in the *Gospel of Thomas* circulated in the successive eddies of an independent-minded tradition, which does not seem to have been governed by the "orthodox"

---

[15] For the discussion, cf. K. Snodgrass, *Parable of the Wicked Tenants,* 52-4. It is surprising, however, that Snodgrass takes no note of the fact that, in the *Gospel of Thomas,* the stone-saying is merely juxtaposed to the parable, not conjoined with it.

NT tradition. The latter insisted on the death and resurrection of Jesus as the lodestone of evangelical communication. Mark, however, probably welded a not dissimilar tradition of distinct, even literarily disparate pieces into one story, imparting to it formal literary and theological coherence.[16]

Partial traces of the Marcan welding can be observed in the introduction and phraseology Mark employs. For the second question (12,10) is correlated with that at the close of the passage on the vineyard in a manner characteristic of Mark's style.[17]

Before proceeding to the third step, that is, to study in detail the movement of the parable, some remarks are in order concerning initial options of interpretation. It should suffice here to preclude two approaches.

First, some scholars might prefer to single out elements treated with considerable freedom by each of the Synoptics. They would do so in order to detect in these more striking alterations a clue to the specific interests of each writer, and to find thereby an opportunity more readily to demonstrate critical control of, say, Luke's use of Mark. Among such elements (cf. the schema given above, p. 62) would figure at least the scriptural reference to the description of the vineyard (no. 2), the sending of a servant or of servants, together with the differing aspects of their rejection (no. 4), and perhaps the way in which Jesus' challenge to infer consequences is answered (no. 8).

This kind of selective, even disjunctive approach, however, which one readily finds in commentaries does not satisfactorily explain the parable as a self-contained, consecutive narrative. For what seems to be omitted from one element may appear more subtly elsewhere. Thus, as we shall see, Luke may seem almost to have abandoned scriptural reference to Isaiah's Song of the Vineyard[18] whereas, actually, he alludes to it more subtly later on in his account (20,13a: τί ποιήσω; cp. Isa 5,4[LXX] and *see below*). Eclectic criticism can be presumed to provide results which are only eclectic, not thoroughgoing or persuasively

---

[16] Snodgrass. ibid., 56-71, argues for the priority of the Matthean text (together with its contested v. 44, bracketed in NA[26]). Towards the end, ibid., 70, he says: "Obviously, to say this does not require the acceptance of Matthean priority overall ..." I do not see how such a conclusion is "obvious" at all. If Matthew is not prior elsewhere, why this exception?

[17] Cf. J. R. Donahue, *Are You the Christ?*, 123. Snodgrass, ibid., 113-18, 63-5 finds the link between the parable and the stone-imagery in a play on words: *bēn* ("son"), *'eben* ("stone"). The distance between the words constituting the alleged wordplay, however, seems to militate against it. Nevertheless, it would not be unlikely on the level of association of ideas in an author like Matthew (who omits ἀγαπητόν in Matt 21,37, and adds τὸν υἱόν in v. 38) or even in Mark; Matthew was certainly acquainted with Hebrew, and Mark may have had a smattering of it—enough to ground a play on simple terms. In Luke, however, the wordplay is not operative.

[18] R. Doran, "Luke 20:18 A Warrior's Boast?" *CBQ* 45 (1983) 61-7, 66, agreeing with J. D. M. Derrett, flatly denies a Lucan reference to Isa 5,1-2, arguing that the vineyard in question is "new." Whence this qualification is derived, especially only in Luke, completely escapes me. It is hardly derived from the text.

plausible in explaining the story as it is progressively told. Each author's most striking freedom of phraseology may appear, moreover, in descriptions which are of secondary interest in themselves but serve mainly to build up to and present in a new light the "traditional climax." Thus, as we shall see in detail later, the sendings of the servant(s) are handled in quite different ways, but so as to shed new light on the father's sending his son, whom he fondly thinks the tenants will respect. The overriding dynamics of the whole story, which unify and impart coherence to all the particular elements, may be described as a deteriorating relationship between the man who planted the vineyard and his tenants, occurring at a critical time: in his sending of his servants and their treatment of them; in his sending his son and their treatment of him; and, climactically, in his own forthcoming action as pointedly noted in the concluding question (fut. tense) and confirmed by the concluding scriptural reference.

Another false option to be avoided in addressing this passage is to ask whether the story of the wicked tenants is to be taken as a parable *or* as an allegory. Adolf Jülicher drew the sharp distinction, at least apropos of this passage.[19] Even granting W. G. Kümmel's forthright criticism of M. Boucher's understanding of Jülicher,[20] Boucher correctly observes that allegory is not a genre in itself, but a mode of interpretation.[21] Indeed, it seems impossible to conceive how allegory could exist as a possible literary form. One finds allegorical biblical interpretations of texts (exposition rather than narratives) like Gal 4,21-5,1, allegorical dramas (notably "morality plays" like *Everyman*), allegorical poems (Edmund Spenser's *The Faerie Queen*), as well as allegorical interpretations of parables.[22] In no small number of works, allegory is subtly intended, at times if only by the circumstances in which, let us say, a play is produced. Jean Anouilh's *Antigone* is a case in point. As K. Snodgrass argues, appealing to X. Léon-Dufour,[23] there is nothing in the parable of the wicked tenants which is not in keeping with the essential nature of a parable, so that a choice need not be made to label it an allegory as contradistinguished from a parable.

Furthermore, one should expect to find implicit in Jesus' parables, notably those classifiable as extended metaphors, an endeavor to render the story relevant to the reader's own need and situation and, thereby, an allegorical bent.

---

[19] A Jülicher, *Die Gleichnisreden Jesu* (Tübingen I, ²1910) 385-406, 402, 406.

[20] W. G. Kümmel, "Jesuforschung seit 1965, IV Teil," *TRu* 43 (1978) 105-61; 233-65; 137-8.

[21] Madeleine Boucher, *The Mysterious Parable. A Literary Study* (CBQMS 6; Washington 1977) 17-24.

[22] For example, that of the sower, Mark 4,13-20 pars. The parallels seem to develop further the process of allegorization, that is, of allusive reflection grounded in the basic, extended metaphor of sowing seed with various results.

Snodgrass, *Parable of the Wicked Tenants*, 25 and n. 55, shows that a rabbinic parable similar to that of the wicked tenants was interpreted allegorically.

[23] Snodgrass, ibid., 25 n. 54.

Understanding the parables (sc., knowing the mystery of the kingdom of God; Mark 4,10.12.24-25 and pars.), in accord with the purpose of Jesus' religious teaching, must imply application of the story to the hearer's life and receptivity to it, not merely a conceptualistic grasp of the "point(s)" of the story.

Since such application supposes reflective thinking, allegorization is implicitly evoked and becomes "more or less" expected of the hearer. Perhaps, as in Matt 13,36-43, reflective thinking prompts a didactic, point-by-point application, although this need not be called for by the parable itself. Even in Matt 13,36-43, didactic allegorization remains a function of a direct appropriation of Jesus' teaching. It is not a product of the evangelist's own, independent speculation. A further mode of allegorizing, along the lines of a Neoplatonic ecclesiastical writer like Origen, spins a new world of ideas out of the story or elements within it. This further mode of thinking (akin to what a Thomist would call "second-intention" thinking, as in logic or mathematics) seems to depart completely from exegesis or exegetical theology, if only because it has departed from the intention of the narrative on which it is based and its inner, narrative cohesion.[24] The new ideas rather than an elucidation of the biblical tradition have become objects of speculation in themselves.

We may now move ahead to the third step of this part of our inquiry, analysis of the progression of Luke's version of the parable. The background for Mark's description of the vine, as all recognize, is Isa 5,1-7, the allegorical Song of the Vineyard. The vineyard symbolizes Israel; its owner and planter, the Lord; its disappointing produce, moral infidelity. Seldom noted are the significant alterations of Isa 5,1-7 which are shared by all the Synoptics, and which figure prominently in the sketch of the dynamics of the story as they tell it (*see above*, p. 62). In the Synoptics, it is not the bad fruit of the vineyard (albeit allegorically characterizing the moral fault later stigmatized as injustice and violence, cf. Isa 5,7) which occasions the owner's just punishment, but rather the hostile conduct of the tenants towards those whom the owner sends them, especially his son. What is more, none of the Synoptics speaks of the destruction of the vineyard, although the theme of demolition figures prominently in Isa 5,5-6. All of them speak instead of the transfer of the vineyard to others, and of the destruction of the tenants. In doing so, at least as directing the parable solely to the Jewish leaders (Matt; Mark), the Synoptics seem to envisage mainly a management-group, although other co-tenants are not excluded. The parable itself makes no such distinction any more than does Isaiah. Nevertheless, its frame-passages, especially in Luke, do so. Lastly, in asking the tenants to pass judgment on themselves, a feature of Isa 5,4 just before Yahweh (vv. 5-7) answers the question he poses, the Synoptics place the question on Jesus' lips, and both Mark and Luke attribute to him the answer.

---

[24] Cf. my criticism of J. Danten, "La révélation du Christ sur Dieu dans les Paraboles," *NRT* 87 (1955) 450-77, 468 ff., in "Structural and Theological Considerations on Luke 15," *CBQ* 24 (1962) 15-31, 26-7 and n. 35.

Luke initially draws little attention to the vineyard, so little, indeed, that some have concluded he makes no reference to Isa 5.[25] Crossan's observation that the phraseology "planted (a vineyard)" rather than merely "had (a vineyard)" still holds as solidly alluding to Isa 5.[26] Further support for the allusion may be found in the reaction the people voice to Jesus' answer to his own challenging question (Luke 20,15b-16a). In replying (v. 16b) "Heaven forbid!" (μὴ γένοιτο) upon hearing him, they must be supposed to have seen themselves implicated in a situation which they construed as implicitly allegorical, based on Isa 5. What is more, Luke's omission of details relevant to the building of the vineyard's installations (its fence, vat, and tower) finds its explanation later, in his description of the planter's attempt to communicate with his tenants. After detailing the various sendings, in which he has twice pointedly used the phrasing "and *went on to send*" (καὶ προσέθετο πέμψαι, vv. 11.12), Luke has the Lord of the vineyard ask himself, "What shall I do?" (τί ποιήσω;).[27] This is the question that the Lord asked himself in Isa 5,4 (LXX, τί ποιήσω ἔτι ...), but with reference there to effort expended in building up the plantation. Luke eliminated all and only what suggested effort expended in construction, retaining solely the necessary allusion to "planting the vineyard," and has turned his reader's attention to the planter's effort to establish communication with the tenants in order to elicit from them a favorable response.

To appreciate Luke's concern to develop the vineyard motif with attention to the owner's efforts to elicit a response, one should note that the planter goes away "for a good length of time" (χρόνους ἱκανούς, a Lucan addition). Then, "at an opportune time" (καιρῷ, no article, otherwise than in Mark, and thus suggesting, perhaps, a less definite situation),[28] he sends a servant. Luke's phrasing of the servant's implied task conveys the note of a quite reasonable, tactfully-stated request, "that they should give him [something] from the fruit of the vineyard." Mark worded the mission more bluntly: "to receive/take from the tenants [a return] from the fruits of the vineyard." Matthew develops the Marcan point in the direction of the owner's unquestionable right (Matt 21,34, τοὺς καρποὺς αὐτοῦ; cp. also his characterization of the owner as οἰκοδεσπότης, v. 33), whereas Luke moves in a contrary direction, hinting at the owner's congeniality.

When he develops the succession of sendings, Luke rewrites Mark considerably. For he has only three sendings, which he states step by step: "went on to send another/a second (ἕτερον)," and "went on to send a third (τρίτον)." Mark speaks of multiple sendings, as is evident from 12,5b, καὶ πολλοὺς ἄλλους.

---

[25] *See above,* n. 18.

[26] J. D. Crossan, "The Parable of the Wicked Husbandmen," *JBL* 90 (1971) 451-65, 452.

[27] This is probably an aor. deliberative subj., or the fut. ind. as its equivalent; cf. Blass–Debrunner–Funk, *Greek Grammar of the New Testament* (Chicago 1961) § 366.

[28] Surely not, as in Matt, a time of reckoning: "to produce *his* fruits," i.e., those to which the owner has a right (Matt 21,34).

Furthermore, Mark depicts the treatment of the servants as predominantly disgraceful. Although some progression in Mark's story may be discerned in the line of increasing disregard for those sent, he does not seem to have worked out this motif consistently. Mark's attention is occupied with the number of servants so treated as much as with the quality of their treatment. The third is killed; many others (sc., later) are either beaten or killed. In Luke's account, none of the three servants is killed. That climactic crime Luke reserves for the treatment of the son. A certain maltreatment is observable, however, in Luke's handling of the servants. The first is sent away empty-handed after a beating. The second, too (κἀκεῖνον) is beaten and sent away empty-handed (for the non-response of the tenants remains Luke's chief interest), but Luke retains the Marcan note of dishonorable treatment. Regarding the third servant, Luke remarks that he was physically, severely wounded (τραυματίσαντες). He also shifts from the main verb he has twice used (ἐξαπέστειλαν) to one which, in context, indicates not just dismissal but brutal dismissal (ἐξέβαλον).

Although the servants in all three Synoptics probably allude to the prophets, the allusion is not to be pressed, as it would be if urged to the point of detracting from the presentation of the owner's action in sending his son and in requiting the tenants for their treatment of his son. For Luke, in particular, treatment of prophets may be expected to end with their murder.[29] Here, however, he does not say that even one of the servants has been murdered and, unlike Mark, does not suggest that the son himself is partly characterized by a servant's role (cf. Mark 12,6a, "He still had one [left]"). A somewhat loose analogy with "God's emissaries" seems to be as much as is called for in order to represent the Lucan thrust and focus of the parable.

After the sendings of the servants, Mark introduces the son as "the one left" (ἔτι ἕνα εἶχεν) whom he sent to them "last of all" (ἔσχατον). In effect, the beloved son figures as "the last chance" for any change in the generally worsening relationships between the owner and his tenants. Luke mutes Mark's note of eschatological urgency. Indeed, he replaces anything that suggests it. He refers to the owner by title (ὁ κύριος) and concentrates on his deliberation, rephrasing Mark's narrative εἶπεν ... ἀπέστειλεν ... λέγων (which latter alone introduces a quoted statement) with εἶπεν δέ ... plus a quotation expressing the Lord's deliberation. In Luke's quotation, the Lord asks himself what he should do; clearly, he is patiently attempting to elicit a reasonable response from his tenants. He goes on to say, "I shall send my beloved son." If only by the addition of a possessive pronoun at this point,[30] Luke's phrasing serves to heighten the tone of personal effort on the part of the owner. Luke further states the owner's

---

[29] Cf. Luke 11,47-51, noting that Luke fastens attention on "prophets" in vv. 47.50 (cp. Matt 18,29.35); 13,33-34; Acts 7,52.

[30] Mark has the pronoun (μου) where it looks to the possible reaction, suggesting the *one* whom they might respect, "my own *son*." Luke links it with the owner's further initiative in the process of communication.

conclusion a bit less ingenuously than Mark does, and with more careful attention to the precise sequence of sendings: "Perhaps (ἴσως) they will respect *this one* (τοῦτον)."

Both in Luke and in Mark, however, the owner is incredibly ingenuous, even to the point of foolishness. Herein lies the principal element of exaggeration in this parable.[31] What reasonable person would ever put his son in jeopardy after such crass treatment of his servants at the hands of his tenants? The Lord already has ample reason to punish them severely. In Mark's account, he risks his son's very life in a last effort to get what he has a right to receive. Although Luke brings out the Lord's cool-headed deliberation in trying to elicit a response, he, too, continues to present him as unbelievably tolerant. Such, however, is the way in which God deals with his people, although this illustration of his patience is probably unmatched even in the OT (e.g., Hosea). The coming judgment, then, will appear as all the more reasonable and even as minimally vindictive.

In response, the tenants decide to kill the heir in order to acquire for themselves the inheritance. Luke sets in sharpest relief their deliberate self-interest. They are provoked upon seeing the son, and then "reason with one another,"[32] not simply "say to themselves" (Mark). Luke goes on to rephrase impulsive animosity in the hope of sudden gain (Mark's δεῦτε ἀποκτείνωμεν... καὶ ἡμῶν ἔσται...) in terms of calculated acquisition (by omitting δεῦτε, and writing ἀποκτείνωμεν αὐτόν followed by a purpose clause, ἵνα ἡμῶν γένηται).

In a manner befitting their thoughts, the tenants then cast the son out of the vineyard (suggesting a kind of symbolic appropriation of it) and slay him (v. 15a). Luke does not intend allegorically to foreshadow Jesus' death "outside the enclosure (sc., the city)," as has often been held.[33] This view, proper to Hebrews (Heb 13,11-13) is one that Luke does not share. For he speaks of the event of Jesus' crucifixion precisely as what transpired "in Jerusalem" (cf. 13,33; 24,18). Nor is E. Schweizer's explanation either helpful or convincing, namely, that Israel had rejected Jesus even before Good Friday.[34] The Marcan order (killing, then casting out) seems intended to convey the idea of "adding insult to injury," a point which Mark already made in describing the treatment of one of the various servants (v. 4). Matthew and Luke independently changed Mark's wording to a less arresting

---

[31] Unconvincingly, Snodgrass, *Parable of the Wicked Tenants,* 31-40, esp. 37-8, tries to argue that this element of the parable (among a list of eight that appear questionable to the twentieth century mind; ibid., 31) would not be considered improbable by Jesus' hearers. Snodgrass fails to consider all the elements together in the context of the *telling of the story.* Elsewhere (ibid., 57), he admits that improbability and hyperbole are features of Jesus' parables.

[32] Needless to say, the term does not always have a pejorative sense (cf. 1,29; 3,15; even 24,38). Nonetheless, Luke often uses it elsewhere (or the nominal form, διαλογισμός) in passages referring to self-interested concerns (5,21.22; 12,17; 6,8; 9,46-47).

[33] E.g., C. H. Dodd, J. Jeremias, E. E. Ellis, Montefiore, Schniewind, as cited by K. Snodgrass, *Parable of the Wicked Tenants,* 60 n. 60.

[34] E. Schweizer, *Das Evangelium nach Lukas* (NTD 3; Göttingen [18]1982) 202.

order of maltreatment. Luke's reason for doing so can sufficiently be explained by his emphasis on the tenants' deliberate moves to appropriate the vineyard.

Underscoring lack of receptivity on the part of the tenants as the cause of the owner's action against them (cf. Luke's addition of οὖν in v. 15b), Luke proceeds to repeat Jesus' question (v. 15b) and have him supply the answer (v. 16a). He notes more carefully than Mark does (by adding "these [τούτους]" to the noun γεωργούς) the transfer of husbandry to another group. This other group is not identified (e.g., as "gentiles") nor does such identification seem to be called for. From the frame-passages placing the parable in its immediate context, one can infer that Luke has in mind mainly the "management group" represented by the high priests and scribes. Admittedly, the people are warned, too, but one would seem to force the point if he viewed them mainly from the standpoint of their ethnicity and read into this passage ethnic diversity as the key to understanding "(the) others."[35] Suffice it to say that the (anarthrous) others are *not these*, malicious tenants.

As noted above (p. 67), Luke's account indicates the people's awareness of implied disaster for themselves, even though Jesus does not direct the parable *against them*. Luke, however, also portrays Jesus as pursuing the warning with a testing look (ἐμβλέψας), the term which recurs in describing the look which Jesus directs at Peter (22,61). Here, his look directly prefaces a questioning reference to a biblical text (Ps 117,22). Luke does not cite this text in order to go on, as Mark does, to speak of the paradoxical process of construction as a marvelous event. Both in Mark and in Luke, as may be supported from the use of this proof-text elsewhere in the NT, the text on the rejected stone made into the cornice-stone[36] of the whole edifice evokes the mystery of Jesus' resurrection. Luke, however, employs the text to bridge a connection with a proverbial saying applied to a further function of that stone, namely, his bringing about unavoidable judgment, whether adverse contact with the stone implies active opposition or not. Applied to the cited text, then (cf. "on *that* stone"), is a proverbial saying expressing devastating judgment.

In a recent study of this proverbial statement, Robert Doran[37] makes a number of valid observations. The saying, he remarks, may remind one of OT

---

[35] Even in Matt 21,41, the "others" are determined qualitatively as a "productive" group.

[36] According to Snodgrass, *The Parable of the Wicked Tenants,* 103, the evidence used to interpret a cornerstone in the Bible as a top stone (= cornice stone) is weak and late. Nonetheless, the point of the saying is evidently that something considered of no value has become a necessary part of the building and (if Ps 117,23 is also taken into account) its crowning glory. The "visual imagery," however, is not pursued by Luke, and must not be pressed literal-mindedly when dealing with his second "stone-text," in 20,18. Somewhat as when dealing with apocalyptic imagery, one must look to thematic associations in otherwise bizarre image-clusters. For Jesus' parabolic images are not presented as sermon-illustrations.

[37] R. Doran, "Luke 20:18: A Warrior's Boast?" *CBQ* 45 (1983) 61-7.

passages like Isa 8,7-15 and Dan 2,45, but requires attention, like that which Bornkamm gave it, to the kind of saying it is,[38] namely, a proverbial statement. He argues that, of the first three sayings adduced by Bornkamm, the closest to the formal structure is the rabbinic proverb:

> "If a stone falls on a pot, woe to the pot!
> If a pot falls on a stone, woe to the pot!
> Either way, woe to the pot!"[39]

On the other hand, Doran's interest in formal structure leads him to seek out closer constructions in texts which strike one as alien to Luke's thought and particularly to this parabolic context. Too readily, he supposes that the essence of a proverb is to be easily comprehensible, and that Luke 20,18 fails the test.[40] For, in this parabolic context, where v. 18 is bonded with v. 17 (by the use of ἐκεῖνον τὸν λίθον in v. 18) and the statement about rejection by the "builders" is expanded to encompass anyone at odds with Jesus, no need arises to determine the "material" which is imperiled (whether pottery, or iron, etc.). Nor is any specifically hortatory application (e.g., "Woe to the pot!") called for; Jesus' testing look suffices to prompt it on the part of the hearers themselves. Furthermore, by omitting v. 23 of Ps 117, Luke does not eliminate reference to the resurrection,[41] for that is already contained in v. 22 (cf. Acts 4,11; 1 Pet 2,4.7). Rather, he moves the reader's thought to the ascension and parousia, when the glorified Jesus functions as ruler of the world and judge.

The literary parallel which Doran alleges is closest to Luke's thought is the one which Bornkamm cited from the Mandean Liturgy:

> "Every devil who rushes against me will be hurled down
> And against whom I rush   will be hurled down."[42]

By tendentiously interpreting Luke's use of πίπτειν ἐπί in both clauses of v. 18 in terms of belligerent action (using words "parallel" to "rush" as middle terms), Doran takes this "warrior's boast" as normative for translating Luke 20,18 thus:

> "Anyone who attacks that stone will be crushed,
> Anyone whom it attacks it will grind to powder."[43]

---

[38] Ibid., 62.

[39] Ibid. The imagery also recurs, perhaps independently, in Cervantes, as an example of peasant wisdom:
"Si da el cántaro en la piedra o la piedra en el cántaro, mal para el cántaro."
"Refranes del 'Quixote'" cap. xx, in *Refranero Español,* Federico Carlo Sáinz de Robles (Colection Crisol 80; Madrid n.d.) 508.

[40] Doran, ibid., 63.

[41] As Doran apparently holds he does; ibid., 66.

[42] Doran, ibid., 63.

[43] Ibid., 65.

He concludes by saying: "Luke has skillfully used this warrior's boast so that Jesus makes clear to the people and to the Jewish authorities just whom they are dealing with. It is a last call to repentance." [44]

That πίπτειν ἐπί even with the accusative (rather than a datival construction, as Doran admits is more usual) may mean "attack" can be conceded. Within the NT, however, notably in Luke's own works, it does not elsewhere have that sense (cp. the description of the fall of the tower of Siloam, Luke 13,4,, or the cry to the mountains, 23,30). Furthermore, is it probable that Luke's Jesus could express a call to repentance as a "warrior's boast," as if he frightened people into repentance with a personal threat? Doran's characterization of the saying seems to be an "over-interpretation." True, at times Jesus does warn of severe judgment for those who have refused to accept him or who fail in expected productivity, and he does so by alluding to himself as the eventually exalted king (as, notably, in the parable of the pounds, 19,11-27). Even so, the parable of the pounds clarifies the perspective of the kingdom; it is not set forth as an appeal for repentance. Much less are even demanding calls to repentance (cf. 13,1-9; 10,13-16; 11,29-32; 16,30-31) cast as threats of what Jesus will do personally, or as self-assertive, boastful expressions of "whom they are dealing with."

Lastly, one must be careful in this passage not to equate in the application of Jesus' statement (as Doran apparently does in his conclusion) the leaders and the people. The very difficult nature of the proverb, of which Doran complains, may be required by nuances which Luke intended in its application. The strongest warning of a final reckoning is intended for the leaders of the people; the people themselves are indeed warned, but hardly "attacked" or personally threatened by Jesus' testing interrogation. Even that testing look, as in the case of his encounter with Peter (22,61–although, in Peter's case, there is a reminiscence of future conversion as well as the warning of betrayal, cp. 22,31-34) is less a suggestion of proximate repentance than a pressing home of the consequences for the murderous tenants and those more or less implicated with them.

To conclude analysis of the Lucan emphasis in recounting this parable: There remains even in Luke a strong allusion to Isaiah's Song of the Vineyard. Although Luke distinguishes the people from their leaders, against whom Jesus specifically directs the parable, he has Jesus pointedly warn the people. As Israelites, and, *in casu*, Jerusalemites, they in turn recognize implied disaster for themselves. Luke takes care, however, to stress the Lord of the vineyard's incredibly patient, deliberative efforts to elicit a favorable response from his tenants. Here, Luke makes use of Isa 5, although in a distinctive way. He also faults the tenants on the score of calculated self-interest. He goes on to find the consequences of their slaying the son not just in a transference of tenancy nor, specifically, a transference occurring only in consequence of the resurrection. Rather, he envisages a forthcoming, ineluctable judgment by the rejected stone, but does not express this in an antagonistic, boastful manner.

---

[44] Ibid., 67.

We should now turn briefly to consider, with a view to this implied judgment and the historical-typological moral which the parable supports, the texts which precede and follow it.

C. The Parable as Contributing to the Historical-Typological Moral

Preceding the account of Jesus' teaching in the temple and his telling this parable, Luke has made quite clear the forthcoming fate of the city. Its inhabitants have not responded (19,41-44) to the coming of the Messiah when they should have done so. In the parable of the wicked tenants, he points out that Jesus alerts the people to consequences for themselves, even though he does not direct the parable against them. Unlike Mark and Matthew, however, Luke strives to make the parable directly relevant to the people, even though he points out that Jesus' intended condemnation is directed precisely against their leaders. In recasting the Marcan parable, Luke has conditioned his reader to perceive God's forbearance in bringing judgment upon the whole group of tenants, and, at the same time, has indicated the ineluctable character of a judgment arising from the slaying of his son. The coming moment of judgment, however, is not depicted as a self-assertive boast nor, univocally, as applicable to everyone in his audience; the term πᾶς ("everyone") in 20,18 remains ambivalent according to the frame-passages of the parable itself. In the wider context of the Jerusalem narrative, Luke has moved from non-recognition of the Messiah (especially by the people—yet notably by some Pharisees among them) to intended violence against the Lord's son (specifically, by the leaders of the people, typed as high priests and scribes) as grounds for judgment affecting the inhabitants of the city (as they themselves perceive). He has also refocused the scope of judgment from "the crowd" mentioned in 19,39 to "the people."

Although the people enthusiastically listen to Jesus, their enthusiasm has not amounted to the kind of recognition he expected at his entry. In the light of foregoing texts in Luke, the people may therefore be regarded as "impressed unbelievers." The extension of the Lucan perspective to include in the scenario of the coming judgment the people themselves will emerge unequivocally from a study of the forthcoming "eschatological discourse." Similarly, the focus on Jerusalem itself, as the capital of the whole nation, and thus representative of the people, will be brought out explicitly later on. In the parable of the wicked tenants, the emphasis falls mainly on "Israel," although, because of the programmatic OT quotation (cf. esp. Isa 5,3, "... men of Jerusalem and of Judah ...") as well as by reason of the temple-forum chosen for Jesus' telling this parable, the fate of Jerusalem is at least implied. In brief, Luke has reworked the Marcan version of the parable of the wicked tenants to stress both God's forbearance and the inescapable judgment to come, though with a marked distinction between the people and their leaders. Thus, he has provided a qualified connection between the oracle of judgment against the city in 19,41-44 and the eschatological discourse. The final qualification, as we shall see, will occur in Jesus' words to the sympathetic daughters of Jerusalem.

VII. Jesus' Final Discourse in the Temple (Luke 20,45 – 21,36)

To avoid slighting the adequate context and scope of Luke's so-called eschatological discourse (21,5-36), it is advisable first to recall the placement of the latter pericope in the narrative sequence which Luke has provided. Jesus' teaching in the temple contains three major sections, each governed mainly by the needs of the particular audience in question. Each also contains a reference to an aspect of his passion, resurrection, or parousia.

The first major section (20,1-26) is devoted to Jesus' teaching the people, with a marked polemic directed against the high priests and scribes. Its central episode consists of the parable of the wicked tenants.

The second major section (20,27-44) deals rather irenically with another group, the Sadducees and some scribes. In this section, Jesus tries to bring the Sadducees not only to accept scriptural testimony concerning the resurrection, but to appreciate a new level of existence proper to God's sons, destined for the resurrection. When commended by some scribes (v. 39), he raises the question of a particular state of sonship, the issue of divine sonship of the Messiah in view of the scriptural presentation of David's son as David's Lord. The people do not seem to be mentioned at all, except perhaps by the plural of indefinite reference, "With what right / in what sense do 'they' say ...?" [1]

As the first major section ends with a passage which prepares Luke's reader to grasp the malice of the charge brought against Jesus before Pilate (cp. 20,20 and 23,2), the second closes by preparing the reader to understand Jesus' testimony about himself when he stands before the Sanhedrin (22,66-71).[2] The third section will close with a pastoral warning concerning what needs to be avoided and done by those who hope successfully to stand before the Son of Man come to judge the world (21,34-36, cp. 21,27).

The third major section (20,45 – 21,36) of the sample day of teaching in the temple introduces still another change in the audience (20,45). Since the disputatious religious leaders have been silenced (20,26b.40), Jesus no longer

---

[1] Cf. Blass – Debrunner – Funk, *Greek Grammar of the New Testament* (Chicago 1961) § 131 (1). On the sense of πῶς, cf. Arndt – Gingrich, *Greek-English Lexicon of the New Testament* (Chicago ²1979) πῶς, 1.a.

[2] The combination of Dan 7,13 with Ps 110 evokes a new image not contained in either text taken by itself, and conveys the notion of divine messiahship: a Davidic Messiah empowered with the divine prerogative of heavenly judgment. From the way Jesus answers the question about his Messiahship (in Luke's account), the Sanhedrists rightly conclude (οὖν) in their further question that he means he is God's Son, not just David's.

reasons with them. He has concluded his discussion even with appreciative religious leaders (20,39) by offering to them further food for thought (20,41-44). Once more the people themselves are expressly introduced as part of Jesus' audience, but secondarily, as those who hear what Jesus addresses to his disciples. Later reference to the remarks of "some" who were speaking about the temple (21,5) is not clearly delimited. One may opt to identify these as disciples (as supposed by the specific exhortations of the discourse, cf. vv, 12-19.28.34-36) or as members of the people (because of the respectful address, διδάσκαλε, in v. 7a, which Luke elsewhere does not place on the lips of Jesus' disciples when they address him).[3] As Paul Minear has observed, Luke regularly determines his audience exactly, notably at the beginning of a discourse.[4] That he does not do so here suggests that a special discourse does not begin with 21,5, but with 20,45. What is more, Luke has eliminated the Marcan restriction of Jesus' words to his disciples not only in 21,5-7 (cp. Mark 13,1.3) but also in 21,1-4 (cp. Mark 12,43a), and has altered the Marcan notation in 12,37b to direct Jesus' words mainly to the disciples (20,45). At the same time, Luke directs Jesus' words in this third major section not just to "a large crowd" but to a representatively universal audience of Jews in their public forum, the temple: "in the hearing of the whole people."

Thus, the so-called eschatological discourse (21,5-36) is squarely situated in the context of the moral conduct which Jesus denounces or commends to his disciples in a public discourse which proves to be his final one, heard by the whole people. Opening this discourse are two models of religious persons. The model to be avoided (20,46-47) is that of ostentatious scribes who devour the homes of widows and will receive very severe judgment.[5] The model commended is that of the poor widow who contributes all that she has, probably a gesture of her totally selfless reliance on God.[6] Luke makes virtually no changes from Mark's version of

---

[3] Elsewhere, Luke replaces the disciples' use of διδάσκαλε (Mark 4,38; 9,38) or ῥαββί (9,5) with ἐπιστάτα (Luke 8,24; 9,49) and employs ἐπιστάτα independently in 5,5; 8,45; 9,34; and (of non-disciples' form of address) in 17,13. In 22,11, however, where Jesus instructs Peter and John to refer to him as ὁ διδάσκαλος Luke shows that he does not reject the use of the title by disciples (*pace* L. Gaston). Nevertheless, Luke's usage here suggests that he surely does not intend that the speakers be assumed to be disciples.

[4] Paul S. Minear, "Jesus' Audiences, According to Luke," *NT* 16 (1974) 81-109.

[5] Since the comparative adjective here is not employed in comparing the judgment of this group with another, it can readily be taken in the accepted sense of a superlative; cf. Zerwick – Smith, *Biblical Greek* (Rome 1963) §§ 146, 151.

[6] Addison G. Wright, "The Widow's Mites: Praise or Lament? – A Matter of Context," *CBQ* 44 (1982) 256-65, takes Jesus' saying in Luke 21,1-4 and Mark 12,41-44 as that of a religious reformer, who regards her contribution as totally misguided, thanks to the encouragement of official religion, and a waste (ibid., 263). Contrary to Wright, the context in both Gospels is not identical. For Luke, in particular, what emerges in the (more closely conjoined) two scenes (20,46-47; 21,1-4) is a contrast of *basic religious dispositions*. Whether the widow was wise or not (or even whether or not she had been an instance of religious exploitation in the past) in giving her last two, thin copper coins – which one could

the model to be shunned, although he does pay more attention to the issue of an interior attitude of mind.[7] He does seem considerably to depolemicize Mark's negative view of the temple-centered religious practices in the contrasted model.[8] In Luke's version, both passages entail contrasts between the rich and the poor. More importantly, however, both deal with Jesus' perception of motives for action and help condition the reader to attend to what follows not mainly as to an awesome scenario of destruction in the end-time, but as to a pattern of conduct required on the part of his disciples, specifically, one that results from discerning the religious meaning of coming events.

Again, without a change of locale, Luke situates Jesus' words about the temple and his explanatory discourse in the temple itself. There appears to be no sufficient reason to suppose for part or all of Luke 21,5-36 a source other than Mark, especially when one has found ample reasons to account for redactional changes which render quite intelligible Luke's own version.[9] To set these in relief, however, it may help briefly to sketch Jan Lambrecht's analysis of the structure of Mark 13.[10] I hasten to add that my theory of the structure of the Lucan discourse is not predicated on acceptance of Lambrecht's analysis of Mark, particularly on the perhaps overly-detailed criteria which he employed in articulating it. Nevertheless, in my opinion, Lambrecht does offer the most intelligible and persuasive outline of Mark's discourse. If only for sweet clarity's sake, it should be a boon to advert to it — albeit in a simpler, adapted form

---

argue were barely enough to sustain her for a day – is not the point of the story. That point is her total reliance on God (like that of "the poor" elsewhere considered by Luke – not as a socio-economic group but rather as a religious type) as shown by her generosity in contrast to what others offered from their abundance.

[7] The most significant alteration is Luke's attention to the interior attitude or disposition, sc., by adding φιλούντων in v. 46.

[8] The term "treasury" recurs repeatedly (thrice) in Mark. He appears to stress the wealth of the temple, and situates Jesus as "seated opposite" the treasury for his address to the disciples. A similar tension appears in 13,3, where Jesus is seated opposite the temple (a massive, fortress-like structure, vv. 1-2, so described on the way out) as his disciples ask him about its ruin.

[9] The stylistic analysis justifying this assumption has been worked out clearly and solidly by Fridolin Keck, *Die öffentliche Abschiedsrede Jesu in Lk 20,45 – 21,36. Eine redaktions- und motivgeschichtliche Untersuchung* (FzB 25, Stuttgart 1976) 36-84, 108-89, 263-82.

In striving to justify calling 20,45 – 21,36 a "farewell discourse," Keck strongly appeals (ibid., 317-27) to O. Michel's criteria (*Brief an die Hebräer* [KEK 13; Göttingen [6]1966] 90 f., 87-9, 100-6, 104, 108). Still, the admitted lack in 20,45 – 21,36 of any explicit note of Jesus' departure or death, which regularly appears in other Lucan eschatological discourses (12,50; 17,25; 22,36-37) suggests that "Open Farewell Address" is an over-interpretation of Jesus' "Final Public Exhortation Regarding the End-Time."

[10] Jan Lambrecht, *Die Redaktion der Markus-Apokalypse. Literarische Analyse und Strukturuntersuchung* (AnBib 28; Rome 1967). Note especially pp. 263-97 and the fold-out page at the back.

offered below — in order to facilitate subsequent comparison with Luke's version. The Marcan schema provided here will be discussed in the course of examining Luke's departures from it. My schematization of the Lucan discourse will be provided below (pp. 85-86).

13,1-4	*Introduction:* address to the first four disciples called.	

13,5-23	*A.*	CONCERNING THE SIGNS
13,5a		Introductory phrase
13,5b-6		*a. Watch out* that you are not deceived!
13,7-8		*b. When you hear* of wars, do not be upset; not the end, but the beginning of birth-throes.
13,9-13		*c. Watch out* for yourselves — betrayal, testimony for my sake, survival in the end.
13,14-20		*b'. When you see* the profanation of the Temple, flee; the tribulation par excellence, but shortened.
13,21-23		*a'.* Do not believe in false Messiahs — *watch out!* I have told you everything beforehand.

13,24-27	*B.*	THE COMING OF THE SON OF MAN
		After that tribulation; gathering of the elect.

13,28-36	*A'.*	CONCERNING THE TIME
13,28-29		*a.* Parable of the fig tree — he is near *at the gates.*
13,30		*b.* Logion assuring imminent coming.
13,31		*c.* Logion assuring the transcendent permanence of Jesus' words.
13,32		*b'.* Logion about not knowing the day or hour.
13,33-36		*a'.* Parable inculcating alertness, especially for *the gatekeeper.*

13,37	*Conclusion:* explanation extended to all.	

Now, when studying Luke's account of Jesus' words concerning Jerusalem (21,20-24), it becomes indispensable to consider them in the whole proximate context (vv. 5-36) into which they have been integrated. Two headings may prove to be sufficient as well as necessary. First (A), we should sketch the articulation of the whole Lucan discourse vis-à-vis Mark, especially to render plausible the link between the destruction of Jerusalem and the catastrophic events in store for the world at large. For our thesis is that the former is a case in point, a historical lesson which looks towards the latter, universal judgment. The first point in establishing this thesis demands attention, therefore, to the articulated unity and coherence of the Lucan discourse. Second (B), more detailed observations in line with the above will show that, while Luke distinguishes the fall of Jerusalem (vv. 20-24) from the end of the world (vv. 25-27), he also interrelates the two events; he does not separate them. They are both components of his eschatological perspective of fulfillment. This interrelationship may be expected to help disclose the reasons for the destruction of Jerusalem as Luke perceives them and to account for his concern with the event for the benefit of his reader.

A. The Over-All Structure of Luke 21,5-36

Rather than debate the wide variety of "outlines" proposed by commentators, but drawing on the best analysis to date, that of Fridolin Keck,[11] I shall discursively present my own. Its principal justification will lie mainly in whether or not it yields fruitful results. The first item to consider is the immediate setting for the discourse, Jesus' prediction, and the question posed to him. The second item is the structural articulation of Jesus' reply.

Much less formally than Mark, Luke sets the stage for Jesus' discourse by noting a remark apropos of which Jesus predicts the dismantling of the temple and then replies to a query posed to him. Without much ado, the topic of discussion moves from Jesus' observations concerning religious types (20,45; 21,4) to his prediction concerning the impermanence of the magnificent religious center itself. He predicts (εἶπεν, ... vv. 5-6) the ruin of this imposing, beautiful edifice.[12] Since his auditors readily perceive his remark as a prophecy, their request for an indication of the time and especially for the sign comes as no surprise. The Lucan discourse proper then begins with a mere ὁ δὲ εἶπεν in v. 8. Mark, on the other hand, notes Jesus' prediction of the fate of this massive structure as Jesus leaves the temple (13,1-2) and then a new, suggestively antithetical location which may bear out an attitude of opposition to the temple and what it represents. The question posed to him in Mark is broached privately by the first four disciples he had called and looks pregnantly to "the fulfillment of all these things." For, underlying their perhaps superficial concern with the fate of this structure may lie the critical religious issue of what the end of this cult-center will mean for their relationship to God and to Jesus. Mark formally begins the discourse proper in v. 5a (ὁ δὲ Ἰησοῦς ἤρξατο λέγειν αὐτοῖς). Thus, Mark conveys the sense that Jesus' prophecy is a

---

[11] F. Keck, *Die öffentliche Abschiedsrede Jesu in Lk* 20,45 – 21,36, 36-84, 108-89, 263-82. Keck (ibid., 8) regards as the "central part" of Jesus' farewell discourse Luke 21,10-28. Concluding warnings (ibid., 10) occur in 21,29-36. Although, admittedly, the discourse as a whole begins with 20,45, Keck's view of the unity of 20,45 – 21,9 as a "Grosse einleitende Paränese" (ibid., 8) should be corrected. For 21,10 refers more proximately to v. 8 and, through that verse, to the new issue introduced in vv. 5-7.

[12] The eschatological note is sounded with ἐλεύσονται ἡμέραι (v. 6; cp. 5,35 [par. Mark 2,20]; 17,22; cp. 19,43).

mystery to be explained, although he takes care at the close of the discourse (13,37) to exclude the note of esoteric teaching.

Both in Mark and in Luke, however, Jesus' answer will prove to transcend the point of view of his questioners. As elsewhere, in all the Gospels, Jesus never gives a pat answer, a merely informational answer, but always an educative one, which imparts a new perspective and demands a further level of reflective thinking concerning religious issues.[13] Even in Mark's version of the discourse, Jesus will recast the prediction of the temple's destruction as its idolatrous profanation during the great tribulation that immediately presages the coming of the Son of Man and the realization of the community of those chosen by God.[14] The genuine focal point of the disciples' religious concerns is to be the coming of the Son of Man and their readiness for it. Luke's version maintains this Christological focus, and further subordinates the importance of the temple to the fate of the city for which, however, the temple has regularly figured as a religious forum. Luke is not concerned with the Christological or anti-Christological significance of the Jewish cult-center, but with the city in whose religious and cultural heart Jesus has been teaching.

Luke articulates both the beginning of Jesus' discourse and its development by marking three stages paced off by noting Jesus' own words. Thus, Luke follows ὁ δὲ εἶπεν (v. 8) with τότε ἔλεγεν αὐτοῖς (v. 10). The latter phrase calls more attention to itself as the real beginning of an "explanation"[15] both of his prophecy (εἶπεν, v. 5) and of his opening warning in replying to his questioners (ὁ δὲ εἶπεν, v. 8). With v. 10 (not in Mark), and also with the omission of ἀρχὴ ὠδίνων ταῦτα in Mark 13,8c, Luke begins strikingly to depart from the Marcan structure. He opens the next and concluding stage of Jesus' discourse with v. 29, καὶ εἶπεν παραβολὴν αὐτοῖς (not in Mark),[16] having in the meantime suppressed a concluding formula in Mark 13,23b, προείρηκα ὑμῖν πάντα.

---

[13] The pattern can be noted regularly in all of the evangelists. Perhaps one of the most striking developments of it is found in John, in four instances where Jesus' action follows upon his own indicated point of view, at odds with a suggestion implying an urgent human need, to which he reacts negatively; cf. C. H. Giblin, "Suggestion, Negative Response, and Positive Action in St. John's Portrayal of Jesus (John 2.1-11; 4.46-54; 7.2-14; 11.1-44)," NTS 26 (1980-81) 197-211.

[14] This would be in line with the Marcan view that Jesus is the builder of a temple not made with hands, the Christian community. Cf. Donald Juel, Messiah and Temple. The Trials of Jesus in the Gospel of Mark (SBLDS 31; Missoula 1977) 208-9. In this text, however, which Juel does not examine, the contrast lies between an idol and the Son of Man, and between profanation prophetically fulfilled and the gathering of the elect at the Son of Man's prophesied coming.

[15] The meaning "explain" is not infrequently supposed by the more general sense of λέγειν, sc., "tell." Moreover, it here begins a longer passage: "In deutlichem Unterschied zum Aorist εἶπεν leitet also bei Luk das Imperfekt ἔλεγεν eine längere und bedeutende Rede ein." F. Keck, Die öffentliche Abschiedsrede Jesu, 111.

[16] The phrase is typically Lucan; cf. F. Keck, ibid., 264. Not infrequently, Luke introduces a parable as the concluding portion of Jesus' words to a given audience (cf. 5,36; 6,39; 12,16; 13,6; 19,11).

Luke's restructuring of Jesus' ongoing discourse entails a number of adjustments to the temporal schema employed by Mark. In the first stage (vv. 8-9), Luke underscores the "non-immediacy" of the parousia. False prophets appear who aver that "the time is at hand" (v. 8b, not in Mark). When wars and rebellions occur, the end is not immediate (v.9). At this point, Mark's discourse looks ahead to when the end (τὸ τέλος) will indeed occur, for he says it is "not yet" (οὔπω, Mark 13,7), whereas Luke cautions that it does not lie in the immediate future (οὐκ εὐθέως τὸ τέλος, v. 9c), because these instances (ταῦτα) of religious deception and political disturbances must occur as a prior condition, not just as an inevitable necessity (adding πρῶτον in v. 9 to Mark's δεῖ γενέσθαι).

After alerting the audience to non-eschatological "signs" and views of "imminence," Luke's discourse, not unlike Mark's, takes a decidedly positive turn. Using the imperfect of λέγειν after τότε, Luke suggests a more important, subsequent stage of Jesus' discourse: "Then he went on to say [explain] to them ..." [17] Here, Luke begins to depart from the Marcan "sign structure," which is dictated largely by a schematized temporal framework: the beginning of birth-pangs (*Aab* in the schema provided above [p. VII/6]), the logically (but perhaps also temporally) prior need to preach the Gospel to all nations and endure until the end (*Ac*),[18] then the period of tribulation in Judea (*Ab'a*) further described as one in which the days are "shortened" because of the elect, and, climactically (*B*) the coming of the Son of Man "after that tribulation."

Luke's perspective is no less eschatological, for all its conscious avoidance of a kind of mechanical schematization of the genuine signs preceding the coming of the Son of Man. He looks forward (vv. 11-12), goes on to state prior, practical concerns for the disciples' relationship to Jesus (vv. 12-19), and then details the end-time scenario (vv. 24-27) which he has announced (vv. 10-11), but combines with it further practical warning (v. 21) or assurance (v. 28) intended for Jesus' audience.

Thus, in vv. 10-11, Luke announces an escalated scenario of the end-time. Significantly, he includes not only the picture of international wars and physical catastrophes (vv. 10--a), but also, *closely conjoined with these* (τε καί, v. 11b), frightening heavenly prodigies as well — whereas Mark has reserved the latter for his § *B*. Luke does not detail the latter here, although he expressly terms them "signs" (σημεῖα). One receives the impression that, in vv. 10-11, Luke is limning the fully eschatological stage of events, but that he sees the "earthly" closely conjoined with the "heavenly," so that the two are not separated, disjunctively related occurrences. Moreover, unlike the warning regarding necessarily prior religious and political confusion (vv. 8-9), the scenario in vv. 10-11 contains no exhortation. In Mark, it did so, at least implicitly, insofar as Mark 13,8 must be

---

[17] Mark's beginning is more formal: ὁ δὲ Ἰησοῦς ἤρξατο λέγειν αὐτοῖς, if only by reason of the reintroduction of the subject of the verb.

[18] Luke omits mention of the end (Mark 13,13b) and stresses the conditions for survival: ... ἐν τῇ ὑπομονῇ ὑμῶν ... v. 19 (cp. 8,15).

joined to 13,5a-7 (because of the way ἀρχὴ ὠδίνων ταῦτα picks up and concludes δεῖ γενέσθαι, and γάρ joins v. 8 to the exhortation in v. 7a, μὴ θροεῖσθε).

Luke supplies the hortatory element with vv. 12-19, and in a manner which undergirds the tentative inference that he intended vv. 10-11 to depict the fully-fledged eschatological scenario. For he opens the exhortation in v. 12 with πρὸ δὲ τούτων πάντων. The term "all" may comprise even vv. 8-9 (the falsely assumed indications of the end-time) as well as vv. 10-11 (the actual, briefly sketched scenario for it) without any appreciable change of scope. It must certainly cover at least vv. 10-11. Placed at this point, the term πρῶτον (perhaps derived from Mark 13,10) helps improve the coherence of the whole exhortation in vv. 12-19. Although Luke does not mention "preaching the gospel to the whole world," his perspective is no less universal than Mark's since he speaks of kings (adding "governors," ἡγεμόνας, v. 12) as well as Jewish religious adversaries. Luke appears to fasten the reader's attention not so much on the disciples' need to beware of what will happen to themselves (he omits, for example, the programmatic phrase introducing the passage in Mark 13,9a, βλέπετε δὲ ὑμεῖς ἑαυτούς), as he does on the disciples' constant relationship to Jesus in face of persecution by authorities or by personal contacts, and in public controversy.

Thus, three linked segments within vv. 12-19 may be discerned. The first (vv. 12-13) and third (vv. 16-19) predict the disciples being betrayed or "handed over": in the first case (by unnamed enemies) to religious and secular authorities; in the second, by relatives and friends. In both cases, what they will suffer is "for my (Jesus') name." The first segment ends with reference to the occasion for their personal testimony (ὑμῖν, rather than the polemically-oriented Marcan αὐτοῖς); the second, with a paradoxical assurance of the survival of the community. In the center (vv. 14-15), Jesus insistently (θέτε οὖν ...) assures them of his personal gift of articulate wisdom effectively to counter all their adversaries. This coherently composed movement (vv. 12-19) of the second stage of Jesus' discourse (vv. 10-28) suggests that the concluding movement (vv. 20-28) of this stage of the discourse and, indeed, other stages of the discourse, have not been composed haphazardly.

The concluding movement of the second stage consists of vv. 20-28. These verses are set off from the third stage by the introductory phrase in v. 29 (καὶ εἶπεν

---

[19] Earlier (12,11-12), Luke referred to instruction by the Holy Spirit, probably with reference to the testimony of the community following the resurrection-ascension (cp. 12,10b). Here, he seems to have in mind situations to be recounted in Acts; cf. Joseph Zmijewski, *Die Eschatologiereden des Lukasevangeliums. Eine traditions- und redaktionsgeschichtliche Untersuchung zu Lk 21,5-36 und Lk 17,20-37* (BBB 40; Bonn 1972) 137. The Lucan rephrasing of Mark 13,11b, referring to the Holy Spirit, redactionally avoids a doublet of Q material; cf. Ruthild Geiger, *Die Lukanischen Endzeitsreden. Studien zur Eschatologie des Lukas-Evangeliums* (Europäische Hochschulschriften Ser. XXIII, Vol. 16; Frankfurt / M. 1973) 179-80. More significantly, this redactional alteration supports R. J. Dillon's arguments against an "absentee Christology" in Acts; cf. Dillon, "The Prophecy of Christ and His Witnesses According to the Discourses in Acts," (forthcoming in *NTS* [his MS pp. 9, 13, and notes 25 and 38]).

παραβολὴν αὐτοῖς), which opens the closing exhortation. Progressively, the element of exhortation tends to dominate the entire discourse: the whole but brief first stage (vv. 8-9), the major, second movement (vv. 12-19) in the second stage (vv. 10-28), and the whole of the concluding stage (vv. 29-36). The apocalyptic scenario, first as announced (sc., in the first movement, i.e., in vv. 10-11) and then as developed (in the third movement vv. 20-28) is more evidently than in Mark subordinated to pastoral instruction (sc., to vv. 12-19). This observation should be borne in mind when addressing what to some may appear as a merely historical prediction regarding the fate of Jerusalem.

With v. 20, Luke returns to the prospect of the approaching end (cf. vv. 10-11), adding ἤγγικεν, but at the same time restricting the perspective to the desolation of Jerusalem. From Mark, he takes over the phrase "When you see ...," but he does not give it the same function as Mark does in the structure of the eschatological discourse. Mark 13,14 ("When you see ...") introduces a sub-unit (vv. 14-20) concerned with the perversion of the temple cult and, along with this momentous event, the greatest tribulation of all time, which will be abridged only for the sake of God's elect. This sub-unit (vv. 14-20, Ab′ in the Marcan schema) structurally counterweights the foregoing, corresponding sub-unit (vv. 7-8, Ab in the Marcan schema) that spoke of the non-imminent sign of the end ("When you hear ...," v. 7a) describing only the beginning of the birth-pangs. Luke has already broken at least once (v. 10)[20] the concentric pattern of the Marcan discourse. True, Luke's phrase, "when you see" (v. 20) recalls "when you hear" (v. 9), but only in such a way as to command awareness (τότε γνῶτε, v. 20) of the arrival of judgment on Jerusalem. In the Lucan structure, vv. 20-24 develop the "earthly signs," notably v. 19 in the general scenario announced in vv. 10-11, with which Luke began the second stage of Jesus' discourse. As he seems to have alluded to Scripture (2 Chr 15,6; cp. Isa 19,2; 8,21; 13,13) in v. 10b (following Mark in this), he now expressly appeals to Scripture in describing the judgment on Jerusalem (v. 22).[21]

Accordingly, "When you see" in Luke 21,20 builds upon the opening movement of the second stage of Jesus' reply. Luke goes on to combine with the scenario of the war against Jerusalem advice to flee and not to enter the city. He does so, however, only to stress the hopelessness of its situation, not to suggest, as Mark does (13,18), a trial for Christians as well. The woe directed towards women in Luke's account (v. 23) is explained by the ineluctable plight of the land and wrath on the city's people. Christians (and others) who heed the warning given in v. 21 will have escaped the catastrophe (cp. φευγέτωσαν, v. 21, and ἐκφυγεῖν, v. 36). Luke's depiction of the calamity, therefore, centers almost entirely on the

---

[20] Other breaks can be noted: in v. 11 (where Mark 13,8 has ἀρχὴ ὠδίνων), in v. 12 (where Mark 13,9 [cp. 13,5.23a] contains the thematic word βλέπετε), in v. 19 (where Mark 13,13b has εἰς τέλος), in v. 19 (where καὶ ὅταν ἄγωσιν in Mark 13,11 [Ac in the Marcan schema] looks back to v. 7 [Ab] and ahead to v. 14 [Ab′]).

[21] The background and scope of this verse will be discussed below (§ B).

historical fate of the city. His grim view of its end is unrelieved. He remains silent about any tempering of the situation attributable to the elect (cp. Mark 13,20, which Luke omits altogether). At the same time, Luke begins to relate Jerusalem's fate as a prophetic fulfillment (v. 22. ἡμέραι ... τοῦ πλησθῆναι πάντα τὰ γεγραμμένα to a fulfillment of times for nations [v. 24b].... ἄχρι οὗ πληρωθῶσιν καιροὶ ἐθνῶν). Without a break in the narrated discourse, he pursues the point in this third movement (vv. 20-28) of the second stage (vv. 10-28) of Jesus' reply.

Once again, it seems apposite to observe how Luke departs from the Marcan structure at this juncture. Mark 13,21-23 is counterpoised to the warning against deception already given in Mark 13,5b-6 (as *Aa* 'to *Aa*). Luke omits entirely Mark 13,21-23. What is more, with the close of vv. 21-23, Mark voices once again the watchword he has used repeatedly, βλέπετε (which figures prominently in his §§ *Aa, Ac, Aa'*), and he concludes the first major part (*A*) of his discourse: "I have told you everything beforehand." Forthwith, he proceeds to describe heavenly prodigies in a further period (*B*), "In those days, after that tribulation, ... the sun ... the moon ... the stars ...," and the coming of the Son of Man to assemble the elect (Mark 13,24-27). To some small extent, Luke's omission of Mark 13,21-23 may be accounted for by noting that he had used similar material in 17,23. There is solid evidence, however, that a further reason is operative for the extensive omission. For, at the beginning of v. 25, Luke avoids the schematic compartmentalization which would have followed from taking over Mark 13,24. Instead, Luke continues with a conjunctive clause (v. 25) mentioning, but not describing, heavenly signs.

The concluding portion (vv. 25-28) of the third movement of stage two (vv. 10-28), at least as clearly as the first portion (vv. 20-24), recalls the programmatic announcement of end-time events given in vv. 10-11, especially the closely correlated but distinguishable "frightening *signs* (which there will be) *from heaven*." Without the Marcan caesura ("after that tribulation," 13,24), Luke's third movement goes on to describe turmoil among the nations and death from fright at the prospect of events coming upon the whole world (vv. 25b-26a). Nevertheless, even earthly upheavals are ascribed to the shaking of the powers of the heavens (v. 26b, γάρ). These things are but the immediate prelude to the sight of the Son of Man coming for judgment (καὶ τότε, v. 27a). The only instructions offered in this concluding portion are comprised in the closing words of assurance that, "when these things begin," Jesus' disciples are to stand up and raise their heads, for their salvation is approaching.

"These things" must include at least what is mentioned beginning with v. 25. More probably, however, they refer to the whole experience described from v. 20 onwards, that is, from "when they see" Jerusalem besieged and are to know that her desolation has come near (ἤγγικεν) to the point at which people see the Son of Man himself, and the faithful are to realize that their own deliverance is near (ἐγγίζει). Luke has introduced this assurance, reminiscent of the assurance of survival in vv. 18-19, closing the "prior necessity" for disciples (vv. 12-19) to replace the Marcan perspective of the gathering of the elect in triumph. Thus, even

vv. 25-28 are situated in an eschatological but "historical" continuity by attention to the phases of the end-time ("has drawn near... is drawing near").

It is in the third and last stage of Jesus' discourse (vv. 29-36) that Luke expressly takes up the motif of the final assizes. The universal day of reckoning will become a snare only for those who face it morally unprepared. The discourse closes on the warning to be ready to stand before the Son of Man (v. 36).

In this third stage, Luke again breaks away from the Marcan concentric pattern. He edits the opening parable of the fig tree (21,29-31) to bring out the nearness of God's kingdom, dropping mention of Jesus' being near, at the gates. For Luke, this nearness has already been made evident in the sight of the Son of Man (v. 27). The point he makes now is the nearness of the exercise of his power in judgment, the fulfillment of God's kingly rule.[22] In Mark, 13,28-29 is linked with a corresponding parabolic lesson (vv. 33-36) containing a special warning for the gatekeeper — a parable which Luke omits altogether at this point. He retains the Marcan logion (13,30) concerning the occurrence of these events in the lifetime of "this generation,"[23] but omits the corresponding, qualifying logion (13,32) concerning nescience of the day or hour.[24] Luke retains unchanged, however, the

---

[22] This kingly rule, of course, is exercised by Jesus, as the parable told immediately before his proximate approach to Jerusalem is made clear (19,11-27). Luke 21,31 directs attention, however, to the execution of judgment (cp. vv. 34-36) rather than, as in Mark, to the arrival of the judge.

[23] "This generation" should not be *delimited* biologically to Jesus' contemporaries, but should be taken typologically. Elsewhere, added phrases or the context put the typed generation in an unfavorable light (Luke 7,31; 9,41; 11,29.30.31.32.50-51; 16,8; 17,25); here, its scope is general, by reason of the audience addressed, Surely Luke, a third-generation Christian, did not intend to preserve in the context of v. 33 as a relic of Jesus' teaching a logion which proved to be untrue (sc., by being taken literal-mindedly of a biologically delimited generation). As in v. 36, the audience addressed is primarily the disciples, whom Luke hardly considered a biologically-delimited group (cf. 1,1-4).

On the other hand, it is also possible to take ἕως... γένηται as an ingressive aorist ("until... begin to occur"); cp. 1,20 (for Zechariah begins to speak again before much of what Gabriel had told him, cp. vv. 14-17, has actually transpired; cf. Blass—Debrunner—Funk, *Greek Grammar of the New Testament,* §§ 331 and 337[1]). But doing so does not accord with the perspective required by v. 36b: "all these things which are going to occur," and seems to be needlessly subtle.

[24] Luke seems to have clarified the sense of the Marcan logion (and to have transferred it to Acts 1,7). Even in Mark 13,32, the basic sense seems to be that the prerogative of controlling the day and the hour belong not to men, not even to the angels (who execute God's will), or to the Son (ὁ υἱός, *sine addito* = "the Revealer"). "No one knows (concerning a given matter) except X" indicates, in apocalyptic language, a personal prerogative (cp. Rev 2,17; 19,12-13). The Father's prerogative (as Matthew's monotheistically insistent μόνος, 24,36 makes clear) is the consummation of his creative activity. The moment is not a matter of revelation, any more than is the number of the saved, especially since "numbers," as known by men, suppose calculation and, therefore, men's *control* of a situation.

major Marcan logion (13,31, which is centrally placed, *A'c* in the Marcan schema) containing Jesus' personal assurance of fulfillment ("*my* words...") and formulated in such a way as to transcend the affirmation which could be given by any merely human prophet.[25] Then, after providing this lesson on the signs and certainty of the events which will transpire (vv. 29-33), Luke composes his own hortatory conclusion to the discourse (vv. 34-36).[26]

Although the phrase "that day" in v. 34 is clearly delimited to the advent of the Son of Man, other expressions seem to have a wider purview, namely: "all these things that are to occur" (v. 36), "these things occurring" (v. 31), and "until everything occurs / takes place" (v. 32). Their immediate antecedent may be found at the very close of the second stage, in v. 28: "when *these things begin to occur*." Even ἐγγύς in vv. 30 and 31 finds its antecedent in ἐγγίζει of v. 28. It would be artificial, however, to restrict "these things" to the heavenly prodigies and their sequel as described in vv. 25-28. For Luke, the eschatological scenario is a continuum; it is announced as such in vv. 10-11 and worked out as such, with distinct but inseparable parts, in vv. 20-28. Moreover, "all these things" is employed in v. 12 to refer at least to the scenario limned in vv. 10-11. Lastly, as noted earlier, the expression "flee (ἐκφυγεῖν) all these things which are to occur," though it may convey the general notion of "escape all catastrophes," finds a verbal antecedent in the warning to those in Judea to flee (φευγέτωσαν) to the mountains (v. 21).

To sum up the foregoing structural observations concerning Luke 21,5-36, the following discursive outline should suffice. Given this framework of the narrated discourse, vv. 20-24 will be subjected to closer examination.

21,5-7   TRANSITION from comparative evaluation of "religious types" of persons (20,46-47; 21,1-4) to the issue of the historical, religious center (the temple) itself. The transition and what precedes in 20,46—21,4 suppose the audience specified in 20,45. The opening remarks of some prompt Jesus'
INAUGURATION OF THE DISCOURSE with a predictive comment about the impermanence of the temple (εἶπεν), which is followed by a question concerning its prophetic verification. His subsequent answer transcends the perspective of the questioners by highlighting genuine signs of the end time and by giving warnings and assurances to the disciples

---

It strikes me as at least an inaccurate use of English to speak of the Son's "ignorance" here. "Ignorance" is the lack of that knowledge which is reasonably expected to be present given a person's age, function, etc.; it almost always has a definitely pejorative connotation. "Nescience," though not commonly used, is theologically much more accurate; Jesus simply did not know the day or the hour, sc., as a point in clock-and-calendar time.

[25] No OT prophet ever claimed that *his own* words would last forever; Isa 40,8 declares that it is *the Lord's* word which remains forever.

[26] Cf. F. Keck, *Die öffentliche Abschiedsrede Jesu,* 270-82.

regarding their role before and throughout what is to come. The religious focal point which emerges is judgment by the Son of Man, whose words alone will not pass away.

21,8-9   **FIRST STAGE OF JESUS' ANSWER** (ὁ δὲ εἶπεν)

Negatively-phrased warning concerning necessary but false signs and indications of the end-time.

21,10-28   **SECOND STAGE OF JESUS' ANSWER** (τότε ἔλεγεν αὐτοῖς)

21,10-11   *First movement:*

Positively-phrased apocalyptic sketch of the (true) end-time scenario (earthly events; heavenly signs)

21,12-19   *Second movement:*

Prior necessities for the disciples:

21,12-13   Persecution (official animosity) for Jesus' name predicted; an occasion for their testimony.

21,14-15   Instruction; assurance of Jesus' assistance in controversy.

21,16-19   Persecution (personal animosity) for Jesus' name predicted; assurance of survival.

21,20-28   *Third movement:*

21,20-24   Development of vv. 10-11a with a brief warning; link between fulfillment for Jerusalem and times for nations.

21,25-28   Development of v. 11b; the lot of nations in the end-time when the Son of Man comes—with a closing assurance (v. 28) recalling vv. 18-19.

21,29-36   **THIRD STAGE OF JESUS' ANSWER** (καὶ εἶπεν παραβολὴν αὐτοῖς)

21,29-33   *First movement:*

The proximity of the kingdom in the light of these things which are to occur, as guaranteed by Jesus' lasting words.

21,34-36   *Second movement:*

Concluding exhortation regarding conditions for successfully avoiding these things which are to occur and for being able to stand before the Son of Man.

B. Luke 21,20-24

In studying the articulation of Luke's version of Jesus' eschatological discourse, a distinction surfaced between false announcements regarding the time and regarding ominous wars (21,8-9) and the genuine aspects of the eschatological scenario (vv. 10-11). Perhaps a partial reason for the difference can be detected in the scriptural allusions contained in the latter (cf. v. 10; *see above*, p. 82). When Luke returns to the eschatological significance of a calamitous war, he not only specifies the site of the catastrophe but also develops the motif of fulfillment. This aspect of fulfillment, not only of Jesus' words but also of Scripture itself, accounts for the difference between signs which do not portend the imminent end and those which do. The determining feature of "fulfillment" is first worked out for Jerusalem herself, and is then applied to a correlated event, the fate in store for the nations—but with a certain polarity in the total perspective of the end-time.

With regard to Jerusalem, what is to be recognized as imminent (ἤγγικεν, v. 20) is her own destruction. In view of this, Jesus emphatically enjoins evasive action (cf. the three-line statement in v. 21abc), explaining his warning by referring in biblical language to "days of vindication" that have as their purpose the fulfillment of all that has been written (v. 22). He follows these two opening statements (vv. 20 and 21-22) with a description of the fate of the inhabitants (vv. 23-24): the woe evoking the lot of women (v. 23a); then the explanation in terms of the inescapable necessity for this land and people (v. 23b); and lastly, a three-line description of the ruin of the inhabitants and the city (v. 24abc), concluding with the much-debated phrase, "until times for nations are fulfilled" (v. 24d).

"Days of vindication" (ἡμέραι ἐκδικήσεως) evokes a host of biblical texts. Of the OT passages containing the term ἐκδίκησις or its verbal equivalent,[27] some apply to Israel herself (Hos 9,7; Ezek 9,1; Sir 5,7). Others, significantly, apply to Israel's enemies (Deut 32,35; Jer 46,10 [LXX 26,10]; 50,31 [LXX 27,31]; 51,6 [LXX 28,6]; Exod 7,4; 12,12; Num 33,4. "Fulfillment of all that has been written" seems to bring to bear on Jerusalem not merely what had been written about Jerusalem, but what was said of other world-cities or cultures. This particular text may not of itself require that perspective. On the other hand, the perspective is not out of keeping with Jesus' standpoint in his remarks concerning the lawyers' conduct, a type of religious perversion summing up a whole line of evildoing (11,46-51).[28] Moreover, Jerusalem has already been typed as a murderess of prophets (13,34) and as a world-city like Babylon (19,41-44). In the immediately following verse (v.

---

[27] Other texts, which do not contain the terms ἐκδίκησις, ἐκδικεῖν or ἐδικάζειν, are sometimes adduced to supplement the notion of scriptural fulfillment; e.g., 1 Kgs 9,6-9; Mic 3,9-12; Dan 9,12.

[28] A judgment for all the violence committed against prophets in the past and against apostles yet to be sent (so W. Grundmann, *Das Evangelium nach Lukas* [Berlin ⁹1981] 249) is brought to bear on "this generation."

23), Jerusalem is not viewed as a strictly local area, but as the capital of the land and its people, representing at least the whole region of Judea from which flight is counseled in v. 21. It will experience as an inner-historical reality the Day of the Lord.[29] Lastly, its fate seems eschatologically to be escalated by being described not as a "tribulation" (θλῖψις), from which there may be some escape, but as an ineluctable necessity (ἀνάγκη).[30]

C. H. Dodd and others[31] have observed that the fate of Jerusalem is not depicted in military or political terms characteristic of the Roman siege of 70 A. D. On the other hand, in appealing to a biblical background, they have judged the event as a kind of recapitulation of the destruction by Nebuchadnezzar. Whether or not Luke was inspired by the Deuteronomic view of history,[32] he may have adverted to the parallel. Nevertheless, his typing of the city's fate (and its relation to what is yet to come, introduced at the close of v. 24), transcends the perspective of historical recapitulation of Jerusalem's destruction in the past.

Is it possible to specify more precisely the reason for the destruction of Jerusalem which is implied in "all that is written" (v. 22)? A partial explanation may lie in the forthcoming persecution of those sent in Jesus' name, especially insofar as they represent the continuance of the biblical tradition of persecuted prophets. But this testimony, as described in vv. 12-19 was given before Jews and gentiles alike (c. v. 12b). Accordingly, Fridolin Keck seems unduly to have restricted this testimony to a "hard-necked Israel," and to have overstated it as the principal reason for the destruction of Jerusalem.[33] It is also unwarranted to separate, as Keck does, the treatment of Jesus' disciples from that of Jesus himself as the reason for Jerusalem's lot.[34] Surely, foregoing texts (19,41-44; 20,9-19) as well as that which is yet to come in Luke's Jerusalem narrative (23,26-32) require that the death of

---

[29] Cf. F. Keck, *Die öffentliche Abschiedsrede Jesu*, 221-4.

[30] In Zeph 1,14-15, the Day of Yahweh is described as ἡμέρα θλίψεως καὶ ἀνάγκης. Accordingly, ἀνάγκη can be synonymous with θλῖψις and complement it (cf. also 1 Cor 7,26-28), but its connoting "necessity" seems to favor the sense of "ineluctable" anguish. This accords well with Luke's omission of any indication of the "shortening of days" of θλῖψις.

[31] Cf. C. H. Dodd, "The Fall of Jerusalem and the 'Abomination of Desolation," *JRS* 37 (1947) 47-54; Fred O. Francis, "Eschatology and History in Luke-Acts," *JAmAcadRel* 37 (1969) 49-63, 55 — although he sees a Lucan concern with the prophecy of Joel, ibid., 57.

F. Keck endorses L. Hartmann's correction of Dodd's view, showing that the passage does not describe recapitulation of Nebuchadnezzar's siege, but rather describes in terms of the "Day of Yahweh" the coming day of retribution; in effect, the description is based on prophetic typology; *Die öffentliche Abschiedrede Jesu*, 221.

[32] F. Keck. ibid., 190-205, especially notes 374 and 375; 249.

[33] Even if Luke has made use of a Deuteronomic view of history (cf. n. 31, *above*), he need not have been preoccupied with Israel alone, as Keck implies.

[34] F. Keck, ibid., 254: "Die Zerstörung Jerusalems (nach der Darstellung Lk 21,20.24) ist damit nicht die Folge der Tötung Jesu, wie man allgemein behauptet, sondern die Strafe für die Hallsstarrigkeit gegenüber den christlichen Verkündigern."

Jesus at the hands of a non-receptive people and especially the religious authorities of Jerusalem be included in accounting for the city's fate—indeed, as the major reason, considering the complexus of texts. Furthermore, in the three occurrences of πάντα τὰ γεγραμμένα elsewhere in Luke's writing (Luke 18,31; 24,44; Acts 13,29) "all that has been written" bears on the passion (and resurrection) of Jesus. Although Luke 21,22 lacks this Christological specification, it is unlikely that Luke would be concerned with the fate of the city independently of its relation to Jesus, especially in the context of a narrative leading directly to the passion. The fulfillment of all that is written finds in this case an adequate explanation only in Jerusalem's rejection of Jesus in line with her rejection of the prophets sent to her. Needless to say, the latter does not exclude Jesus' own disciples in the days ahead, before judgment against the city.[35]

The tragic ruin of Jerusalem at the hands of the nations is linked intrinsically, by a subordinate clause in the same sentence (v. 24), to "fulfilling/accomplishing times for nations." The clause ἄχρι οὗ πληρωθῶσιν καιροὶ ἐθνῶν has usually been understood as referring either to a period for preaching the Gospel to all nations,[36] or as time for Israel's own repentance and conversion,[37] or as a hint of vindication against her oppressors.[38] In any event, it has been construed as setting a limit to the time for gentile domination. True, Luke does not elsewhere deny the possibility of Israel's conversion. Rather, the call to repentance in view of "times for refreshment from (ἀπό) the face of the Lord" in Acts 3,20 may look precisely to a "period of grace" before the parousia.[39] Neither the restoration nor the

---

[35] Elsewhere, Keck admits that a rejection of the disciples is a rejection of Jesus himself; ibid., 123-34, esp. 133, 126.

Cf. David Tiede, *Prophecy and History in Luke-Acts* (Philadelphia 1980) 87: "The rejection of God's agents by God's people in connection with God's sanctuaries (synagogue and temple) is the plot device by which the movement of the narrative as a whole is motivated." Tiede misstates the analysis; for the movement of the plot-line is Jesus' concern for the fidelity of his disciples and their final salvation.

[36] Plummer, *Gospel According to S. Luke* (ICC; Edinburgh ⁴1913) 483, admits the possibility of the meaning: "for themselves becoming subject to Divine judgments." On the basis of Rom 11,25, however, he prefers to interpret καιροὶ ἐθνῶν of possessing the privileges which the Jews had forfeited.

F. Keck, *Die öffentliche Abschiedsrede Jesu*, 230-1 combines various aspects: "Damit haben die 'Zeiten der Heiden' eine dreifache Aufgabe: (a) Sie überbrücken die Zeit vom Ende der Judenmission bis zum Endgericht. (b) Sie bezeichnen vor allem die Zeit, in der die Heiden das von Gott bestimmte Instrument sind, das Bedrängnis und Strafe über das jüdische Volk bringt. (c) Nachdem die Zeit Israels vorbei ist, bedeuten die 'Zeiten der Heiden' auch die Epoche, in der die schon längst begonnene Heidenmission weitergeführt wird." Keck "absolutizes" the "times for nations," however, in the light of OT and Jewish apocalyptic traditions (ibid., 230, n. 509; 225, 224-30) rather than assesses it in the light of Luke' own structured composition and its grammatical, philological aspects (in v. 24c).

[37] *See below*, n. 45.

[38] *See below*, n. 45.

[39] For the discussion, cf. J. A. Fitzmyer and R. J. Dillon in *The Jerome Biblical Commentary* (London 1969) 45:27.

conversion of Israel need be excluded in Lucan theology, though each would be conditioned upon recognition of Jesus as God's personal representative, "the one who comes in the Lord's name" (13,35). Nevertheless, to interpret 21,24 in that optimistic light does violence to the text.

First, the end to which καιροί refers is that for the nations. One people's fate is related to that of others,[40] not one stage of Jerusalem's being built to a consummation of the same (as in the often-adduced Tob 14,4-5: καιροὶ αἰῶνος).[41] The plural (καιροί) may reasonably be explained on the score of the plurality of the nations.[42] The anarthrous defining gentive (ἐθνῶν) may be paralleled by phrases referring to a definitive end. Thus, before the flood, God speaks to Noah of "(the) time for every man" (καιρὸς παντὸς ἀνθρώπου, Gen 6,13). That time for man is the day of his end (cf. Qoh 9,12; Lam 4,18; 1 Macc 9,10). One may also note the further interpretation of the Greek translation of Ezek 30,3 (yôm 'ānān 'ēt gôyīm yihyeh) in the description of the Day of the Lord (MSS A, Q, and θ) not as πέρας ἐθνῶν but as καιρὸς πέρας ἐθνῶν. In all these texts, καιρός sounds the knell of a time of reckoning. In the Lucan context of vv. 25-28, there is no basis to suppose anything else.

Second, the conjunction ἄχρι οὗ followed by the subjunctive does not indicate mere termination (surely not of a period of Jerusalem's affliction, particularly given Luke's omission of Mark 13,20), but rather fulfillment or completion of one event, that described in the main clause, in the event described by the subordinate clause and its narrative sequel.[43] The term πληρωθῶσιν, moreover (instead of, say, ἥξουσιν), appropriately underscores the prophetic perspective of the end in

---

[40] As already noted by W. Nicol, "Tradition and Redaction in Luke 21," *Neot* 7 (1973) 61-71, 70, and Helmut Flender (against Conzelmann), *St. Luke. Theologian of Redemptive History* (Philadelphia 1967) 112-4.

Others, ignoring the eschatological perspective of vv. 20-24 as well as of vv. 25-28, and appealing to "imminent expectation of the parousia" as the basis for separation of events, find a disjunction between the two sets of verses; e.g., G. Baumann, "Die Lukanische Interpretation der Zerstörung Jerusalems," *NT* 6 (1963) 120-7, 121. Cf. also A. George, "La Construction du troisième évangile," *Études sur l'oeuvre de Luc* (EB; Paris 1978 [cf. ETL 43 (1967) 100-29]) 15-41, 27.

[41] Cf. Plummer, *Gospel According to S. Luke*, 483; E. Schweizer, *Evangelium nach Lukas* (NTD 3; Göttingen, [18]1982) 211; F. Keck, *Die öffentliche Abschiedsrede Jesu*, 226. Keck adduces Tob 14,4-5 in the context of many apocalyptic texts and claims (ibid., 228) that Luke writes against the background of a tradition which delimits the time of God's punishment.

[42] The plural "times" may also reflect a single time, considered complexively, with its various aspects, as in the case of the "days of the Son of Man," "days of Noah," "days of Lot," where the alternation between singular and plural seems to have been strained in many interpretations (Luke 17,22-35); the narrated discourse closes with paradoxical, dramatic reference to a single night (17,34-35).

[43] Cf. Blass–Debrunner–Funk, *Greek Grammar of the New Testament* (Chicago 1961) § 383 (2).

accordance with what was said of Jerusalem in v. 22. The narrative sequel, which continues without the sharp Marcan caesura (13,24) pointedly introduces into the cosmic signs the dismay of nations (ἐθνῶν—again anarthrous) and men's dying of fright at the prospect of things coming upon the inhabited world (οἰκουμένη).[44]

Third, one should avoid interpreting this Lucan text in the light of non-Lucan theology like Rom 11 (the prospects for Israel's conversion) or Mark (shortening of the time of tribulation). As has already been indicated, Luke describes Jerusalem's plight as an inescapable constraint (ἀνάγκη) unrelieved by any shortening of days. Even later, Luke allows for the possibility of Israel's conversion on a personal, individual basis, rather than in the framework of a general, nation-wide movement, which Paul's own writings seem to envisage.[45]

In v. 24b, apropos of the concisely rephrased description borrowed from Zech 12,3, one may be tempted to suppose the OT theme that the destroyers of Jerusalem will in turn themselves become the objects of God's wrath.[46] For Luke does assign to "all the nations" (v. 24) a share in the booty of the war. In two respects, however, Luke's statements do not accord with the theme. First, he makes no mention of a remnant or of restoration. Second, he does not speak of God's manifesting his concern for Israel or for his personal holiness, but concludes the whole sequence of calamitous events with the vision of the Son of Man (v. 27) and the hope of the faithful (v. 28). Thus, the fate of Jerusalem is not reversed by the subsequent plight of the nations; rather, it stands as a bitter foretaste of worse to come for the world. The only escapees in either situation are the faithful (21,19.28.36).

Jesus' final public discourse, given within the temple precincts, highlights practical religious concerns for his disciples. After predicting the coming ruin of the religious center of Israel and of Jerusalem, Jesus proceeds to give his disciples

---

[44] The background for the anxious fears of mankind at the raging of the elements seems in Luke ultimately to be ascribed to heavenly signs and heavenly powers. Thus, the parousia is preceded, as Helmut Koester has noted, not by a physical collapse of the cosmic order, but by astrological signs which terrify men in general; cf. art. συνοχή in *TDNT* VII, 886-7, 887.

[45] Cf. W. Grundmann, *Evangelium nach Lukas*, 383 n. 4. Similarly, E. Franklin, *Christ the Lord* (London 1975) 13, who finds "a hint of future restoration." Luke 13,34, on which Grundmann bases his argument, does indeed still offer hope for conversion, but it cannot be read into 21,23-24 without considering the course of the *narrative*, especially the developments in 19,28-44.

It is true that "... [the] picture of Yahweh leading foreign hosts against his city and then turning against the foreigners to punish them is a familiar one in the Old Testament (e.g., Is 10:5 ff.; Jer 25:8-14; Is 29:1-8; Ezek 38:1-23)." P. Hanson, *The Dawn of Apocalyptic* (Philadelphia 1975) 361. The covenant-context, or the theme of the manifestation of God's holiness, which is assumed or expressed in the OT texts, is notably absent in Luke 21. Nor do Luke's correlated texts supply a hint of such factors suggesting vindication. Among NT scholars who see an end to Jerusalem's subjection are David Tiede, *History in Luke-Acts*, 89 (cf. 92-3), "... the elusive hint of an end to Jerusalem's subjection"; and L. Gaston, *No Stone on Another*, 36.

an eschatological discourse in three stages, the first two of which (vv. 8-9 and 10-28) highlight fidelity to himself and the third (vv. 29-36) acceptable moral conduct in readiness for his coming. Enclosing his attention to the disciples' forthcoming, successful endurance of persecution (vv. 12-19), presented within the second stage, stand a general, programmatic scenario of the earthly and heavenly signs of the end-time (vv. 10-11a. 11b) and their successive exposition (vv. 20-24 and 25-27), concluding with a word of encouragement (v. 28). The sign of Jerusalem's destruction (vv. 20-24) stands as an interpretation of the event and instruction to the disciples rather than as an oracle of judgment (for it is not addressed to the city itself). Furthermore, it is distinguished from but not separated from the correlated development of the theme of cosmic judgment to come upon the whole world (vv. 25-27).

Closer examination of vv. 20-24, with regard for its structural integration into the discourse and its relationship to other, foregoing texts in Luke's narrative, discloses that Jerusalem's fate is a concrete forecast or type of the day of reckoning for nations. The city's lot, as implied by "fulfillment of all that has been written," befalls it by reason of its treatment of Jesus in particular and of his disciples. The picture of its judgment is unrelieved by prospects of a shortening of days, of conversion, or of restoration.

No special reason is set forth for the judgment on the whole world. Nevertheless, one may infer from the concluding reassurance (v. 28, which recalls vv. 18-19) that the beginning of all these things constitutes the approach of the disciples' deliverance, and that non-reception of Jesus, who is present in his disciples' testimony (cf. v. 15) — but not, for instance, the nations' treatment of Jerusalem — figures as the basis for the catastrophe.

Again, however, the "type" of the end as eschatological judgment ordered to a still wider, universal judgment, is provided by Jerusalem. The "type" retains its own specificity. It does not resemble a universal concept, predicable in exactly the same way of two or more individual persons, things, or situations. Nor is it like any concept, even an analogous one, since it is not an abstraction. As a kind of concrete analogate, however, it is not only meaningful in itself, but also sheds light on a further, climactic event to which it is ordered.

Confronted with the type which was by his day historical reality, Luke's reader would reasonably be expected to ponder not only the ultimate deliverance of Jesus' disciples (v. 28) but also the basis for judgment of the inhabited world that he knows. The next and last passage to be examined (23,26-32) will set forth more clearly the need to consider the consequences of injustice. That passage, however, will prove richer in the light of the connection established in 21,10-27 between the fate of Jerusalem as a world-city and that of the inhabited world.

VIII. The Judgment Oracle on the Way to the Cross (Luke 23,26-32)

After Jesus' teaching in the temple, Luke mentions the fate of the city only once more. He places Jesus' judgment oracle to the daughters of Jerusalem in the context of his last public journey, the way to Calvary, just before the climactic end of the passion narrative, Jesus' crucifixion and death. Several features of the earlier portions of the passion narrative require attention here, for they will have a bearing on a careful examination of the scope of the judgment oracle in its immediate context (23,26-32).

First, as the passover approaches, it remains evident that Jesus is still in favor among the people. Not public disorder (Mark 14,2) but antipathy to themselves [1] poses a difficulty to the high priests and scribes. To their joy, however, their problem is resolved by Judas's offer of betrayal.[2]

Second, the scene of the supper closes with a final passion prediction (22,35-38), which highlights Jesus' role as the just man who is about to suffer unjustly, considered as a criminal. The motif of the just sufferer will be worked out during the remainder of the passion narrative, notably in the trial before Pilate and in the crucifixion scene, but it will underlie v. 32 in the intervening way of the cross as well.

Third, on Mt. Olivet, Jesus' adversaries, the high priests, temple police, and elders, openly led by Judas, come to arrest him. The arrest takes place at the beginning of the next scene (22,54). With mention of the arrest, Luke begins to introduce five major passion scenes by varying the journey motif. Thus, in 22,54, which is insistently phrased, αὐτὸν ἤγαγον καὶ εἰσήγαγον εἰς ... (contrast Mark's simple ἀπήγαγον ... πρός ...), others determine his route. Luke 22,54 places Jesus in the high priest's house, where he is denied by Peter and disgracefully mocked by those who hold him. Luke then consistently introduces successive scenes with a form of ἀπάγειν: the daytime hearing before the Sanhedrin, 22,66, καὶ ἀπήγαγον αὐτόν; the scene before Pilate, 23,1, καὶ ἀπήγαγον αὐτόν (where Mark has ἀπήνεγκαν);[3] the way to the cross, 23,26, καὶ ὡς ἀπήγαγον αὐτόν[4] (with ἤγοντο

---

[1] This is clear in Mark, too, but Luke 22,2b apologetically eliminates the possibility of inferring that Jesus leads a popular movement (sc., as a demagogue).

[2] By using an apocalyptic expression ("Satan's entering into Judas"), Luke places the course of events above the mere level of individual disaffection or a series of socio-politically inspired events. He pursues this point in describing the passion as a cosmic conflict engaging supra-human powers (22,31.41-44.53b).

[3] The intervening episode, an interrogation before Herod, is set off by the use of ἀναπέμπειν (23,6.11.15).

[4] Mark noted this movement earlier, at the beginning of the scene of mockery (15,16), which Luke omitted.

δὲ καί at its close, 23,32). The whole line of movement comes to its term with arrival on Calvary, 23,33, ὅτε ἦλθον (altering Mark's καὶ φέρουσιν αὐτόν).

The literary unit (23,26-32) containing Jesus' words to the women of Jerusalem consists of three portions, each of which places Jesus in the forefront of the reader's attention: putting Jesus' cross on Simon of Cyrene to carry it behind Jesus (v. 26), a multitude's following him and his turning to address the daughters of Jerusalem (vv. 27-31), and the concluding reference (v. 32) to two criminals who are being led to death along with him.

Discussion of this unit may best begin (A) by dealing briefly with Luke's redaction of Mark in the opening verse (v. 26) and with his own composition at the close of the scene (v. 32). Subsequently (B) Luke's composition and use of the prophetic judgment oracle will command attention, together with the way Jesus' following is presented in vv. 27-28a. Further considerations will then be in place concerning Luke's distinctive use of the judgment oracle in the narrative context which he has provided.

A. The Opening and Closing Verses

Luke 23,26 revises Mark in such a way as to suggest the model function of the stranger. In Mark's account, Simon of Cyrene figures mainly as the father of two men who were probably known in Marcan circles as disciples of Jesus and may be intended to suggest the fruitfulness of Jesus' passion in the subsequent development of the Christian community.[5] Simon's impressment by the soldiers may also be intended in Mark (and more so in Matthew)[6] to continue the motif of the previous scene, mockingly conveying the image of the triumph of the king of the Jews over foreigners impressed into his service. Luke recasts the verse in such a way as to recall to the reader's mind the function of one who is himself a disciple (cf. 9,23 and 14,27; cp. esp. ὀπίσω μου in 14,27 and ὄπισθεν τοῦ Ἰησοῦ in 23,26).[7] Here, of course, it is Jesus' cross which is carried, and Simon probably represents quite unwittingly the personal association with Jesus that the sayings in 9,23 and 14,27

---

[5] In Mark's crucifixion narrative, for instance, the profession of faith put on the centurion's lips (15,39) follows the rending of the temple veil and a loud cry of Jesus which seems to echo his prayer for a sign of God's *purpose* (εἰς τί, v. 34) in letting him suffer so. The mockery of unbelievers (vv. 35-36) in answer to his citing Ps 22 is counterbalanced by the positive answer to God's purpose in the centurion's profession of faith, which follows upon the very moment of Jesus' death.

[6] Matthew 27,27 speaks of the soldiers' taking Jesus into (εἰς) the pretorium (rather than inside [ἔσω] the courtyard, as in Mark 15,16) and then, unlike Mark, notes their going out (ἐξερχόμενοι, 27,32). The intervening verses in Matthew are held together by an inclusion (ἐκδύσαντες, v. 28; ἐνέδυσαν, v. 31). An analogous Matthean framing of a whole passage in terms of "entrance" and "exit" can be found in Matt 26,58b (εἰσελθών) and 26,75b (ἐξελθών).

[7] Cf. E. Schweizer, *Das Evangelium nach Lukas* (NTD 3; Göttingen [18]1982) 237.

supposed. Nevertheless, Luke significantly eliminates the note of imposed necessity by dropping the term for impressment (ἀγγαρεύειν) in favor of ἐπιλαβόμε-
νοι... ἐπέθηκαν αὐτῷ ("taking hold of... they placed on him...") and by stressing
the action of carrying the cross rather than the demanded service (φέρειν not ἵνα
ἄρῃ). The pregnant allusion to discipleship makes good sense, then, as a Lucan re-
vision of Mark's attention to the relevance of this scene to the theme of discipleship. It also fits with the following, contrasted portions of the scene, which deal
with the fate of the Jerusalemites and of the criminals to be executed with Jesus.

The extent of Luke's own composition of vv. 27-31, which do not depend on
Mark, continues to be debated. At least v. 32 should be ascribed to Luke. The
vocabulary surely points in this direction.[8] What is more, v. 32 is linked to other
portions of the Lucan narrative. It prepares for Luke's reference to "the criminals"
(with the definite article, as speaking of persons already mentioned) in v. 33 (a
Lucan composition, cp. Mark's later, anarthrous reference to δύο λῃσταί, Mark
15,27). It also reflects the final passion prediction (23,35-38), as did the previous
scene of the trial before Pilate, which proclaimed Jesus' innocence but entailed his
being accused and scourged as a malefactor. Lastly, it may provide an ironic
context for taking the imagery of "green wood" in v. 31 as referring to those
regarded as guilty, but less imperiled than the dry wood (see below). This
concluding verse will have to be reexamined in the context of Jesus' address to the
daughters of Jerusalem. It is enough to note here that v. 32 functions as the
narrative close to the whole passage. It may well echo the tenor of the address in
vv. 28b-31, in that the fate of Jesus is less than that which those not so guilty (as he
apparently is) will suffer because of what has been done to him.

B. Luke's Prophetic Judgment Oracle

Regarding vv. 27-31, W. Käser has argued[9] that only vv. 27-28 and 31 come
from Luke's source, and that Luke himself added vv. 29-30. His analysis is
attractive, for it helps account for the double use of ὅτι (vv. 29 and 31) and the
escalation of a word of warning into a judgment oracle. It seems to suffice,
however, to rest content with Jerome Neyrey's explanation,[10] namely, that this
passage should be form-critically described as Luke's own compilation of diverse
popular and biblical sayings, which amounts to a prophetic oracle of judgment.

Calling vv. 27-31 a "prophetic word of doom" (prophetisches Drohwort), as
Klostermann does, appealing to Isa 3,16,[11] fails to account for the comparisons

---

[8] Cf. especially the use of δὲ καί, ἕτεροι, κακοῦργοι, ἀναιρεθῆναι.

[9] W. Käser, "Exegetische und theologische Erwägungen zur Seligpreisung der
Kinderlosen Lc 23:29b," ZNW 54 (1963) 240-54.

[10] Jerome Neyrey, "Jesus' Address to the Women of Jerusalem (Lk. 23.27-31)—A
Prophetic Judgment Oracle," NTS 29 (1983) 74-86, 74.

[11] E. Klostermann, Das Lukasevangelium (HNT 5; Tübingen ³1975) 227.

with Jesus' own fate, both in Luke 23,28 and in the explanatory clause (v. 31), particularly since the latter is not apparently directed against these sympathetic women at all. Nor does the interpretation of Jesus' address as a "word of compassion" [12] accord with the note of guilt implied by mention of the "dry wood" in v. 31 and the amplifications of the scenario to come (vv. 29-30), especially if the latter are to be attributed to Luke's redaction. For, as Neyrey remarks,[13] vv. 29-30 seem to convey a dreadful message like "better that we and our children had never been born." Lastly, the interpretation of the passage as a call to repentance [14] flies in the face of the lack of any concession (as in the parable of the unfruitful fig tree, Luke 13,6-9) or appeal with an *a fortiori* conclusion (13,1-5) on Jesus' part. Besides, it hardly accords with the foregoing, markedly repeated theme in the Jerusalem narrative concerning the devastation to come on Jerusalem and its people.

Rather, Luke 23,28b-31 follows the pattern of the judgment oracle against the nations, with an acceptable variation in the order of the announcement of judgment (which Luke places first, v. 28b, together with its expansion, vv. 29-30) and the grounds for the coming judgment (which he indicates at the end, v. 31, but in a single sentence, pithily, without any expansion).[15] When examining the passage in detail, it will prove necessary to account for some significant alterations, particularly the way in which the "accusation" is phrased. For the latter, with its subject of indefinite reference ("they"), does not seem to be directed against those addressed, even though they are liable to the dreadful consequences to come.

The crowd which follows Jesus seems to be sympathetic rather than curious, much less hostile. Even as constituting a large multitude (πολὺ πλῆθος) of the people, the crowd is not neccessarily to be equated with the people assembled by Pilate (along with the high priests and rulers) who are said to have figured in accusing Jesus (23,13-14) and who subsequently cry out as part of a whole throng (23,18, παμπληθεί) for Jesus' death and Barabbas's release. Admittedly, "the people" are involved in this condemnation (cf. also Acts 2,23b), and a strained attempt to exclude them by reading τοῦ λαοῦ in 23,13 instead of καὶ τὸν λαόν, without a shred of evidence in the MSS, may be dismissed. Luke retains the traditional element of popular participation in demanding Jesus' death, if only because, ultimately, the appeal to repentance requires he do so. At the same time, Luke does not present the people as a concerted group acting by itself except when he depicts them in a favorable light (cf. "all the people" in 21,38). Subsequently, the people (23,35), equivalently the "crowd" which had come together for the

---

[12] Gustav Dalman, *Jesus—Jeshua* (New York 1971) 193.

[13] Neyrey, "Jesus' Address to the Women of Jerusalem," 77.

[14] Cf. W. Grundmann, *Das Evangelium nach Lukas* (THKNT 3; Berlin ⁹1981) 429; F. W. Danker, *Jesus and the New Age* (St. Louis 1972) 236-7; E. Schweizer, *Das Evangelium nach Lukas*, 238.

[15] For treatment of the formal elements of the judgment oracle, *see above*, pp. 37-40.

spectacle (23,48), merely watch the events on Calvary once Jesus has been crucified. In Luke's account of the crucifixion, they do not mock Jesus (contrast the passersby in Mark 15,29-30). Their presence forms an inclusion framing the scene of the crucifixion [16] and they serve to direct the reader's contemplation and reaction, especially by their final gesture of repentance (v. 48, beating their breasts; cp. 18,13b).

Although the people as a whole have reason to repent, given their role in 23,13-14.18 and their non-recognition of Jesus, noted upon his entry into the temple (22,39-44), this particular group shows no sign of hatred or even of antipathy. It is not a group which heckles, but one which follows him. Luke may well have mentioned them to make plausible, especially in view of the forthcoming scene of the crucifixion, the point that, in spite of the members of the people summoned by Pilate (συγκαλεσάμενος, 23,13), a goodly number were not alienated from Jesus.[17] Their basically sympathetic disposition may further be inferred from the way certain women, members of the same group, demonstratively bewail Jesus' fate.

The women, indeed, are singled out not as distinct from the crowd, but as particularly representative of it. Some, like J. Neyrey, regard the women as a distinct group or sub-group, going even so far as to characterize them as "that element in Israel which consistently rejected God's messengers." [18] Neyrey's view is even antecedently improbable, since women are seldom represented in the Gospels, and never in any text of Luke (except for this alleged instance), in an unfavorable light — either personally or typologically. The only notable exceptions are found in Matthew and in Mark (e.g., Herodias and Salome, Mark 6,17-29; Matt 14,3-12.

What is more, the phraseology of the text does not warrant Neyrey's conclusion. For the singular verb (ἠκολούθει) is followed by a collective (πολὺ πλῆθος) which is further defined by two genitives governed by a single article (τοῦ λαοῦ καὶ γυναικῶν).[19] Thus, the whole group of followers includes the people and

---

[16] The inclusion, based on words proper to Luke's version of the event, is evident in the use of θεωρῶν (23,35) as the beginning and θεωρίαν ... θεωρήσαντες (v. 48) at the end. Reenforcement of the inclusion may be found in the repetition of the pf. ind. εἱστήκει (v. 35, predicated of the people) in εἱστήκεισαν (v. 49, predicated of Jesus' friends, immediately after mention of the contrite crowd).

[17] Surely, women are not to be supposed to have been among those summoned by Pilate (23,13). Still, as noted earlier, there exists a certain ambiguity about the people's reaction even when they are represented as enthralled by Jesus' words, as they were during his teaching in the temple. For they may be "impressed unbelievers," — not disbelievers, but people who do not fully understand Jesus or commit themselves to following him.

Luke 24,20 clearly supposed that those mainly responsible for the death of Jesus were "our high priests and rulers / leaders."

[18] Neyrey, "Jesus' Address to the Women of Jerusalem," 75-6.

[19] Cf. Blass–Debrunner–Funk, *A Greek Grammar of the New Testament* (Chicago 1961) § 276 (1).

(καί) women. Logically, one may take καί in an emphatic, partly epexegetical sense, sc., "particularly." Surely, Luke is not contrasting two different groups, or mentioning "the people" in an otiose way, as though they were irrelevant to Jesus' subsequent address to the women. Helpfully, a close parallel to the phraseology of v. 27 occurs at the end of the very next Lucan scene (v. 49): εἱστήκεισαν δὲ πάντες οἱ γνωστοὶ αὐτῷ [20] ἀπὸ μακρόθεν, καὶ γυναῖκες αἱ συνακολουθοῦσαι αὐτῷ ἀπὸ τῆς Γαλιλαίας, ὁρῶσαι ταῦτα. One main verb (here in the plural because of πάντες ...) is followed by mention of two correlated subjects. Most likely, the variant reading of the article (αἱ) before γυναῖκες is not authentic,[21] so that a single article serves to unify both Jesus' friends and the women from Galilee. Similarly, the καί preceding γυναῖκες serves to single out these women as particularly well-known acquaintances or friends. The two groups are hardly to be contrasted, as if the reader were to suppose that Jesus' friends, not the women, were at a distance (ἀπὸ μακρόθεν) or that the women, not his acquaintances, were the ones who saw (ὁρῶσαι) these things. Both were distant; both watched the scene from a distance.

To complete the analysis of vv. 27-28a, the following observations are in order. First, in Luke 23,27, the phrase describing the women's action is expressed by a relative clause, not by participial modifiers, a variation from the evidently redactional addition by Luke in v. 49. Whether or not this indicates a special source for v. 27, which is unlikely,[22] the dependent clauses of v. 27 continue the narrative in the imperfect tense, and describe an ongoing demonstration of sympathy.

Second, the narrative placement of the participle (στραφείς) opening v. 28a, which describes Jesus' "turning," should be taken in *this* narrative context, not as a term freighted with connotations derived from other contexts. Thus, it is unwise to press the ptc. to convey the notion of an appeal to conversion, as in the case of Peter's denials. For there, the narrative context suffices to convey a special connotation. Peter's face is towards the fire (22,55-56); he is interrogated by one individual after another; finally, Jesus himself "faces him" by turning (στραφείς) towards him.[23] Nor is it methodologically sound to take Jesus' "turning" in 23,28

---

[20] A variant reading, the gen. αὐτοῦ, does not appreciably affect the sense.

[21] Even with the added feminine article, the two distinct subjects would be unified by the same verb. Perhaps the added article (in witnesses of the Alexandrian tradition, especially B) represents an attempt to improve the style.

One may also compare Luke 1,2, οἱ ἀπ' ἀρχῆς αὐτόπται καὶ ὑπηρέται γενόμενοι τοῦ λόγου, which does not contrast two different groups but, in this case, two stages or aspects of their importance; cf. R. J. Dillon, *From Eye-Witnesses to Ministers of the Word: Tradition and Composition in Luke 24* (AnBib 82; Rome 1978) 269-72.

[22] The participial construction in the narrative of v. 49 is dictated by the "stative" perfect, εἱστήκεισαν; the imperfects in the narrative of v. 27, on the other hand, fit with the progressive movement of the scene as a whole, especially with the main verb, ἠκολούθει.

[23] If the word has any further connotation in 22,61, it may be an ironical allusion to the need for Peter's own "turning [back]" (ἐπιστρέψας) in the prediction of his denials

as hinting at an act of judgment.[24] For, in this narrative context, Simon carries the cross behind Jesus, and the great multitude follows him; στραφείς merely introduces Jesus' direct address to the vocal, demonstrative members of the crowd, the women, who are members of the cortege.

Third, the singling out of the women as representatives of a larger group related to Jesus (*see above*) proves to be common to this scene and to the subsequent scene of the crucifixion. A contrast between the two groups has been noted by several commentators. The contrast is not evident, however, except in the course of a wider narrative progression in which Jesus' journey to Jerusalem works out with advertence to the reputation of Jerusalem as the murderess of prophets, and his Galilean following appears as devoted, but not emotionally demonstrative adherents. Interestingly, however, the contrast lies on the level of Luke's historically plausible narrative. Devoted women from Galilee who had followed him, especially since a number of them are named (cf. 8,2-3), are hardly fictitious. One need not suppose that the women of Jerusalem are a fictitious addition, particularly since women were known to exercise the function ascribed here to the daughters of Jerusalem.[25] Historicity in the sense of facticity (sc., an event of this nature in the given time and place) is not by any means at odds with symbolic representation, especially in the dimension of typological thinking.[26]

Now, in the judgment oracle proper (23,28b-31), Jesus addresses the women as "Daughters of Jerusalem," The formula is not neccessarily pejorative.[27] Nor does it correspond with the "messenger formula" of the judgment oracle. Rather, it types the audience not as these individual women or as a sociological group, but as a body representing the people, especially those of its capital city.

Immediately consequent upon Jesus' address there occur in v. 28 a comparative formulation of the judgment motif (μὴ κλαίετε ... τέκνα ὑμῶν) and in vv. 29-30 its explanatory expansion. Jesus' injunction not to weep for him but for themselves and their children should not be construed as a harsh rejection of the women's sentiments. As on other occasions (when the woman called his mother blessed, 11,27; when the Pharisees warned him about Herod, 13,31 ff.; and when the people of his home town welcomed him, 4,22), Jesus does not acknowledge

---

(22,32b). It suffices, however, to note that, at the beginning of this scene, Jesus is being led; his "turning" represents a dramatic pause in this movement, both in 22,61 and in 23,28.

[24] As Neyrey does, "Jesus' Address to the Women of Jerusalem," 76. The term "turning" is not a technical term; its interpretation rests decidedly on the immediate context; that context here is clearly one of narrated movement.

[26] Cf. Klostermann, *Lukasevangelium*, 227.

[26] Neyrey makes the facile (and false) distinction between the "real" and the "symbolic" character of the women; "Jesus' Address to the Women of Jerusalem," 74. Even abstract concepts like "evil" represent real situations, and may be expressed in highly symbolic language, like "your hour," that is, the working out of the *power of darkness*."

[27] E.g., Cant. 1,5; 3,5.10; 5,8.16; 8,4; cp. 2 Kgs 19,21.

sympathy, but rather takes the occasion to make a prophetic declaration. Here, the Jerusalemites are to consider their own lot, suggestively as bad as or, rather, worse than his, for it will affect their children, too. Furthermore, even as a judgment oracle, the text reflects his own concern for those who compassionate him. It cannot be read as a condemnation any more than can the two earlier texts which likewise speak of the fate of children (19,41-44.44a; 21,20-24,23a). In the first, Jesus even demonstrated painful concern for his people's fate. In the second, his most severe statement, intended mainly for the benefit of his disciples, he phrased the judgment as a fulfillment of Scripture. Its near brutality consisted in matter-of-fact prediction, not in personal denunciation.

The explanatory expansion (vv. 29-30) bears out the dire prospects matter-of-factly stated in v. 28b. The phrase "days will come" (ἔρχονται ἡμέραι) establishes the eschatological framework.[28] Here, it introduces an ironic reference to days of woe, a tristych beginning with the word "blessed." These woes concerning their children and their own future reduced to futility will be succeeded by appeals for an alternative to enduring the affliction (τότε ἄρξονται λέγειν..., followed by a distych). Of the two portions of the expansion, the second has borrowed heavily from an OT passage (Hos 10,8) which speaks of the consequences of the religious perversity of Israel (Samaria). The first echoes the anguish expressed apropos of a mother's children, for which a certain parallel occurs in Luke 21,23a. That verse repeats almost verbatim Mark 13,17, except for the precise scope of the context. Luke reformulates the preceding Marcan verse to the effect that this plight is the kind of thing identified with the judgment on Jerusalem, and eliminates Mark 13,18 ("pray that..."), which implied that Christians would be included.

A second ὅτι, at the beginning of v. 31, introduces the grounds for the coming events stated above. The reason is formulated as a question, indeed, one of a parabolic,[29] proverbial quality, and therefore demands special reflection: "For if they do these things in [i.e., to] the green wood, what should [is to] happen to the dry?" Although the reason is obviously given to the women, it is phrased almost in such a way as deliberately to avoid condemning them as the people responsible for the predicted catastrophe. One should perhaps remind oneself of the "double audience" for Luke's version of the parable of the wicked tenants; it was spoken to the people, but against their leaders, not against the people themselves.

The following observations should help clarify the proverbial statement. First, the protasis of the conditional clause (εἰ + pres. ind.) looks to a real, present situation. The apodosis, of an *a fortiori* nature (deliberative subjunctive), poses the consequent prospect for the future.

---

[28] The present tense (ἔρχονται) is here equivalent to the future, as the following future tense (ἐροῦσιν) makes clear. Nonetheless, this future is "in the making" thanks to current action (cf. v. 31a).

[29] One may compare the conditional parabolic expressions in Luke 11,13-36; 12,28.

Second, in the protasis, the 3rd per. pres. ind. (ποιοῦσιν) has an unspecified subject ("they"). Although God himself has been suggested as the agent intended,[30] such an interpretation is theologically ill-founded.[31] Where Luke refers to the plan of God in the death of Jesus, he formulates it in such a way as to exclude God's intending the death of Jesus as something in itself (for example, severe pain like that described in the verses for which v. 31 provides the reason) and, not seldom, as supposing the agency of evil men.[32] Lastly, it is more likely that God's action is alluded to in the apodosis (τί γένηται ...;) because it is the apodosis which states the specific reason proper to the judgment oracle. This reason is given in the form of a deliberative subjunctive, "What ought to happen / what should happen?" and entails a change of subject from that of the protasis. If God is intended as the logical agent behind the plural of the protasis, why the change of subject in the apodosis, not to mention the change of mood?

More plausibly, other subjects have been suggested for ποιοῦσιν: the Jews (notably, their leaders), the Romans (particularly those immediately involved, Pilate's troops), or a combination of both.[33] The latter option, if indeed any such precise option need be made, accords better with the vague introduction to this scene (ἀπήγαγον, v. 26). For Pilate has handed over Jesus to the demanding crowd consisting primarily of the high priests and their allies, and v. 26 follows immediately upon Pilate's handing Jesus over "to their will," which, in effect, means that of the Jewish leaders. On the other hand, it is obvious that those who have Simon carry Jesus' cross and (as *mandati*, not *mandantes*) "are doing these things" to Jesus are not members of the high priesthood, much less members of the great crowd of people who are following him. They are Pilate's soldiers, who crucified him and the two criminals (v. 33b).

Even though a combination of "Jews and Romans," particularly the powerful among them, fits as the logical subject of ποιοῦσιν, a generic qualification suggesting "responsible persons" would best suit both the grammatical vagueness and Luke's intention to make his account relevant to his intended audience. His typed readership ("Your Excellency, Theophilus") should find here, as in foregoing texts of the passion narrative, the consequences of power-politics which entail committing injustice. Luke need not spell out the consequences at this point. "What should happen" can readily be construed: a severe judgment on the guilty,

---

[30] Cf. F. W. Danker, *Jesus and the New Age,* 237.

[31] Grammatically, it seems to be possible. According to Zerwick – Smith, *Biblical Greek* (Rome 1963) § 236, Luke seems to use the indefinite plural instead of the theological passive in 16,9; cf. § 2, which refers to Lk 12,48 and 6,38, and, with an indication of doubt, to Lk 23,31. H. Schürmann, *Das Gebet des Herrn,* n. 88, is cited as holding a contrary opinion.

[32] There is question of the salvific plan of God (εἰ βούλει) in 22,42; cf. Acts 2,23 (a plan achieved through the actions of wicked men).

[33] A. Plummer, *Gospel According to S. Luke* (Edinburgh [4]1913) 529-30 indicates the variety of opinions, but wrongly supposes the same logical subject both for protasis and for apodosis.

amounting to the destruction of the nation's capital city and what it stands for, but including inevitably even the destruction of those who are not actively participants in the carryng out of unjust practices or policies; for example, as yet unborn children and infants, the women of the city, and a multitude of the people among whom they stand. Such is historical reality, even in a religious history of Jesus' work on earth among his own people. Those who are innocent (actually or relatively) suffer because of the guilty.

A major problem in the proverbial statement may now be studied in terms of the formulation itself. The problem centers on the contrast between "green wood" and "dry wood." As the examples given below both from the OT and from rabbinic literature will indicate, the contrast always concerns groups of persons rather than impersonal situations.

One text which illustrates this contrast but turns out to be irrelevant on other grounds is Ezek 17,22-24. The Lord dries up the green (high) tree and makes the dry (lowly) one flourish. The green tree, a symbol of the "high and mighty" obviously cannot be applied to Jesus on the way to his crucifixion, nor can the lowly tree to be exalted apply to the Jerusalemites who face the catastrophe just described in vv. 29-30.

Another text from Ezekiel initially seems to be quite relevant, for it contrasts the righteous and the wicked. First, an oracle against the south (Ezek 20,45-49) speaks of a fire which will scorch every green tree and every dry tree.[34] Second, the opening portion of oracles on the sword (Ezek 21,1-7.2-4) applies this judgment specifically to Jerusalem and pursues the contrast in terms of the destruction of righteous and wicked alike.[35] In bringing this to bear on Luke 23,31, one must allow, of course, for the difference of perspective: Ezekiel speaks of a single judgment or destruction, whereas Luke refers to two different situations: the crucifixion of Jesus and the days of woe for Jerusalem. Even so, the judgment in Ezek 20,45 – 21,7 strikes all alike; there is no *a fortiori* argument as in Luke 23,31. What is more, in the passage in Ezek 20, the Lord's action is supposed regarding both the righteous and the wicked, whereas Luke 23,31 distinguishes agency in each portion of the argument (εἰ ... ποιοῦσιν, ... τί γένηται;). Regarding the narrative of Luke's text itself, one may well doubt that, in v. 31a, Jesus is implicitly asserting his own innocence. From the close of the Last Supper (22,37), he has announced the fact that he is to be reckoned with the lawless. Subsequently, even

---

[34] Ezek 20,47 speaks of ... *kol 'ēṣ laḥ wᵉkol 'ēṣ yābēš;* Ezek 21,13 says: *wehirattî mimmāk ṣaddîq wᵉrāša'.* The LXX, however, morally equates both, translating *ṣaddîq wᵉrāša'* as ἄδικον καὶ ἄνομον. Since Luke relies regularly on the LXX, it seems doubtful that he would have in mind this text.

Other texts, of course, contrast the judgment of the wicked in an *a fortiori* context of comparison with the righteous (Prov 11,31; 1 Pet 4,17-18), but the specific imagery is lacking, and the contexts are not persuasively comparable.

[35] Cf. Arnold Tkacik in *The Jerome Biblical Commentary* (London 1968) §21:47-48. Interestingly, the text stands in tension with Ezekiel's emphasis on personal responsibility.

before Pilate, he has offered no defense of his own innocence. The reader, of course, knows that Jesus is indeed innocent. Now, however, he can appreciate the irony of the fulfillment of the final passion prediction and the shameful reality of the suffering which Jesus has accepted. Jesus is being pitied as a malefactor, although he really is not one. As if to underscore the irony, the verse resuming the narration and concluding this scene is phrased not in such a way as to distinguish the two malefactors from Jesus, but rather so as strongly to suggest his being (to all appearances) *identified* with them: "two *other* malefactors ... with him.[36] Clarification of the difference between Jesus and the others will appear by implication in 23,33b, and explicitly in the prayerful confessions made in the course of the crucifixion narrative (23,39-43.47).

Turning to rabbinic parallels, one finds a much closer approximation to the Lucan saying. According to *Seder ElijR* 14 (65),[37] because of the water of contention (cf. Num 20,12 f.) Moses and Aaron were punished. The scholars said: "If fire seized what is fresh (moist, green wood, *laḥīm*), what may one expect it to do to what is dry (*yebāšīm*)?" The comment does not distinguish between the righteous and the wicked since, to have been punished, even Moses and Aaron must have done wrong. Rather, the comparative liability to judgment looks to greater danger for the dry wood. In Billerbeck's translation, the Jewish argument looks to possible deliverance from dire consequences for the dry wood by suggesting self-improved conduct ("... what should the dry do?"), in which case the parallel would be less pertinent.[38] Luke 23,31 requires that one consider what should or must happen to the dry wood. In any event, it becomes easier to see in the light of this rabbinic language how the imagery of green wood can be used by

---

[36] As Plummer notes, with a keen sensitivity for the meaning of Luke's Greek, *Gospel According to S. Luke,* 530, the order of the best MS reading "has been corrected to ἕτεροι δύο κακοῦργοι, to avoid the implication that Jesus was a κακοῦργος." Plummer's further evidence points strongly in the direction of Lucan irony in the light of Isa 53,12, but, perhaps to preserve doctrinal insistence on Jesus' innocence, he dodgingly opts for what Field called "a negligent construction." He should have stuck to his guns.

Even the further σὺν αὐτῷ bears out Jesus' identification, to all appearances (and rightly so, in view of the course of the narrative from 22,27 onwards), with malefactors. Also, δὲ καί is a stronger connective than δέ; F. Keck, *Die öftentliche Abschiedsrede Jesu,* 38-9.

[37] The text is not able to be dated; "the wise said" is not the formula used in Tannaitic literature. The translation given is that by W. G. Braude and J. J. Kapstein, *Tanna Děbe Eliyyahu. The Lore of the School of Elijah* (Philadelphia 1981) 187; they refer to the saying as a cited, popular proverb.

[38] Cf. Str-B, II, 263. Further rabbinic references translated by Billerbeck evidence the same mentality, albeit without the same imagery, ibid., 263: *MQ* 25b (a saying dated about 426 C.E.). The oldest dated saying, again without the imagery of "green wood / dry wood," but ascribed to a Jew crucified about 150 B.C.E., speaks of the relative, albeit harsh suffering (in terms, however, simply of what happens, not of implicitly different agents) of those who do God's will and those who irritate him; ibid., 263-4.

Luke of Jesus not as one who is innocent, but as one considered to be a wrongdoer.

For the benefit of his typed readership, Luke reenforces in 23,27.31 a historical moral: the fate of Jerusalem is an instance of what will happen to the city and people which does not accept Jesus as the Messiah and whose leaders commit injustice in bringing about his death. The particular force of this passage is to underscore the point that even those sympathetic to Jesus, but not accounted among his disciples, will suffer for what others do. These unfortunate people, including those (at least the children and, likewise, the women) who have committed no personal wrong against him, will nevertheless be swept up in the catastrophe. Such is historical reality, even from the prophetic perspective. If crucifixion is the fate of one reputed to be a criminal, what must be going to happen to those who are less innocent than he? Once more, Jesus avoids attacking the people themselves, represented at least to a large extent by the women in this great multitude of the people. The "sentence" of the judgment oracle does not indict those to whom the oracle is spoken. Rather, it suggests somewhat indeterminately, but in a way which can be construed from previous portions of the Jerusalem narrative, the responsibility of those who have brought Jesus to his death, notably the high priests of the people. The perspective of the role of Jesus' own disciples (cf. v. 26) remains in view here, under the figure of one who shares his cross — although the passage as a whole ascribes the judgment against Jerusalem to what "they do" to Jesus himself.

For the intelligent reader of Luke's Gospel-as-religious-history, the lesson, the historical-typological moral can be inferred once again: if this is what is to happen to Jerusalem because of the way Jesus has been treated, what will happen to my city and people if he is not acknowledged by them or if his disciples are treated as was their Lord, especially by those responsible for the government of the city and people?

IX. Concluding Reflections

The principal thesis of this study and the way in which it is worked out have been set forth from its outset (PREFACE and CH. I.). Concluding reflections offered here will briefly consider the topic from a complementary, retrospective standpoint.

From Jesus' immediate point of approach to Jerusalem, indeed, as he came in sight of it, to the last stage of his passion journey, Luke has presented his concern for the city's fate. No other NT author approximates Luke's salient interest in this tragic event. In four major texts of the Jerusalem narrative (19,28-44; 20,9-19; 21,20-24; 23,26-32), Jesus' concern, according to Luke, ranges from compassionate weeping over the city's unawareness of the terms for peace, and nonetheless an oracle of judgment, through measured warning of forthcoming judgment given to the people (but directed against their leaders), to matter-of fact prediction to his disciples, and, once again, to an oracle of judgment given to an albeit sympathetic throng of people represented by the women of the city. The possibility of conversion is neither excluded nor envisioned. From the tenor of the narrative, however, it is evident throughout that the reason for the forthcoming destruction of Jerusalem is surely not Jesus' personal hostility to the inhabitants of the city. Major reasons which do emerge are injustice committed by the rulers and, secondarily, the Jerusalemites' own failure to recognize the time of their visitation. Although they are quite favorable to his teaching in the temple, they remain even there, in effect, impressed unbelievers. For example, they have not done that which his disciples have done on the occasion of his entry.

The issue of "guilt," however, especially as individually assessed, is not Luke's principal concern. Even where Luke states or implies Jesus' references to the responsibility of the authorities (in the parable of the wicked tenants; in the words to the women of Jerusalem), he does not render them apologetically explicit. In at least one instance, where Jesus instructs his disciples concerning the significance of the fall of Jerusalem, responsibility must be construed from a number of other passages regarding both Jesus and those whom he will empower as his witnesses. Rather, Luke's major concern lies in further educating his reader in line with the historically-oriented development of a pastoral-hortatory approach, as indicated in the distinctive preface he has written for his Gospel (1,1-4).

Luke's preface types both his intended readership and the general character of the work which he addresses to his reader. The sort of reader Luke has in mind —

as his audience, not merely as an acquaintance to whom he "dedicates" his composition — is a man of the Hellenistic world who is affluent, educated, and influential. Such a typed person would readily construe Luke's work as a kind of history, albeit a religious history, and would reasonably recognize how such a literary composition should be read. Accordingly, he would be alert to the good to be admired and imitated and to the evil to be avoided.

As Luke's narrative proceeds, the reader would become conditioned to consider the purpose of its chief character, Jesus, and the way in which this purpose takes on concrete shape in the course of his journeys and personal interchanges. Luke regularly conditions his intended audience to reflect on the words and actions of Jesus in a manner relevant to his own cultural situation, although Luke himself does not moralize (as do many Hellenistic historians, including Josephus). Rather, he disposes his reader to a parabolic mode of thinking, which necessarily challenges his own powers of reflection, as did Jesus' own thinking for the people of his day.

From Jesus' inaugural address at Nazareth onwards, Luke disposes his reader to consider the rejection of Jesus' public ministry. Only with the second part of that ministry, however (9,51 - 19,27), are Jesus' movements as a prophet focused on Jerusalem. This part opens with a statement of Jesus' decided purpose, but without any indication of a threat to Jerusalem. In the middle of this portion of Luke's Gospel a warning is sounded regarding that city itself, but without a note of condemnation calling for destruction of the city. At the same time, in the foregoing context of judgment awaiting Chorazin, Bethsaida, and Capernaum (in view of Jesus' ministry and the universal mission of the seventy-two disciples, 10,1-16). the apostrophe to Jerusalem (13,34-35) should be seen in a typological context. Jerusalem, not unlike the towns mentioned earlier, is a type of world-city, and indeed, a special type. Unlike pagan cities, although typed as their equivalents, these towns did not accept Jesus; Jerusalem is already the murderess of prophets. With Jesus' entry into Jerusalem in 19,28-44, where he is acknowledged only by the disciples who accompany him, the knell of coming judgment on the city is finally sounded, and its typing as a world-city (like Babylon) comes to the fore.

In the course of the Jerusalem narrative, Luke's intended reader can become even more keenly aware of the metahistorical typing of the city and, therefore, of its parabolic reference to his own situation. In particular, Jesus' closing public discourse in the temple, directed mainly to his disciples, depicts the destruction of Jerusalem in prophetically typological terms and relates the city's fate to the end of the inhabited world. Accordingly, the reader finds himself in a position to ask what will happen to his own "city," sc., his own civilized culture and society, if it rejects Jesus (and his disciples, through whom he testifies) as did Jerusalem. Furthermore, reflecting on the injustice, especially on the part of those in authority, in treating the innocent Jesus as guilty, he should be prompted to consider the standards of justice in his own society and, of course, the way he may personally share these or correct them.

I submit that the text of Luke's Gospel and an attentive reading of Luke's ongoing narrative in the light of his preface persuasively support the foregoing interpretation of his view of the destruction of Jerusalem. I would admit, however, that it does not necessitate or definitively *demand* the interpretation as given here. For I hold that Luke himself does not treat his reader in a didactically insistent way. Like any skilled narrator, Luke suggests but does not impose interpretations, and often allows for several complementary modes of interpretation. Such narrative skill does not foster nebulous ideas; observations must be grounded in the carefully-written text. Doctrinaire positions or narrowly delimited and honed interpretations, however, are not counseled or admitted, I think, by the kind of composition which Luke has offered to an intelligent, sensitive reader for his further education in the Gospel truth. If the new interpretation offered here contributes to a fuller understanding of the unity, coherence, and over-all individual and personal relevance of Luke's Gospel, and helps to exclude some faulty, short-sighted views, it will amply have served its purpose.

APPENDIX

The Reticence of Acts Concerning the
Judgment Against Jerusalem

Luke's second volume, the Acts of the Apostles, is virtually silent about the destruction of Jerusalem. The fate of the temple figures in one context only: expressly in the charges leveled against Stephen at the instigation of Hellenistic Jews in Jerusalem, and perhaps implicitly in Stephen's reply (Acts 7,2-60). Although the fate of the temple may well suggest the fate in store for the whole city (as in Jesus' last public discourse), the lot in store for the city is nowhere specifically mentioned, and the significance of the temple itself is seen in a light quite different from that of Luke's Gospel. Both the charges against Stephen and the relevance of his response to them need briefly to be considered. For they may provide some rationale for the different way in which the fate of Jerusalem is treated in Acts.

Those who instigate accusations against Stephen are Hellenistic (that is, Greek-speaking) Jews in Jerusalem.[1] Most likely, as G. Schille argues, Stephen is depicted as confronting not members of a single synagogue but Hellenistic Jews representative of the entire diaspora.[2] For these conservative Jews, the city and its temple no doubt represented the spiritual center of the world. Furthermore, they would probably have regarded the diaspora, a "scattering" or "sowing" of Israel among the Gentiles, as a national and religious catastrophe. Accordingly, it is not unlikely that they would have considered Jerusalem and its temple as the focal point for Jewish worship, though perhaps not of messianic restoration.[3] Reconstruction of their cast of mind, however, lies mainly in the inferences made from Stephen's polemic reply, which Luke has made his own.

Why Stephen's adversaries did not themselves state the charges against Stephen may be discerned from their inability to resist him in debate (6,10). Hypothetical reconstruction of Stephen's position in prior controversy with them need not be predicated to discuss the charges as Luke presents them. It may well be

---

[1] Martin Hengel, "Zwischen Jesus und Paulus. Die 'Hellenisten', die 'Sieben' und Stephanus (Apg 6,1-15; 7,54-8,3)." *ZTK* 72 (1975) 150-206, 185.
[2] Gottfried Schille, *Die Apostelgeschichte des Lukas* (THKNT 5; Berlin 1983) 174-5.
[3] Cf. Johannes Bihler, *Die Stephanusgeschichte im Zusammenhang der Apostelgeschichte* (Münchener Theologische Studien I/30; Munich 1963) 23.

that Stephen had employed a saying of Jesus regarding the temple, and that he had done so in line with Hellenistic Christian *Enthusiasmus* concerning the irrelevance of the temple as the necessary center for the worship of God.[4] Perhaps his view did not much differ from the pejorative Marcan view of the temple and its cult. Be that as it may, Stephen's response as Luke presents it offers the best avenue to determining both the position of Stephen and the mind-set of his accusers in line with the over-all scope of Acts.[5]

The narrow-minded accusations which Stephen's adversaries instigated serve to indicate to Luke's reader their point of view. In effect, it is that point of view to which Stephen responds, a place-centered and thing-centered outlook more nationalistic than religious in conception.

Luke clarifies the scope of the charges by stating them and by then providing an interpretation placed on the lips of false witnesses. The charge (v. 11), "We have heard him speak blasphemous words against Moses and God," is ostensibly a strictly religious charge. The testimony of the false witnesses, however, even as it becomes more precise,[6] discloses the cast of mind behind the accusation: (a) he has not ceased speaking against the [this][7] holy place and the law (v. 13), for (b) they had heard him saying that this Jesus of Nazareth would destroy this place and change the customs Moses gave them (v. 14). That Stephen had said Jesus himself would destroy the temple was no doubt false; Luke's reader could hardly construe the charge otherwise. That Stephen had repeated Jesus' polemic statements about some Jewish practices (e.g., what is allowed on the sabbath) may have had some foundation. Even so, it proves irrelevant to the charge as stated. For the specification of the charges discloses the view that an absolute value is given to *this place*. Even the term "sanctuary" (ναός), which occurs in the false charges brought against Jesus (Mark 14,58; Matt 26,61), is altered here to τόπος.[9]

---

[4] Gerhard Schneider, "Stephanus, die Hellenisten und Samaria," *Les Actes des Apôtres. Traditions, rédaction, théologie* (ed. J. Kremer) (BETL 48; Leuven 1979) 215-40, 238-9.

[5] The scope of Acts may be indicated as the confirmation of the Gospel, articulated by showing how the word of God went forth from Jerusalem, the center of the Jewish world, to Rome, the center of the world at large, under the guidance of the Holy Spirit and through the instrumentality of those whom Christ chose to be his witnesses. Cf. W. C. van Unnik, "The 'Book of Acts' the Confirmation of the Gospel," *Sparsa Collecta* (ed. W. C. van Unnik *et al*) (NTS 29; Leiden 1973) 340-85; G. W. H. Lampe, "Luke," *Peake's Commentary on the Bible* (ed. M. Black and H. H. Rowley) (Edinburgh 1962) §715ef.

[6] John Kilgallen, *The Stephen Speech. A Literary and Redactional Study of Acts 7,2-53* (AnBib 67; Rome 1967) 31-2.

[7] The authenticity of the demonstrative pronoun remains an open question; cf. Schille, *Apostelgeschichte,* 176; B. M. Metzger, *A Textual Commentary on the Greek New Testament* (New York 1971) 341.

[8] *Contra* J. Kilgallen, *The Stephen Speech,* 33.

[9] Earl Richard, *Acts 6:1-8:4. The Author's Method of Composition* (SBLDS 41; Missoula 1978) 325.

In v. 13 as well as in v. 14, direct reference to God is dropped. In v. 14, the term "holy" is omitted, and the "law" itself is presented in a more nationalistic, cultural sense as "customs" which Moses had given.[10]

Stephen's reply has been said to ignore the charges.[11] It contains no defense about what Jesus said, nor does it (initially) deal with the law of Moses. On closer inspection, however, the reply is a counter-accusation which, though it takes the form of an interpretative history of Israel,[12] may be characterized as the interpretation of an apocalyptic vision. In recounting God's past dealings with his people, Stephen's face is "like that of an angel." Both his appearance and his thematic opening, "The God of glory appeared ..." become intelligible in the light of the vision which Luke describes at the end of the speech: being filled with the Holy Spirit and looking intently into heaven, Stephen sees the glory of God and Jesus standing at God's right hand (v. 55).[13] The final words of his address (v. 56) attest this vision, interpreting Jesus as the Son of Man.[14]

Throughout his speech as a whole, Stephen has emphasized God's direction of his people to the places he has determined for them, contrasting this with their attempted "localization" of him and progressive opposition to the norms given them. God moves Abraham from place to place, tying his inheritance to the progeny he promised (7,2-8). Joseph was providentially delivered to provide for his people in Egypt, but was later acknowledged by his brothers (7,9-16); a certain tension between rejection and recognition appears in this transitional passage. As the time for fulfillment of the promise to Abraham approached, Moses was prepared to liberate his people (7,20-22), but was at first rejected by them and became a sojourner in Midian (7,23-29). Through a vision in a place which God's communication to him made holy (7,30ff.), he was again sent to Egypt, this time with a clearly divine commission, but was not obeyed. The divinely-appointed ruler and redeemer was rejected by an idolatrous people who were happy with the works of their own hands. The consequence was a punitive, prophetically-announced displacement to Babylon. Insofar as it was associated with heavenly guidance, an earthly sanctuary like the tabernacle in the desert is not disparaged, nor is a stable dwelling intended for the

---

[10] As Gerhard Schneider observes, *Die Apostelgeschichte I. Teil* (HTKNT 5.1; Freiburg 1980) 439: "Lukas bezieht die ἔθη wohl primär auf die kultische Gesetzgebung."

[11] For the discussion, cf. Ernst Haenchen, *Die Apostelgeschichte* (MeyerK; Göttingen [14] 1965) 238-9.

[12] Cf. Earl Richard, *Acts 6:1 - 8:4. The Author's Method of Composition*, 306-11, 357.

[13] Cf. G. Schneider, *Apostelgeschichte*, 440.

[14] Mention of Jesus' "standing" at God's right hand may be intended to suggest only his being there (not a precise function); cf. E. Richard, *Acts 6:2 - 8:4. The Author's Method of Composition*, 294-9. M. Sabbe finds no new significance in the change of the participle, "The Son of Man Saying in Acts 7,56," *Les Actes des Apôtres. Traditions, rédaction, théologie* (ed J. Kremer) (BETL 48; Leuven 1979) 241-79, 256-79. Nevertheless, if the simple point is being *there* (a point which does not seem to be at odds with Sabbe's study), then Jesus' "place" is effectively contrasted with the nationally delimited cult-center.

benefit of the people ("a house for Jacob"[15]) (7,40-46). But a house for God, conceived as a humanly-designed limitation of the Lord of creation, is out of keeping with the prophetic vision (7,47-50). Disregard for the guidance of the Holy Spirit by their forebears is repeated in Stephen's accusers' own disregard for the Just One announced particularly by Moses, and in their not keeping the heavenly-given law.

Thus, the speech as a whole may coherently be construed as a prophetic-apocalyptic counter-indictment of disregard for God and Moses. What Stephen attacks, notably as his speech moves precipitately towards its climactic conclusion with the resumption of direct address (7,51; cp. 7,2a), is his adversaries' idolatrous, anti-prophetic (and therefore anti-Mosaic) outlook and action. Stephen does not attack the temple but attacks a state of mind according to which that building and institution, divorced from response to God's guidance, stands as a pseudo-religious absolute. Equivalently, this attitude constitutes idolatry.

Such an attitude may presage national calamity, as it did before the Exile (7,39-43). Curiously, however, even apropos of the Solomonic temple itself (7,48-50), Stephen does not restate this penalty for the nation. If the point is implied, it would be reasonable to infer it regarding the Second Temple as well, since Stephen expressly identifies his accusers' mentality with that of their forebears. His polemic, however, targets their religious ideology in terms of the specific form it has taken in the contemporary situation. It is their rejection of Jesus himself, the prophesied Just One, specifically their role in the crucifixion, and also their rejection of the Holy Spirit (now testifying prophetically through Stephen himself) which constitutes their sin. Whether a forthcoming catastrophe is implied for the nation, city, and temple remains unclear. It is surely not rendered explicit by the speech itself.

If a forthcoming catastrophe of such proportions is implied, however, it would accord with the major reasons for that calamity as already discerned in Luke's Gospel, although it would at the same time elaborate them. The murder of the Just One would, in both cases, figure as the salient reason. The rejection of God's spokesmen, here typified by the disciple Stephen, fits with the theological position taken in the Gospel (cf. Luke 21,15 and 10,16). Although those who are hostile to Stephen do not include the high priests, they do comprise members of the people and Jewish religious leaders.[16] On the other hand, the polemic against an idolatrous regard for the temple and the counter-charge of rejection of Moses move considerably beyond the perspective of Luke's Gospel.

---

[15] Notwithstanding E. Richard's preference for "for the God of Jacob," ibid., 130-3, the reading "for the house of Jacob" is more probable, cf. B. M. Metzger, *A Textual Commentary on the Greek New Testament*, 351-3. Besides, David had in mind something akin to the σκηνή of the desert sojourn (v. 44), namely, a σκήνωμα which, moreover, "he asked to find." The contrast with Solomon's "man-made edifice" (vv. 47-48a) would be perceptible even if τῷ θεῷ Ἰακώβ were read in v. 46.

[16] Cf. M. Hengel, "Zwischen Jesus und Paulus," 187.

Reasons for the development of perspective cannot be detailed here. Suffice it to note that the historical tensions to which Luke draws attention in the context of the selection of the deacons and its sequel serves, in accordance with the Lord's word (1,8), to move the Christian community beyond Jerusalem. The "Christian diaspora" which follows (cf. διεσπάρησαν, 8,1; διασπαρέντες, 8,4; 11,19) proves to be productive. It becomes the antithesis of the kind of movement which is not of God's doing (cf. 5,35-39). In introducing and in developing the reactions to Stephen's discourse, Luke shows no concern for the fate of Jerusalem and its temple. The general rejection of the Gospel by the Jews between Jerusalem and Rome is ultimately accounted for by a refusal to listen. Contrary to C. van der Waal's opinion,[17] no connection obtains between this refusal and the judgment upon Jerusalem or its temple. For the closing quotation from Isa 6,9-10 in Acts 28,26-27, as elsewhere in the NT, is not exploited with an eye to Isa 6,11-13.

Why Acts says so little about the forthcoming catastrophe for the city and the temple is not difficult to construe. First, Luke's account closes with Paul's preaching in Rome before the actual fall of the city. Notation of its actual destruction would have been grossly anachronistic. Second, it probably suffices for Luke to leave on the Lord's lips the certain prediction of coming events regarding the judgment of Jerusalem. Luke's own temperament would probably have disinclined him from any vindictive insistence on the Lord's own non-vindictive prophecy. Stephen's speech itself is not vindictive, much less so his prayer for those who lynch him (7,60). The protomartyr's brash polemic, a novice-like instance of apostolic παρρησία, is not necessarily endorsed by Luke, even in this provocative situation. His later accounts of Paul's polemic against idolatry (17,22-31) as well as of Paul's rejoinder to a charge quite similar to that brought against Stephen (21,28; cf. 22,1-22) become both more eloquent and more tactful. Once the emphasis on forthcoming judgment has been made tellingly by the Lord himself, Luke progressively draws attention to the message of salvation for all nations. In fine, the only situation in Acts in which Luke mentions the fate of the temple occurs while the Church is still located in Jerusalem and its immediate vicinity. It deals with a false charge, according to which Jesus allegedly expressed hostility towards the temple. As the reader of Luke's Gospel knows, he did not do so. Rather, he expressed compassion for the doomed city (Luke 19,41-44). Stephen's speech itself makes no direct reference to the forthcoming fate of the city and its temple, but indicts a pseudo-religious reverence for the cult-center, a narrowly nationalistic, thing-centered outlook. That point had to be made to provide a rationale for the movement of the Church beyond Jerusalem to accord with its prophetic character and Christological focus.

---

[17] C. van der Waal, "The Temple in the Gospel According to Luke," *Neot* 7 (1973) 49-59, 53.

Select Bibliography

Both the footnotes and the bibliographical entries are given according to the conventions adopted by *Biblica, 1982.*

Arndt, W. F., *The Gospel According to Luke* (St. Louis 1956).

Bachmann, Michael, *Jerusalem und der Tempel. Die geographisch-theologischen Elemente in der lukanischen Sicht des jüdischen Kultzentrums* (BWANT 109; Stuttgart 1980).

Barrett, Charles Kingsley, *Luke the Historian in Recent Study* (Philadelphia 1970 [repr. of 1961 ed. with supplemental references]).

Baumann, G., "Die lukanische Interpretation der Zerstörung Jerusalems," *NT* 6 (1963) 120-7.

Beck, B. E., "*Imitatio Christi* and the Lucan Passion Narrative," *Suffering and Martyrdom in the New Testament* (FS. G. M. Styles; [ed. W. Horbury and B. McNeil] Cambridge 1981) 28-47.

Benoit, Pierre, "'Et toi-même, un glaive te transpercera l'âme!' (Luc 2,35)," *CBQ* 25 (1963) 251-61.

Betz, Hans Dieter, "The Cleansing of the Ten Lepers (Luke 17:11-19)," *JBL* 90 (1971) 314-28.

Bihler, Johannes, *Die Stephanusgeschichte im Zusammenhang der Apostelgeschichte* (Münchener Theologische Studien I/30; Munich 1963).

Boucher, Madeleine, *The Mysterious Parable. A Literary Study* (CBQMS 6; Washington 1977).

Bovon, François, "Du côté de chez Luc," *RTP* 115 (1983) 175-89.

———, *Luc le Théologien. Vingt-cinq ans de recherches (1950-1975)* (Neuchâtel 1978).

Braude, W. G., and J. J. Kapstein, *Tanna Děbe Eliyyahu. The Lore of the School of Elijah* (Philadelphia 1981).

Brongers, H. A., "Die Wendung *bešēm ywhw* im Alten Testament," *ZAW* 77 (1965) 1-20.

Brown, Schuyler, "The Role of the Prologues in Determining the Purpose of Luke-Acts," *Perspectives in Luke-Acts* (ed. C. H. Talbert) (Edinburgh 1978) 99-111.

Bultmann, R., *History of the Synoptic Tradition* (trans. John Marsh) (Oxford 1963).

Busse, U., *Das Nazareth-Manifest Jesu. Eine Einführung in das lukanische Jesusbild nach Lk 4,16-30* (SBS 91; Stuttgart 1977).

Cadbury, Henry J., "The Purpose Expressed in Luke's Preface," *Expositor* 21 (1921) 431-44.

Cassidy, R. J. and P. J. Scharper (editors), *Political Issues in Luke-Acts* (Maryknoll 1983).

Creed, J. M., *The Gospel According to St. Luke* (London [1930] 1965).

Crossan, J. D., "The Parable of the Wicked Husbandmen," *JBL* 90 (1971) 451-65.

Dalman, Gustav, *Jesus–Jeshua* (New York 1971).

Danker, F. W., *Jesus and the New Age* (St. Louis 1972).

Danten, J., "La révélation du Christ sur Dieu dans les Paraboles," *NRT* 87 (1955) 450-77.

Davies, J. J., "The Purpose of the Central Section of St.Luke's Gospel," *SE* II (= TU 87 [1964]) 164-9.

Derrett, J. Duncan, "Law in the New Testament: The Palm Sunday Colt," *NT* 13 (1971) 241-58.

Dillon, Richard J., "Easter Revelation and Mission Program in Luke 24: 46-48," *Sin, Salvation, and the Spirit* (ed. D. Durken) (Collegeville 1979) 240-70.

————. *From Eye-Witnesses to Ministers of the Word: Tradition and Composition of Luke 24* (AnBib 82; Rome 1978).

————, "Previewing Luke's Project from His Prologue (Luke 1:1-14)," *CBQ* 43 (1981) 205-27.

————, "The Prophecy of Christ and His Witnesses According to the Discourses in Acts," *NTS* (forthcoming).

Dodd, C. H., "The Fall of Jerusalem and the 'Abomination of Desolation,'" *JRS* 37 (1947) 47-54.

Donahue, John R., *Are You the Christ? The Trial Narrative in the Gospel of Mark* (SBLDS 10; Missoula 1973).

Doran, Robert, "Luke 20:18. A Warrior's Boast?" *CBQ* 45 (1983) 61-7.

Dupont, Jacques, *Les béatitudes* (3 vols.; Louvain 1958, 1969, 1973).

————, "Les pèlerins d'Emmaüs (Luc XIV, 13-35)," *Miscellanea Biblica B. Ubach* (ed. Romualdo Ma. Díaz) (Montserrat 1953).

Evans, Craig A., "'He Set His Face': A Note on Luke 9,51," *Bib* 63 (1982) 545-8.

Feldkämper, Lüdger, *Der betende Jesus als Heilsmittler nach Lukas* (St. Augustin bei Bonn 1978).

Fitzmyer, Joseph A., *The Gospel According to Luke (I-IX)* (AB 28; Garden City 1981).

Flender, Helmut, *St. Luke, Theologian of Redemptive History* (trans. R. H. and I. Fuller) (Philadelphia 1967).

Flückiger, Felix, "Luke 21,20-24 und die Zerstörung Jerusalems," *TZ* 28 (1972) 385-90.

Francis, Fred O., "Eschatology and History in Luke-Acts," *JAmAcadRel* 37 (1969) 49-63.

Gaston, Lloyd, *No Stone on Another. Studies in the Significance of the Fall of Jerusalem in the Synoptic Gospels* (NTS 23; Leiden 1970).

Geiger, Ruthild, *Die lukanischen Endzeitsreden. Studien zur Eschatologie des Lukas-Evangeliums* (Europäische Hochschulschriften Ser. XXIII, Vol. 16; Frankfurt /M. 1973).

George, A., "La Construction du troisième Évangile," *Etudes sur l'oeuvre de Luc* (EB; Paris 1978 [cf. *ETL* 43 (1967) 100-29]).

————, "Le sens de la mort de Jésus pour Luc," *RB* 80 (1973) 186-217.

Giblin, C. H., "Reflections on the Sign of the Manger," *CBQ* 29 (1967) 87-101.

————, "Revelation 11, 1-13: Its Form, Function, and Contextual Integration," *NTS* 30 (1984) 433-59.

————, "Structural and Thematic Correlations in the Matthean Burial-Resurrection Narrative (Matt. xxvii. 57-xxviii. 20)," *NTS* 21 (1975-76) 406-20.

————, "Structural and Theological Considerations on Luke 15," *CBQ* 24 (1962) 15-31.

————, "Suggestion, Negative Response, and Positive Action in St. John's Portrayal of Jesus (John 2. 1-11; 4. 46-54; 7. 2-14; 11. 1-44)," *NTS* 26 (1980-81) 197-211.

————, "Theological Perspective and Matthew 10:23b," *TS* 29 (1968) 637-61.

Gilmour, S. MacLean, "The Gospel According to Luke," (IB 8; New York 1952).

Grelot, Pierre, "Étude critique de Luc 10,19," *RSR* 69 (1981) 87-100.

Grundmann, W., *Das Evangelium nach Lukas* (THKNT 3; Berlin ⁹1981).

Haenchen, Ernst, *Die Apostelgeschichte* (MeyerK; Göttingen [14]1965).

Hanson, Paul D., *The Dawn of Apocalyptic* (Philadelphia 1975).

Harvey, Julien, *Le Plaidoyer prophétique contre Israël après la rupture de l'Alliance. Étude d'une formule littéraire de l'ancien Testament* (Studia 22; Bruges 1967).

Hengel, Martin, "Zwischen Jesus und Paulus. Die 'Hellenisten', die 'Sieben' und Stephanus (Apg 6,1-15; 7,54 - 8,3)," *ZTK* 72 (1975) 150-206.

Hill, David, "The Rejection at Nazareth," *NT* 13 (1971) 161-80.

Hubaut, Michel, *La Parabole des Vignerons homicides* (Cahiers RB 16; Paris 1976).

Jeremias, Joachim, *Die Gleichnisse Jesu* (Göttingen [6]1962).

Juel, Donald, *Messiah and Temple. The Trial of Jesus in the Gospel of Mark* (SBLDS 31) Missoula 1977).

Jülicher, A., *Die Gleichnisreden Jesu* (Tübingen I, [2]1910).

Käser, W., "Exegetische und theologische Erwägungen zur Seligpreisung der Kinderlosen Lu 23:29b," *ZNW* 54 (1963) 240-54.

Keck, Fridolin, *Die öffentliche Abschiedsrede Jesu in Lk 20,45 - 21,36. Eine redaktions- und motivgeschichtliche Untersuchung* (FzB 25; Stuttgart 1978).

Kilgallen, John, *The Stephen Speech. A Literary and Redactional Study of Acts 7,2-53* (AnBib 67; Rome 1976).

Klein, G., "Lukas 1,1-4 als theologisches Programm," *Zeit und Geschichte* (FS. R. Bultmann; [ed. Erich Dinkler] Tübingen 1964) 193-216.

Klostermann, E., *Das Lukasevangelium* (HNT 5; Tübingen [[2]1929] [3]1975).

Koester, H., art. συνοχή in *TDNT* VII, 886-7.

Kümmel, W. G., "Jesuforschung seit 1965, IV Teil," *TRu* 43 (1978) 105-61; 233-65.

van der Kwaak, H., "Die Klage über Jerusalem (Mt 23,37-39)," *NT* 8 (1966) 156-70.

Lambrecht, Jan, *Die Redaktion der Markus-Apokalypse. Literarische Analyse und Strukturuntersuchung* (AnBib 28; Rome 1967).

Maddox, Robert, *The Purpose of Luke-Acts* (Göttingen 1982).

Marshall, I. Howard, *The Gospel of Luke* (NICNT; Exeter 1978).

de Meeus, X., "Composition de Lc., XIV et genre symposiaque," *ETL* 37 (1961) 847-70.

Metzger, Bruce M., *A Textual Commentary on the Greek New Testament* (New York 1971).

Minear, Paul S., "Jesus' Audiences, According to Luke," *NT* 16 (1974) 81-109.

Miyoshi, Michi, *Die Anfang des Reiseberichts, Lk 9,51 - 10,24. Eine redaktionsgeschichtliche Untersuchung* (AnBib 60; Rome 1974).

Neyrey, Jerome H., "Jesus' Address to the Women of Jerusalem (Lk. 23. 27-31) — A Prophetic Judgment Oracle," *NTS* 29 (1983) 74-86.

Nicol, W., "Tradition and Redaction in Luke 21," *Neot* 7 (1973) 61-71.

Nolland, John, "Impressed Unbelievers as Witnesses to Christ (Luke 4:22a)," *JBL* 98 (1979) 219-29.

Patsch, Hermann, "Der Einzug Jesu in Jerusalem. Ein historischer Versuch," *ZTK* 68 (1971) 1-26.

Plümacher, Eckhard, *Lukas als hellenistischer Schriftsteller. Studien zur Apostelgeschichte* (Göttingen 1972).

Plummer, A., *The Gospel According to S. Luke* (ICC; Edinburgh [4]1913).

Rengstorf. K. H., *Die Re-Investitur des Verlorenen Sohnes in der Gleichniserzählung Jesu Luk 15,11-32* (AFLNW 137; Cologne 1967).

Richard, Earl, *Acts 6:1 - 8:4. The Author's Method of Composition* (SBLDS 41; Missoula 1978).

de Roche, Michael, "Yahweh's *rîb* Against Israel: A Reassessment of the So-Called 'Prophetic Lawsuit' in the Preexilic Prophets," *JBL* 102 (1983) 563-74.

Sabbe, M., "The Son of Man Saying in Acts 7,56," *Les Actes des Apôtres. Traditions, rédaction, théologie* (ed. J. Kremer) (BETL 48; Leuven 1979) 241-79.

Schille, Gottfried, *Die Apostelgeschichte des Lukas* (THKNT 5; Berlin 1983).

Schneider, Gerhard, *Die Apostelgeschichte I. Teil* (HTKNT 5.1; Freiburg 1980).

———, *Das Evangelium Nach Lukas* (Ökumenischer Taschenbuchkommentar zum NT 3/1, 3/2; Würzburg ²1984).

———, *Die Passion Jesu nach den drei älteren Evangelien* (Munich 1972).

———, "Stephanus, die Hellenisten und Samaria," *Les Actes des Apôtres. Traditions, rédaction, théologie* (ed. J. Kremer) (BETL 48; Leuven 1979) 215-40.

Schottroff, Luise, "Das Gleichnis vom verlorenen Sohn," *ZTK* 68 (1971) 27-52.

Schürmann, Heinz, *Das Lukasevangelium: Erster Teil: Kommentar zu Kap. 1,1-9,50* (HTKNT 3/1; Freiburg 1969).

Schweizer, Eduard, *Das Evangelium nach Lukas* (NTD 3; Göttingen ¹⁸1982).

Snodgrass, Klyne, *The Parable of the Wicked Tenants* (WUNT 27; Berlin 1983).

da Spinetoli, Ortensio, *Luca, il Vangelo dei Poveri* (Assisi 1982).

Steck, Odil Hannes, *Israel und das Gewaltsame Geschick der Propheten. Untersuchungen zur Überlieferung des Deuteronomistischen Geschichtsbildes im Alten Testament* (WMANT 23; Neukirchen-Vluyn 1967).

Steele, E. Springs, "Luke 11.37-54 — A Modified Hellenistic Symposium?" *JBL* (1984) 379-94.

Sylva, Dennis D., "*Ierousalēm* and *Hierosolyma* in Luke-Acts." *ZNW* 74 (1983) 207-29.

Talbert, Charles H., *Luke and the Gnostics* (Nashville 1966).

Thériault, J. Y.,"Les dimensions sociales, économiques et politiques dans l'oeuvre de Luc," *ScEs* 26 (1971) 205-31.

Tiede, David, *Prophecy and History in Luke-Acts* (Philadelphia 1980).

Toynbee, A. J., *Greek Historical Thought. From Homer to the Age of Heraclius* (New York ¹⁰1952).

van Unnik, W. C., " 'The Book of Acts' The Confirmation of the Gospel, *Sparsa Collecta* (ed. W. C. van Unnik *et al*) (NTS 29; Leiden 1973) 340-85.

———, "Éléments artistiques dans l'évangile de Luc," *L'évangile de Luc. Problèmes littéraires et théologiques* (Mémorial Lucien Cerfaux; [ed. F. Neirynck *et al*] Gembloux 1973).

———, "Once More St. Luke's Prologue," *Neot* 7 (1973) 7-26.

Vanhoye, Albert, "Structure et théologie des récits de la Passion dans les évangiles synoptiques," *NRT* 89 (1967) 135-63.

Völkel, Martin, "Der Anfang Jesus in Galiläa. Bemerkungen zum Gebrauch und zur Function Galiläas in den lukanischen Schriften," *ZNW* 64 (1973) 222-37.

van der Waal, C., "The Temple in the Gospel According to Luke," *Neot* 7 (1973) 49-59.

Weinert, Francis D., "Luke, the Temple and Jesus' Saying about Jerusalem's Abandoned House (Luke 13:34-35),"*CBQ* 44 (1982) 68-76.

———, *The Meaning of the Temple in the Gospel of Luke* (Fordham University Dissertation 1979; available from University Microfilms International, Ann Arbor, MI 48106).

Westermann, Claus, *Grundformen Prophetischer Rede* (EEvT 31; Munich 1960).

Wijngaards, J., "Saint Luke's Prologue in the Light of Modern Research," *Clergy Monthly* 31 (1967) 171-9; 251-8.

Wright, Addison G., "The Widow's Mites: Praise or Lament? — A Matter of Context," *CBQ* 44 (1982) 256-65.

Zmijewski, Joseph, *Die Eschatologiereden des Lukasevangeliums. Eine traditions- und redaktionsgeschichtliche Untersuchung zu Lk 21,5-36 und Lk 17,20-37* (BBB 40; Bonn 1972).

Index of Texts

A. Old Testament

GENESIS

6,13: 90
10: 33 n. 15
48,11: 49

EXODUS

7,4: 87
12,12: 87

NUMBERS

19,2: 49
20,12f.: 103
33,4: 87

DEUTERONOMY

21,13-14: 49
32,35: 87

1 SAMUEL

6,7: 49
8,17: 49

1 KINGS

1,33: 50
9,6-9: 87 n. 27
17,28: 53
19,4-18: 54 n. 22
21,17-19: 39
22,13-28: 54 n. 22

2 KINGS

1,3-4: 39
9,13: 50
17,5-23: 54 n. 22

2 CHRONICLES

15,6: 82
23,20: 50

TOBIT

14,4-5: 90

PSALMS

22 (LXX 21): 94 n. 5
110: 74 n. 2
117 (MT 118),22-23: 42,
    53 n. 19, 62, 70-71
121: 55
122: 55
137,9: 56

PROVERBS

11,31: 102 n. 34

QOHELETH

9,12: 90

SIRACH

5,7: 87
48,22: 52

ISAIAH

3,1-11: 39
3,26: 56
5,1-7: 62, 66-67
5,4 (LXX): 64
6,9-10: 112
6,11-13: 112
8,5-8: 39

8,7-15: 71
8,21: 82
10,5: 91 n. 45
13,13: 82
14,11-15: 34
19,2: 82
29,1-8: 91 n. 45
30,12-16: 39
38,5: 52
40,8: 85 n. 25
51,2: 52
53,12: 103 n. 36
58,14: 52
63,16: 52

JEREMIAH

2,26-28: 39
22,5: 42
25,8-15: 91 n. 4
46,10 [LXX 26,10]: 87
50,31 [LXX 27,31]: 87
51,6 [LXX 28,6]: 87

LAMENTATIONS

4,19: 90

EZEKIEL

4,1-2: 56
9,1: 87
17,22-24: 102
20,45-49: 102
21,1-7: 102
30,3: 90
38,1-23: 91 n. 45

DANIEL

2,45: 71
7,13: 74 n. 2
9,12: 87 n. 27

HOSEA

2,7-9: 39
9,7: 87
10,8: 100

AMOS

4,1-3: 39
7,6-17: 39
9,8-18: 39

MICAH

3,1-4: 39
3,9-12: 87 n. 27

HABAKKUK

2,11: 55

ZEPHANIAH

1,14-15: 88 n. 30

ZECHARIAH

9,9: 49 n. 12, 50

1 MACCABEES

9,10: 90

B. New Testament

MATTHEW

5,20: 36 n. 21
8,10: 27 n. 23
10,23b: 43 n. 50
12,3-40: 35
13,36-43: 66
14,3-12: 97
16,1-4: 35
19,20: 22
21,5: 50
21,23 – 23,36: 41
21,33-46: 62 ff.
23,13-16: 40, 41
23,25-36: 41
23,37-39: 40, 41
23,39: 42, 43
24,1: 40
24,2: 42
24,15: 42
24,36: 84 n. 24
26,58: 94 n. 6
26,61: 109
26,75: 94 n. 6
27,27-32: 94 n. 6

MARK

1,2: 3 n. 1
1,5: 3
1,14-15: 28
1,22: 26

1,23-38: 58
2,24: 55 n. 26
2,25: 27
3,8: 2
3,22: 3
3,20-30: 27-28
4,13-20: 20, 65
4,26-32: 28
6,17-29: 97
7,1: 3
8,15: 27
8,27: 26 n. 19
9,9-50: 2 n. 8
9,47: 28
10,17-31: 22
10,32: 48, 51
11,1-13: 48-49
11,5: 50
11,8: 50
11,9: 51
11,15-18: 59-60
11,27: 60, 60 n. 10
12,1-2: 62
12,4-44: 75 n. 6
12,12: 61
12,13: 60 n. 10
12,18: 60 n. 10
12,28: 60 n. 10
12,35: 60 n. 11
12,37: 75
13,1-37: 75 ff.

13,17-18: 100
13,20: 90
13,24: 91
13,32: 84
14,2: 93
14,56-59: 58 n. 6, 109
14,62: 42 n. 49
15,6-15: 52
15,16: 93 n. 4
15,29-30: 97
15,34: 94 n. 5
15,37: 52

LUKE

1,1-4: viii, 6, 8, 10-18, 101,
   105
1,2: 98 n. 21
1,5 – 2,52: 1,3
1,18: 53
1,20: 84 n. 23
1,32-33: 54
1,34: 53
1,78-79: 56
2,10-14: 53-54
2,18-22: 5 n. 8
2,34-35: 54
2,49: 59
3,1 – 9,50: 1
3,1-38: 1
3,1-18: 60 n. 12

3,23-38: 25
4,1-13: 1
4,8: 3
4,9: 2, 4
4,13: 4
4,14-44: 1
4,16-30: 25
4,18-19: 29
4,22-23: 25, 90
4,30: 24 n. 14
4,31-44: 58
4,33: 52
4,43-44: 26, 29
5,1 – 7,5: 2
5,14: 3 n. 12
5,16: 3 n. 12
5,17-26: 2, 3, 26, 31, 41 n.
   43, 54
5,19: 19
5,27-39: 20, 26
5,36: 79 n. 16
6,1-5: 3 n. 11
6,3: 3 n. 11, 26
6,6-11: 27
6,10-11: 3 n. 11
6,17: 2, 3, 30 n. 6, 31
6,20: 29
6,39: 79 n. 16
6,46: 40 n. 41
6,48: 19
7,15-19: 53, 56
7,18-23: 29
7,29-35: 17
7,31: 84 n. 23
7,36-50: 20
8,1-21: 2, 26
8,9-10: 27
8,11: 14
8,11-15: 20-21
8,16: 19
8,22-56: 2, 26
8,24: 40 n. 41, 75 n. 3
8,28: 52
8,37: 27
9,1-17: 2, 26
9,2-11: 19
9,5-6: 33
9,7-9: 33 n. 17, 38

9,18-50: 2
9,22: 26, 28
9,23: 94
9,27: 28
9,28-36: 2
9,31: 2-4, 28
9,37-50: 2
9,41-44: 5
9,41: 84 n. 23
9,44: 28
9,49: 75 n. 3
9,51 – 19,27: vii, 1, 4, 30-
   46, 106
9,51 – 10,37: 4 n. 4
9,51-55: 31-32
9,51: 33 n. 6
9,52-53: 32 n. 14
10,1-16: 32 n. 4
10,1: 33 n. 16, 33-34, 56
10,10-16: 33-34, 72, 106,
   111
10,13-14: 3 n. 13
10,18: 54
10,19: 54 n. 23
10,38: 31 n. 8
11,13-36: 100 n. 29
11,14-28: 34-35
11,17-20: 28 n. 26
11,22: 99
11,29-32: 34-36, 72
11,29-54: 84 n. 23
11,37-54: 20, 54 n. 25
11,46: 87
11,48b-49: 27, 32 n. 14
12,1 – 13,9: 44 n. 57
12,1: 31 n. 7, 36 n. 23
12,8-12: 32 n. 14, 81 n. 19
12,14: 36 n. 23
12,16: 79 n. 16
12,28: 100 n. 29
12,36: 43 n. 52
12,50: 76 n. 9
12,51: 54
12,54 – 13,9: 36
12,58: 19 n. 1
13,1-9: 34-37, 72, 79 n. 16
13,10-17: 54
13,22: 40

13,31-33: 4, 37-43, 69
13,31: 30, 99
13,33: 25
13,34-35: 4, 87, 90, 91 n.
   45, 106
14,1-24: 20
14,15-24: 25 n. 16
14,25: 31 n. 7
14,27: 94
14,32: 55 n. 30
15,1-32: 22-24
16,8: 84 n. 23
16,9: 101 n. 31
16,14-15: 54 n. 25
16,22-29: 37 n. 24
16,30-31: 72
17,11: 30
17,15-16: 52
17,20 – 18,8: 44
17,22: 78 n. 12
17,23: 83
17,22-35: 90 n. 42
17,25: 76 n. 9, 84 n. 23
17,37: 43-44
18,9-14: 54 n. 25
18,13: 97
18,18-30: 22
18,31: 89
18,32: 4
18,35-43: 54
18,38-49: 55
19,9: 45
19,11: 79 n. 16
19,11-27: 4, 43-48, 52, 54,
   72, 84 n. 22
19,28 – 24,53: viii, 1, 5, 45,
   47-56, 91 n. 45, 105-
   106
19,28-44: 5, 45, 47-56, 91
   n. 45, 105-106
19,41-44: 38, 73, 87, 109,
   112
19,41: 8
19,46-47: 58, 61 n. 14
20,1-26: 57-58, 74
20,1: 61 n. 14
20,9-19: 5, 57-73, 100, 105
20,20: 74

20,27-44: 57-58, 74
20,39-44: 75
20,41: 60
20,45 – 21,36: 5, 57-58, 74-92
21,5-36: 44 n. 57
21,15: 111
21,20-24: 100-105
21,22: 44 n. 57
21,23: 100
21,24-26: viii
21,38: 57 n. 2
22,1-13: 49 n. 9
22,2: 93 n. 1
22,11: 75 n. 3
22,15: 41
22,31-34: 40 n. 41, 72, 94
22,35 – 23,49: 7
22,35-38: 50 n. 13, 93
22,36-37: 79 n. 9, 102
22,39-44: 97
22,41-44: 93 n. 2
22,53: 58, 93 n. 2, 99 n. 26
22,54: 93
22,55-56: 98
22,61: 70, 72, 98 n. 23
22,66-71: 74, 93
22,69: 31 n. 9
23,1: 93
23,2: 45, 74
23,6-15: 38, 93 n. 3
23,13-14: 96
23,13-18: 96-97
23,26-32: 93-104, 105
23,27-31: 5, 38
23,30: 72
23,35-38: 45, 95-96, 97 n. 16
23,39-43: 103
23,46: 52

23,47: 103
23,48-49: 97-98
23,50 – 24,53: 58
23,56: 58 n. 3
24,1: 58 n. 3
24,13-35: 20, 24
24,18: 69
24,20: 97 n. 17
24,25-49: 50 n. 13
24,44: 89
24,53: 57 n. 2

JOHN

2,1-11: 79 n. 13
4,46-54: 79 n. 13
7,2-14: 79 n. 13
11,1-44: 79 n. 13

ACTS

1,1-2: 16 n. 22
1,7: 84 n. 24
1,8: 112
2,23: 96
2,32-36: 15, 31 n. 9
3,20: 89
4,11: 71
4,25: 52
5,35-39: 112
6,4: 14
6,10: 108
6,11-15: 109-110
7,2-60: 108-111
7,57-60: 52 n. 17
8,1: 112
8,4: 112
8,7: 52 n. 17
10,37-38: 1 n. 4
11,19: 112

13,29: 89
14,10: 52 n. 17
16,28: 52 n. 17
17,22-31: 112
18,25: 15 n. 20
21,28: 112
22,1-22: 112
26,24: 52 n. 52
27 – 28: 31 n. 7
27,9a: 51 n. 14
28,26-27: 112

ROMANS

11,25: 89 n. 36, 91

1 CORINTHIANS

7,26-28: 88 n. 30
12,24: 49

GALATIANS

4,21 – 5,1: 65

HEBREWS

13,11-13: 69

1 PETER

2,4-7: 71
2,12: 56
4,17-18: 102

REVELATION

2,17: 84 n. 24
11,1-13: 5 n. 18
19,12-13: 84 n. 24

C. Other

BEDE THE VENERABLE,

In Luc. Ev. Expositio
2,41: 1

CERVANTES,

Don Quixote: 71

DANTE ALIGHIERI,

De Monarchia I, xvi. 2:
vii
Ep. VIII, 14: vii

DIO CHRYSOSTOM,

Discourses VI, §60: 25
n. 14

DIODORUS OF AGYRIUM,

Universal History I, 1-5:
17

DIODORUS SICULUS,

Historical Library I, 1.5:
17

DIONYSIUS OF HALICARNASSUS,

Roman Antiquities:
I, 6. §5: 16-17
I, 11. §§2-3: 11 n. 8

2 Esdras 5,5: 55 n. 27

Gospel of Thomas §§65-66:
63-64

JOSEPHUS,

Antiquities XVIII, 58-
89: 37 n. 25
Jewish War:
I, 1-5 §§1-16: 11 n. 8
II, 13: 37 n. 25

Against Apion:
I, 1. §1: 8, 14
II, 1. §§1-2: 14

JUSTIN,

Apology I, 32: 49 n. 8

LUCIAN,

How to Write History
§55: 28

POLYBIUS,

World History:
I, 1: 17
IX, 1-2: 11 n. 9, 17

Seder ElijR 14 (65): 103

Test. Jud. 9,7: 55 n. 30

Index of Authors

Arndt, W.F., 7

Bachmann, M., 59
Barrett, C.K., 11
Baumann, G., 90
Beck, B.E., 7
Benoit, P., 54
Betz, H.D., 52
Bihler, J., 108
Blinzler, J., 37 n. 25
Boucher, M., 65
Bovon, F., 16
Braude, W.G., 103
Brongers, H.A., 53
Brown, Schuyler, 16
Bultmann, R., 24, 48
Busse, U., 24

Cadbury, H.J., 7
Conzelmann, H., 30, 90
Creed, J.M., 22, 34, 47
Crossan, J.D., 67

Dalman, G., 96
Danker, F.W., 96, 101
Danten, J., 66
Davies, J.H., 4
Derrett, J.D., 49, 64
Dillon, R.J., 7, 10, 13, 15, 81, 89, 98
Dodd, C.H., 69, 88
Donahue, J.R., 58, 64
Doran, R., 64, 70-72
Dupont, J., 24, 29

Ellis, E.E., 69
Evans, C.A., 4, 31-32

Feldkämper, L., 3
Fitzmyer, J.A., 1, 3, 4, 8, 10, 12, 13, 15, 21, 26, 29, 30, 32, 47, 89

Flender, H., 54, 90
Flückiger, F., 56
Francis, F.O., 88
Franklin, E., 91

Gaston, Lloyd, 6, 37, 43, 44-45, 75, 91
Geiger, R., 81
George, A., 1, 7, 90
Giblin, C.H., 5, 23, 35, 43, 53, 66, 79
Gilmour, S. MacLean, 7
Grelot, P., 54
Grundmann, W., 3, 21, 44, 47, 52, 55, 87, 91, 96

Haag, H., 40
Haenchen, E., 110
Hanson, P., 91
Harvey, J., 37, 39
Hengel, M., 108, 111
Hill, D., 25
Hubaut, M., 57

Jeremias, J., 19, 69
Juel, D., 79
Jülicher, A., 65

Käser, W., 95
Kapstein J.J., 103
Keck, Fridolin, 5, 15, 76, 78-79, 85, 88-90, 103
Kilgallen, J., 109
Klein, G., 13
Klostermann, E., 21, 22, 48, 95, 99
Koester, H., 91
Kümmel, W.G., 65
van der Kwaak, H., 40

Lambrecht, Jan, 76-77

Lampe, G.W.H., 109
Léon-Dufour, X., 65
Loisy, A., 48

Maddox, R., 8
Marshall, I.H., 3, 21, 35, 40, 47, 49, 55
de Meeüs, X., 20
Metzger, B.M., 109, 111
Michel, O., 76
Minear, P.S., 8, 75
Miyoshi, Michi 4, 31
Montefiore, C., 69

Neyrey, J.H., 4, 61, 37, 38, 39, 95-99
Nicol, W., 90
Nolland, John, 25, 51

Patsch, H., 47
Pesch, R., 55
Plummer, A., 6, 49, 89, 90, 101, 103
Plümacher, E., 16

Rengstorf, K.H., 23
Richard, E., 109-111
de Roche, Michael, 37

Sabbe, M., 110
Schille, G., 108
Schneider, Gerhard, 7, 8, 13, 22, 47, 109-110
Schniewind, J., 67
Schottroff, Luise, 23
Schürmann, H., 13, 101
Schweizer, E., 67, 90, 94, 96
Snodgrass, Klyne, 57, 63-65, 69-70
da Spinetoli, O., 50
Steck, O.H., 26

Steele, E. Springs, 20
Sylva, D. D., 2

Talbert, C. H., 8
Tiede, D., 89, 91
Tkacik, A., 102
Toynbee, A. J., 17

van Unnik, W. C., 10, 11,
13, 16, 109
Vanhoye, A., 7
Völkel, M., 26

van der Waal, C., 112
Weinert, Francis D., 1, 41-

42, 58
Wellhausen, J., 48
Westermann, Claus, 39
Wijngaards, J., 11
Wright, A. G., 75-76

Zmijewski, J., 81

FINITO DI STAMPARE NEL MESE DI GIUGNO 1985
DALLA TIPOGRAFIA POLIGLOTTA
DELLA PONTIFICIA UNIVERSITÀ GREGORIANA
PIAZZA DELLA PILOTTA, 4 - ROMA